Reclaiming Authorship

Reclaiming Authorship

Literary Women in America, 1850–1900

SUSAN S. WILLIAMS

PENN

University of Pennsylvania Press

Philadelphia

Copyright © 2006 University of Pennsylvania Press
All rights reserved
Printed in the United States of America on acid-free paper

10 9 8 7 6 5 4 3 2 1

Published by
University of Pennsylvania Press
Philadelphia, Pennsylvania 19104-4112

Library of Congress Cataloging-in-Publication Data

Williams, Susan S.
    Reclaiming authorship : literary women in America, 1850–1900 / Susan S. Williams.
        p. cm.
    Includes bibliographical references and index.
    Contents: Defining female authorship — Writing in and out of the home : parlor
culture and authorship — Authorizing reception : Maria Cummins and *The Lamplighter* —
Revising romance : Louisa May Alcott, Hawthorne, and the Civil War — Contractual
authorship : Elizabeth Keckley and Mary Abigail Dodge — Elizabeth Stuart Phelps's
ethical authorship — Epilogue : amateurs and professionals in Woolson and James.
    ISBN-13: 978-0-8122-3942-3
    ISBN-10: 0-8122-3942-3 (cloth : alk. paper)
    1. American literature—Women authors—History and criticism. 2. American
literature—19th century—History and criticism. 3. Women and literature—United
States—History—19th century. 4. Authorship. I. Title.

PS217.W64W55 2006
810.9'928709034—dc22

                                                                                    2005058496

For Jeff and Alex

Contents

Preface

When I first began this study of female authors, I had in mind relating the key term "authorship" to some other critical category: realism as a literary mode, or the formation of women's professional life in the United States, or the nineteenth-century literary marketplace and its production of cultural hierarchies of taste. And indeed, this book takes up all of these categories in one way or another, thinking in particular about realism as an authorial practice as well as the way in which the women studied here constructed their professional relations to the marketplace. But in the end I have realized that I am ultimately most interested in the category of authorship itself: how it was defined and what it teaches us about American literary history in the second half of the nineteenth century.

My approach to this topic is largely historical, focusing on the complex ways in which five nineteenth-century women—Maria Susanna Cummins, Louisa May Alcott, Mary Abigail Dodge, Elizabeth Keckley, and Elizabeth Stuart Phelps—foregrounded the issue of authorship in their manuscript and published writing. Their understandings of this term were necessarily influenced by the literary culture of which they were part, including ongoing debates about romance and realism, literary nationalism, literary property and copyright, and professionalism. These debates were shared by male and female authors alike, and for that reason I situate these women authors alongside their male counterparts, understanding Alcott and Dodge in the context of Nathaniel Hawthorne, for example, or Phelps in the context of William Dean Howells. Yet, this is fundamentally a study of female authorship. By grouping these women together, I hope to give them increased critical visibility while also highlighting their various models of authorship.

In offering case studies of women authors, this book follows the scholarly trend, over the past several decades, of studying nineteenth-century women's writing as a distinct literary tradition. Much of this scholarship, inspired by seminal works such as Nina Baym's *Women's Fiction* (1978) and Josephine Donovan's *New England Local Color Literature* (1983), focuses on sentimental and domestic fiction in the antebellum period and on regionalism in the postbellum period. This work has had the important effect of highlighting the particular contributions of women's writing to nineteenth-century American history and helping to consolidate the study of American women writers as a field of study. My own reason for focusing on women authors, however, is not to claim a specific "women's literary tradition," as Judith Fetterley and Marjorie Pryse describe regionalism in their recent comprehensive study.[1] Instead, I propose, first, to help close the gap between antebellum sentimental and postbellum regionalist writing by giving attention to authors who wrote throughout the period 1850–1900 (and who do not always fit into a single tradition) and, second, to claim—or, more accurately, to reclaim—female authorship as serving as what Michel Foucault terms "a means of classification" within this period.[2] Its features were not wholly separate from those associated with male authorship, but they were discussed and utilized in distinct ways. Moreover, these features did not lead to a single definition of "the female author," but rather opened up a variety of practices and authorial personae.

My interest in filling in some of the gaps between sentimentalism and regionalism is reflected in two other recent studies, both of which were published as I was completing the manuscript for this book. The first, Anne Boyd's *Writing for Immortality* (2004), also seeks to challenge a "pattern of women's writing that advances from sentimentalism to domestic fiction to local color" and "perpetuate[s] the narrow view of late-nineteenth- and early-twentieth-century canonizers who sought to elevate a few writers above all others." Boyd suggests that we focus instead on the generation of women—writing primarily in the 1860s and 1870s—who contributed to an emerging high literary culture by "clearly adopting models of authorship that previously had been considered available only to men."[3] This interest in high culture is echoed in Naomi Sofer's *Making the "America of Art"* (2005). Sofer sees the second half of the nineteenth century as witnessing an important shift from moral and religious to aesthetic goals in a "transitional generation" of women writers, a shift that is accompanied by a high art that is specifically tied to American nationalism. Sofer's main interest is in the "emergence of the self-consciously literary American woman writer" and the connection of that emergence to ongoing conversations about the utility of art in the post-Civil War nation.[4]

Reclaiming Authorship differs from these other studies in its emphasis on how women theorized their own authorship, a theory that did not produce a unified conception of authorial practice (as, for example, of "high art") or trajectory of authorial careers. To be sure, the women studied here were influenced in various ways by constructions of sentimentality and/or of high culture. And the overall trajectory of their careers moves, broadly, from the domestic and personal to the contractual and cosmopolitan. Furthermore, as I show in Chapter 1, discussions of female authorship as a general category—discussions that occurred primarily in the pages of American periodicals—did help to define its general features. Yet each individual author related to these general features in various ways. Maria Cummins adapted a reader-centered parlor authorship, while Louisa May Alcott re-created Hawthorne's notion of the author as romancer. Elizabeth Keckley and Mary Abigail Dodge presented a contractual model of authorship, and Elizabeth Stuart Phelps utilized a carefully constructed ethical model.

Some of these models apply to male authorship as well, one obvious example being the case of Alcott and Hawthorne. In this sense, I am sympathetic to Catherine Gallagher's claim, in her study of eighteenth-century British women writers, that "the 'feminine' aspects of their authorial personae only intensified contradictions implicit in authorship generally." In this view, women do not belong "to a separate tradition" but instead are "representatives of the condition of the author" in general.[5] Rather than argue that American authorship as a whole was a feminized construct, however, I want to single out the classificatory function of female authorship for particular analysis. In part, this is because nineteenth-century authors and critics did so; to recover the cultural field of nineteenth-century definitions we are required to consider women's authorship as a distinct, if not exclusive, category.

Pierre Bourdieu's explication of the competing principles of cultural hierarchy—the "heteronomous" and the "autonomous"—is useful here. The first refers to a notion of authorship ("the established definition of the writer") that arises from market demand and is therefore subject to external forces; its primary values are social utility and wide recognition. The second, which is the ideal aspired to by many high-art authors, sees "temporal failure as a sign of election and success as a sign of compromise." This autonomous principle supports an internal recognition of value (analogous to modern peer review) and can be a force both of radical experimentation (since it is not dependent on market "success") and of disciplinary policing (reinforcing the borders of values that have already been established). However, the main point of Bourdieu's analysis, I take it, is that, while competing in a "battlefield over taxonomy," these two principles are also inherently interconnected and reciprocal. One principle defines success as popular and the other as elite, but the idea of the elite would not exist without the popular. Although cultural production often exists as a struggle for a "monopoly of literary legitimacy," in other words, both sides of the struggle are fundamental to the production of that legitimacy.[6]

In general, contemporary studies of American women's authorship in the second half of the nineteenth century have understood women as

moving up in the literary hierarchy by proceeding from the heteronomous to the autonomous, or from writing for economic necessity to writing as artists for art's sake. This is, broadly, the progression traced by
Boyd and Sofer as well as by the scholars who influenced them, particularly Elizabeth Ammons, who sees the autonomous principle as leading to a coherent "pioneer generation" of women artists at the end of
the century, and Richard Brodhead, who traces the move toward high-
art authorship in Alcott and Jewett.[7] The complicating factor, however, is
that many of the female (and male) authors during this period assumed
different positions in relation to the literary field at various times in
their careers, and not necessarily in a coherent movement. Alcott, for
example, wrote a philosophical novel about the value of art, *Moods*,
before writing the market-driven *Little Women* and its sequels and then
moved to revise *Moods* near the end of her career. Phelps wrote a wildly
popular spiritualist novel, *The Gates Ajar*, and then a "high-art" novel, *The
Story of Avis*, only to move back at the end of her life to what she referred
to as hack writing. If such works are "position takings," as Bourdieu calls
them, they reflect ever-changing and variable positions in the literary
field. It is for this reason that Bourdieu cautions against "universalizing
the particular case," stating that analysts "will only ever encounter historical definitions of the writer, corresponding to a particular state of
the struggle to impose the legitimate definition of the writer."[8] By iso-
lating various examples of such historical definitions, *Reclaiming Authorship* investigates the historical functions of the category of female
authorship while also being attentive to its local practices.

   One effect of such a study is to recover the multiple terms under which
female authorship was defined and practiced in the second half of the
nineteenth century. Another effect is to question an oppositional mode
of scholarship that pits competing modes of authorship against each
other. Some such competition is, as Bourdieu makes clear, fundamental
to literary production. Indeed, literary critics and scholars also operate
within this inherently competitive "playing field," vying for the cultural
authority of their particular views. In the scholarly field of American
women's writing, this point has been historically evident in studies that
oppose literary value and cultural work, or artistic experimentation and
social justice, or professionalism and artistry. These struggles have the
effect not only of replicating debates that have already been waged on
behalf of male authors (note Boyd's emphasis on women taking up authorial positions formerly available only to men) but also of impeding new
ways of conceiving the field.

   Oppositional criticism does not have to be, I think, fundamental to
our own scholarly practices. Bourdieu suggests this when he defines his
methodology as helping to resolve tensions between close or "internal"

readings of cultural products and external or sociological ones.[9] By proposing models of authorship that do not fall neatly into either of Bourdieu's categories (or rather that partake aspects of both), I hope to move
the conversation beyond opposition and toward alternate ways of conceptualizing authorial labor. I do so in part because I think such alter-
natives more accurately reflect the lived experiences of the women I
study here, women who, while aware of the competing principles operating in the larger cultural field, did not necessarily define themselves
in terms of that competition.

For the purposes of this book, the most fundamental competing principles that I will be investigating are those embedded in the terms
"woman writer" and "female author." As we will see in Chapter 1, discussions about the relative status of these terms formed a key element
in the historical construction of authorship. On the whole, writers in the
nineteenth century were seen as occupying a lower (heteronomous) cultural plane than autonomous authors since they were defined as those
who wrote from experience or observation rather than from unique
genius or imagination. Authors, on the other hand, were associated with
a discrete, original, and prophetic imagination, a proprietary model of
production, and a personality anterior to the work of art.[10] In this scenario women were often cast as writers rather than authors, as having a
natural strength of observation and attention to detail that sometimes
precluded their imaginative range.

At the same time, the category of the "female author," particularly as
it was discussed in periodical columns and stories, recast this opposition
by embracing the experiential power of observation while also defining
writers as being less controlled and disciplined in their use of it. Authorship and writing, that is to say, had similar origins but different outcomes.
This idea of "universal exceptionalism," as Jennifer Cognard-Black has
put it, posited that authorship, as a profession, was broadly accessible—
available to anyone who wished to be trained into it—but also subject to
"structural limitations on who qualified as an appropriate trainee."[11] By
establishing criteria for what constituted authorship, professional female
authors—those who were paid for work that showed a particular level of
expertise—served as disciplinary gatekeepers. Yet, they did so, I think,
less to establish a "monopoly of literary legitimacy," as Bourdieu puts it,
than to give a realistic sense of the distance to be traveled between experiential observation and aesthetic production. The representation of such
distance, in turn, demystified the concept of artistic "genius" and, by the
end of the century, consolidated authorship as a category that could be
applied to women as well as to men.

Given this history, it is significant that contemporary criticism, influenced by postmodernism, has come to privilege the term "writer" rather

than "author." Within the field of nineteenth-century American women's writing, even scholars interested in the relation of women to "high art," such as Sofer and Cognard-Black, use the term "writer" or "artist," whereas in the nineteenth century "author" would have been the requisite term. The Society for the Study of American Women Writers (SSAWW), the field's main scholarly organization, also reflects this shift, as do the two most influential publishing ventures for American women in the past two decades: the Rutgers American Women Writers series (1986–93) and Oxford's Schomburg Library of Black Women Writers (1988–2002).

Taken together, the Schomburg and Rutgers series constitute a new canon of women's literature, one that scholars and the general public can line up on their bookshelves. The Rutgers series was, as coeditor Judith Fetterley puts it, "recovery made visible," a "notable dream" despite its "innocent" assumption that it could "provide in one collectible book-shelf all the significant texts of prose fiction produced by American women in the nineteenth century."[12] Oxford University Press issued the complete forty- volume set of the Schomburg series in 2002 so that it too could be lined up in a row. The blue binding and gilt lettering on the covers of these volumes resemble nothing so much as the house style of the nineteenth-century Boston publisher Ticknor and Fields, which in 1856 began to use blue and gold to distinguish its pocket editions of high-art publications.[13] Oxford, like Ticknor and Fields, is publishing a distinctive, library-quality series that helps give prestige to previously neglected authors. In this sense, it serves as an important counterpart to another recent (and ongoing) series, the Library of America, which seeks to provide "handsome, enduring volumes" to individuals and institutions and defines itself as being "dedicated to preserving the works of America's greatest writers." Writers, not authors, can now be associated with high art, greatness, and longevity, whatever their previous status.

To some extent this shift has operated more as a disciplinary unconscious than as a polemical practice. Despite the critical currency of the term "writer," much of the recovery work done on these writers has of necessity utilized traditional modes of single-author study, focusing on such issues as biography and publishing history.[14] Early covers of *Legacy* (now the official journal of the SSAWW) included a list of individual names of women (repeated in various patterns), a graphic display both of the presence of what had previously been an absence in American literary history and of the controlling idea of the journal (see Figure 1). These early issues also featured profiles of individual women as well as photographs of their historic homes. By focusing on the recovery of these women's personal lives, the journal was implicitly working to recover their status as personalities—authors—behind particular works.

Figure 1. Cover of *Legacy*, vol. 3 (spring 1986).

At the same time, since the records and archives for some women were more available than others, these biographical profiles lifted up certain women over others—something that the use of the term "writer" (and the cover of *Legacy*) seemed to want to guard against. Although the generation of scholars who first did the work of recovery found new ways of conceptualizing literary value, the succeeding scholarship has in fact shown that some writers have appealed more to current critical taste than have others. There have been special issues of *Legacy* devoted to Emily Dickinson and Willa Cather, and the first major conference of nineteenth-century American women writers was prompted by and organized around the centenary of Harriet Beecher Stowe. At the SSAWW's first international conference in 2001, the most frequently talked about nineteenth-century figures were Dickinson, Fuller, and Jewett, and in 2003 Stowe, Dickinson, and Gilman were the focus of discussion. In part this is because each of these women (except for Jewett) has a scholarly society devoted to research on her works, and these societies are signs in themselves of continuing interest in individual authors. Ironically, the only panel at either of these conferences to use the word "author" was one in 2001 entitled "Historicism and the Present: A Discussion of Lesser-Studied Nineteenth Century Authors." The wording of this panel title suggests that more frequently studied figures can safely be called "writers" but that understudied ones are still fighting for the legitimacy that the term "author" provides.[15] (It is instructive, in this regard, that scholars in digital media studies currently speak of "web authors" rather than "web writers.")

I note these phenomena not to criticize either *Legacy* or the SSAWW conference, both of which have been crucial to the formation and growth of American women's writing as a field. Rather, I want to note that despite the wide use of the term "writer," there are still certain women whose lives and works receive the lion's share of critical attention and who are treated as individual "authors." They are for the most part the usual suspects, the figures who have been visible in twentieth-century American literary history the longest. Appropriately enough, Harriet Beecher Stowe and Emily Dickinson—each of whom was the focus of a total of fifteen papers over the two conferences—are also featured on the "American Women Authors Card Game," currently manufactured by U.S. Games Systems, Inc. (see Figure 2). In this respect, my call to talk about women as "authors" may diverge from current critical terminology more than it does from actual practice. However, I want to suggest that we need to synchronize practice and terminology, particularly given the fact that so many nineteenth-century women worked hard to claim themselves as "authors."

If the actual study of American women has often taken an author-centered approach, why has "writer" become the privileged term in the

DOROTHY PARKER | HARRIET BEECHER STOWE | SARAH ORNE JEWETT

AMERICAN WOMEN AUTHORS
CARD GAME

Portraits by Virginijus Poshkus
Edited by Carolyn P. Karwoski

EDITH WHARTON | EMILY DICKINSON | PHILLIS WHEATLEY

Printed in Belgium

U.S. GAMES SYSTEMS, INC.

Copyright © 1994 by
U.S. GAMES SYSTEMS, INC.
Stamford, CT 06902 USA

Figure 2. Title card of the "American Women Authors Card Game."
Reproduced by permission of U.S. Games Systems, Inc., Stamford, Conn.
Copyright 1994. Further reproduction prohibited.

scholarly field? The main answer to this question is that the use of the term has achieved some salutary political and scholarly functions. First, it has reclaimed a "master" term, shifting attention from the myth of a God-like single creator by converting the "damned mob of scribbling women" (made famous by Hawthorne's phrase in a letter to his publisher) into writers of great variety, complexity, and depth.[16] Second, use of the term has expanded the literary field to include writing of all kinds—not only prose, drama, and poetry but also letters, diaries, advice books, travel accounts, and anything else that women wrote. (In the case of the Library of America, however, this expansion has not led to increased access to women's writing; as of 2005 there are titles by sixty-one male authors and twelve female ones, with only three of these being offered in "college editions" suitable for classroom use.) Third, use of the term "writer" has bracketed issues of canonicity. Since the term "author" is taken to be more privileged than "writer," calling all women "writers" means not having to discriminate among different kinds of literary production.[17] Fourth, it has highlighted the political aims of women's writing, allowing for a criticism based on identity politics that is not as easily open to the proprietary term "author." Last, use of the term "writer" has created a synergy between the women being recovered and the women doing the work of recovery. Few scholars that I know would call themselves "authors," but almost all of us do talk about our writing (or lack of it). A roundtable discussion at the 2003 SSAWW conference examined "Twenty-First Century Working Women Writing on Nineteenth-Century Women Writing Work," thereby stressing the continuity between the women doing the work of literary recovery and the women writers they are recovering.[18] The hard work of writing scholarship and the hard work undertaken by nineteenth-century women writers are mutually reinforced by the homologous term "writer."

Underlying all of this is the general shift, in literary study, from authorship to writing in the wake of theoretical debates about the "death of the author." To be sure, the emergence of book history as a critical field has helped to resurrect the importance of authorship to what Robert Darnton calls "a full understanding of the transmission of texts."[19] Yet, the influence of Roland Barthes's claim that the reader, not the author, is the originator of textual meaning remains strong. Barthes's notion that texts could be made of "multiple writings" shifts the focus away from a hypercompetitive and possessive "authordoxy," as one critic puts it, that "does not allow . . . for that which may be authoritative without being authoritarian."[20] Yet, as feminist critics have shown, Barthes declared the author dead just at the moment when women had again become culturally visible in that position. "For the author to die," as Christine Battersby puts it, "he must first have lived." Barthes saw the author as a kind of imperialist category—as a concept that "still reigns" and "tyran-nically" limits the play of language—but his willingness to dismiss the category was itself an act of male privilege and patriarchal oppression that was, in Battersby's words, "parasitic on the canons of 'great texts' and 'great authors' established by Modernism."[21] Michel Foucault, in his response to Barthes, supports this view when he notes that the concept of writing (*écriture*) "sustains the privileges of the author through the safeguard of the a priori."[22] Foucault's solution to this is the concept of a discursive "author function" and the related idea that authorship is a necessary cultural construction that is usefully applied to some works but not to others. As such, it serves a "certain functional principle."

Understanding authorship as a functional principle—a principle that both converges and diverges with actual literary practice—necessitates reclaiming it from its romantic, modern, and postmodern constructions. Doing so allows us to think about female authorship as its own func-tional principle (if not tradition) and about the specific ways in which it enabled and sometimes disabled women who wanted to adapt it to their own ends. This does not mean dismissing the various critiques of author-ship waged in contemporary criticism; it is crucial to understand the structures of privilege surrounding the term and to be attentive to the ways in which it functioned to deny access to certain kinds of literary production. However, it does mean being aware of our own use of the term and remembering the great lengths to which some nineteenth-century women went to claim the title "author." Foucault acknowledges the significance of "a sociohistorical analysis of the author as an individ-ual persona" that would include a study of the "status" of authorship at particular historical moments.[23] It is this status that I seek to unpack in this book and reclaim as an important lens through which to understand the history of women's literary production.

A corollary of this claim is that it is important to continue to support single-author studies of American women. This goes against the grain of current publishing trends, which support studies (like this one) that think about literary and cultural formations and an array of authors and texts. But just as feminist scholars were right to complain that the death of the author came before the birth of the female author, so too should we worry about the death of single-author and bibliographical studies just at the moment when they are most needed in the feminist project of recovery. For the most part, women authors lack the authoritative tex-tual and bibliographic information that has been given to many of their male peers. This lack, in turn, means that it is difficult to do some of the basic work involved in studying the history of authorship. The Modern Language Association's Center for Editions of American *Authors* (my emphasis), for example, is now subsumed into the work of the Committee on Scholarly Editions. No longer does it exist to fund and coordinate editorial work for standard editions of American works, as it did in 1968, when director William Gibson was able to report in the *New York Review of Books* that he was overseeing the preparation of authoritative editions of Emerson's works, the Centenary Hawthorne edition published by Ohio State University Press (which ended in 1994 without a projected volume of Sophia Hawthorne's letters), a complete Thoreau, the Mark Twain Papers, the Indiana University Howells project, and the Northwestern-Newberry Edition of Melville. Instead, its main function is advisory and evaluative, providing guidelines for editors of scholarly editions, both digital and print. This broadening makes it applicable to all periods, nationalities, and languages but does not provide focused help—both financial and editorial—for scholars seeking to establish appropriate copy texts for, say, the complete works of Elizabeth Stuart Phelps.[24]

Although there are some fine scholarly editions of female authors available—examples include Jean Fagan Yellin's edition of Jacobs's *Incidents in the Life of a Slave Girl* and her new digital Jacobs archive; R. W. Franklin's edition of Dickinson's poetry (published, like the Jacobs text, by Harvard); and the Willa Cather Scholarly Edition published by the University of Nebraska Press—there are no complete authoritative scholarly editions of the works even of such canonical authors as Alcott, Stowe, or Jewett, not to mention of more newly emergent ones. I hope that my study will inspire in-depth, single-author studies and editions of the women, in addition to Alcott, presented here: Cummins, Dodge, Keckley, and Phelps.[25]

Although these authors are known, studied, and in print, they have not received as much attention as some of their peers have, despite the fact that they were better known in the nineteenth century. Cummins's *The Lamplighter* sold more copies than Susan Warner's *The Wide, Wide World,* and yet it is often conflated with Warner's work as an exemplum of the domestic and/or sentimental novel (the terms shift). Alcott, although a figure of continuing fascination, has on the whole received less critical attention than has another key mid-century figure, Harriet Beecher Stowe. Dodge ("Gail Hamilton"), as a humorist and cultural critic, is now less well-known than her friend Fanny Fern. Elizabeth Keckley's narrative has been overshadowed by Harriet Jacobs's *Incidents in the Life of a Slave Girl.* Phelps, one of the most prolific and varied authors of the nineteenth century, has been seen primarily in tandem with other authors who correlate to various parts of her career: Rebecca Harding Davis in terms of her depiction of the working class; George Eliot in conjunction with *The Story of Avis;* Sarah Orne Jewett in the depiction of the woman doctor. The regionalist contributions of Constance Fenimore Woolson, whose story "Miss Grief" I consider in the epilogue, tend to be subordinated to those of New Englanders such as Jewett and Mary Wilkins Freeman. My aim, however, is to depict these authors as key proponents of certain practices of women's authorship more than as forgotten influences.

Each of the authors presented here highlights a particular practice of female authorship in the second half of the nineteenth century. Although I make no claims that these women provide an exhaustive history of authorship between 1850 and 1900, I do believe that they represent some of the key models available to women at this time. As shown in Chapters 1 and 2, all of these models worked within the context of prevailing definitions of authorship put forward in magazines, advice books, letters to aspiring writers, and literary accounts of authors. It is notable, for instance, that Mrs. A. J. Graves's 1847 list of the ideal subject matter for female novelists reads as a template for much of the fiction discussed in this book. Graves advised that women write not about "artificial women of fashion" but rather about a "humble seamstress," "the experience of the solitary female orphan," "the struggle of the widowed mother," or "the trials of the much-enduring, neglected, and oppressed wife of the brutal inebriate"—a list that we can see in practice in Elizabeth Keckley's account of her work as a seamstress, Maria Cummins's depiction of the orphan Gerty, and Alcott's and Phelps's representations of the lives of wives and mothers.[26] Yet, even as these writings correspond to Graves's list, the authors who produced them demonstrate a range of approaches and concerns.

Maria Cummins, with whom I begin, exemplifies the link between the amateur manuscript culture of the parlor and professional authorship. Writing initially to her nieces, in *The Lamplighter* she converts what is essentially a private parlor performance into an international best-seller. Such "parlor literature" emphasizes the moment of telling between narrator and reader, thereby highlighting the importance of reception to any construction of authorship.

My study of Louisa May Alcott in Chapter 4 explores how she reanimates the well-worn notion that literary realism emerged as a response to the Civil War. By examining some of Alcott's Civil War writing, I show how she created a form of domestic realism that was synonymous with— not a delayed reaction to—the war. This realism reanimated the model of romance practiced by her Concord neighbor Nathaniel Hawthorne while at the same time reaching toward a vision of revolution as an alternate model of civil conflict. These concerns, I argue, characterize Alcott's "sensational" writing as well as her domestic writing, leading to a model of authorship that is fluid and dynamic rather than internally divided.

Elizabeth Keckley and Mary Abigail Dodge, the subjects of Chapter 5, represent a different form of authorial conflict: that between an author and her male mediators, particularly publishers. Although both of these women experienced such conflict, their writings remain optimistic about the ability of legal obligations and what I term "contractual authorship" to provide material support for writing. Assimilating preindustrial models (personal letters and collaborative female friendships) into their exposés of the business of the marketplace, they did not oppose the market and "private" writing but rather defined authorship as a way of constituting both. Their racial differences influenced their relations to legal rights, but they represent authorship in similar ways as both a right and an obligation.

In Chapter 6, I offer a comprehensive case study of Elizabeth Stuart Phelps, who in many ways merges the parlor writing of Cummins, the domestic realism of Alcott, and the business sense of Keckley and Dodge. In doing so, she redefines creative isolation as a form of productive citizenship. Although she advocates attending to the details of the business of publishing, she sees this business as integral to her construction of an ethical model of authorship.

The final chapter, an epilogue, presents thoughts about Constance Fenimore Woolson as an example of an author who was attracted to romantic authorship but also understood it to be inherently solipsistic and self-absorbed, as excluding those who most needed to hear its words. It is not surprising that she is often thought of in concert with (or as a footnote to) Henry James, who perhaps more than any other late nineteenth-century author was both attracted to and frightened by the models of female authorship he saw around him. I end with a short meditation on James, not to label him a "female author" or to say that the payoff of studying women authors is to better understand James, but rather to point to ways in which the model of authorship I trace might be applied well beyond the immediate cases put forward here.

In turn, these case studies challenge us to rethink the primacy of an oppositional, resistant model of authorship in the second half of the nineteenth century. Foucault has taught us that authorship is founded on transgression; books needed real authors at the historical moment "when the author became subject to punishment and to the extent that his discourse was considered transgressive."[27] To be sure, some authors, males and females, thrived on such an oppositional model, particularly insofar as it defined itself as resisting the popular marketplace or conventional literary form. One of the most long-standing metanarratives of American literary history (one that is currently being questioned by transnational studies) defines American literature as arising out of a need to detach itself from its British "mother" and create literary heritages that would befit the new nation. The qualities of self-reliance, orphaning, and individualism that enabled literary nationalism have in turn

informed many histories of American authorship. As Nina Baym has persuasively argued, there is an entire strain of American literary history
that defined the best writing (and authors) as presenting "melodramas
of beset manhood."[28] In recent years the critical emphasis has been less
on "beset manhood" (the way in which male heroes are troubled by and
resist the civilizing influences of maternal women) than on "beset womanhood" or "beset commodity culture." In the former, the texts (and
the women producing them) that are most valued are those that either
critique patriarchal literary tradition through a poetics of irony or anger,
or that are themselves shown to be complicit in imperialist and nationalist violence. In the latter, virtually every American author—whether
male or female—is seen both as catering to and resisting an increasingly
variegated and growing literary market.[29]

I suspect that part of this oppositional relation has to do with scholars'
own contested relations to the market and to their own writing. We work
to preserve time for our "real work" of writing—which in turn deter-
mines our tenure, promotion, and professional standing—even while
hearing from the Modern Language Association and other sources that
there may soon be no market for our books. Yet the most remarkable
thing about these women's authorial manifestos, to my mind, is that
they are not particularly beset by anything. That is not to say that they
do not recognize the challenges they have getting into print and with-
standing the criticism sometimes leveled against them. But they imagine
a kind of authorship in which productivity is not inherently linked to
alienation or violence.

My goal in offering such a corrective is not simply to invert the gender
hierarchy by arguing that male authors were the insecure, marginalized,
and alienated artists who were vying for readers alongside the successful
"scribbling mob" of women. Such an inversion is suggested in Michael
Davitt Bell's remark that "we should also recognize that if there was anxiety or antagonism between these male and female 'traditions,' it flowed
almost exclusively in one direction. Writers like Hawthorne and Melville
aroused little professional anxiety in popular women writers."[30] Bell's view
of male anxiety is supported, in turn, by nineteenth-century commentaries such as an 1851 *North American Review* essay, "Female Authors."
This essay cites a "witty satire" of Marmontel, *La Femme Auteur*, in which
two lovers, Natalie and Germeuil, are perfectly content until Natalie
achieves success as an author, at which point Germeuil begins to affect
"an obstinate opposition to every thing she said."[31] The very fact of
Natalie's success leads Germeuil to adopt a defensive oppositional stance.
An 1853 article in the *United States Review* makes a direct appeal for men
to convert this defensiveness into active competition for the literary
market: "American authors, be men and heroes! Make sacrifices, . . . but

publish books . . . for the hope of the future and the honor of America. Do not leave its literature in the hands of a few industrious females."[32]

In the end, however, such a blame game spirals in on itself: nineteenth-century men were envious of women's success, then twentieth-century women were envious of men's success in the process of canonization, and so on. Such formulations do not move us beyond familiar oppositions between the high and the popular or the male and the female; instead, they simply shift their terms. *Reclaiming Authorship* encourages us to move beyond such oppositional thinking and to focus instead on the thoughtful commentaries that specific women offered about the trajectories, practices, and even pleasures of authorship. These commentaries, I trust, will ultimately illuminate the history of authorship for men as well as for women.

Chapter 1

Defining Female Authorship

In recent years, one of the most frequently cited critical shorthands for the plight of women writers in the United States has been Fanny Fern's assertion, in *Ruth Hall* (1854), that "no happy woman ever writes."[1] Fern's immediate context for this statement is the fact that Ruth, like Fern, was initially forced to write out of economic necessity, not artistic passion. A quick survey of nineteenth-century American fictional writers supports Fern's statement. Mrs. James, in Elizabeth Stuart Phelps's "The Angel over the Right Shoulder," becomes happy only when she abandons her idea of writing in her study two hours each day. St. Elmo, in Augusta Evans's novel of that name, ends his wife's writing career by saying, "To-day I snap the fetters of your literary bondage. There shall be no more books written! No more study, no more toil, no more anxiety, no more heartaches!"[2] Jo March, in Louisa May Alcott's *Little Women*, starts writing with a vengeance after she has broken off relations with Laurie, but she stops writing altogether after her marriage to Professor Bhaer, at least until the sequels. The unnamed narrator of Charlotte Perkins Gilman's "The Yellow Wallpaper" writes herself into madness. Even when women were not forced to write out of financial necessity, the story would seem to go, writing was not a happy activity, leading instead to isolation, bondage, and even madness. At the same time, unhappiness was supposed to produce greatness. As one advice book for women put it in 1883, "Books written under difficulties are nearly always the most successful, as the friction of adverse circumstances brings out more freely the sparks of genius."[3]

Reclaiming Authorship will give plenty of evidence of the difficulties faced by female authors throughout the nineteenth century, particularly having to do with receiving adequate compensation for literary production. But in many ways, this book is meant to be a corrective to Fern's idea, or at least a modification of it. *Ruth Hall* is not, of course, a transparent index of Fern's own ideas toward authorship, given her ironic tone and multilayered use of literary veils. Although the other examples given above could also be seen as ironic critiques of nineteenth-century cultural devaluations of female artistry, the fact that the phrase has been so frequently cited also reflects our own critical preoccupations. To some extent we need writing to have been unhappy for nineteenth-century women. It is still a struggle to find time to write, and we empathize with these women. In addition, the male authors of the period most talked about now were the most unhappy or tortured ones—Nathaniel Hawthorne, Herman Melville, Henry James; it is politically important to register the fact that women were just as unhappy. The gradual movement from unhappy nineteenth-century to happy (or at least happier) twenty-first-century women authors also creates a cultural success story that we love to tell. In 1854 no happy woman wrote; in 2002 Carol Shields, a Pulitzer Prize-winning novelist, could write a book about a female novelist who is for the first time moving beyond "the useful monotony of happiness." This character, Reta Winters, does go through a period of unhappiness because of a struggle with her teenage daughter, but it does not have to do with her writing. By the age of forty-three, Reta has published ten books while also raising three daughters, for whom she prepares three meals a day. If she has had anxiety about her marriage interfering with her writing, it has been "unnecessary" anguish; her husband's "ego was unchallenged" by her success.[4] A period of a century and a half has led us from happy endings to happy beginnings, from an unhappy woman moving into authorship to a too-happy woman moving away from it.

And yet the story is obviously not as neat as this formulation would suggest. Although there were many struggles attendant to nineteenth-century authorship, clearly it could also bring great satisfaction and even happiness to its practitioners. "I am happy, very happy tonight," Alcott wrote to her mother after finishing *Moods*, "for my five years work is done, and whether it succeeds or not, I shall be the richer and better for it, because the labor, love, disappointment, hope and purpose that have gone into it, are a useful experience that I shall never forget."[5] Later in the century Sarah Orne Jewett wrote to a friend, "I have been delightfully well and busy with work and play ever since I came home"; Rebecca Harding Davis described literature as "an easy, respectable way" of earning a living; and Edith Wharton characterized her writing of *Ethan Frome* as a "state of fatuous satisfaction."[6] It was not that writing did not involve "labor" and "disappointment," as Alcott put it, but that such labor was balanced by satisfying "love" and "purpose."

When women did take the time to think about authorial anxiety, it was more in the name of equal rights than aesthetic ideals, and even then they realized that the biggest losers were themselves. As shown in Chapter 5, Mary Abigail Dodge spent more than two years fighting against and writing about her mistreatment by Ticknor and Fields, but in doing so she ultimately lost not only about $750 of her own money but also valuable writing time. It is better, she argued, for an author "to take what a publisher chooses to give than to make an ado about it afterwards. Even if successful in regard to the particular sum he claims, it is at a cost of time and trouble altogether disproportionate to it. He plays an un-equal game at best, because the publisher's business goes on serenely, during all the difficulty, while the author's must be at a stand-still. The very instrument that he uses in defending his works is the instrument which he ought to be using in producing them."[7]

Dodge maintained high standards for her writing and recognized the discrimination in pay that some women faced. But she also understood the importance of the literary market in enabling her to do the work she loved and in circulating her ideas. It is in this sense that I think Michael Davitt Bell is right to say that the anxiety between male and female "tra-ditions" of authorship "flowed almost exclusively in one direction," with men projecting their anxieties onto women.[8] Literary historians have often associated such anxiety in the second half of the nineteenth cen-tury with the conversion of high art into a more rigidly masculine field that would escape the "contaminating" effects of women.[9] Yet even at high-water moments of such cultural stratification, such as the all-male 1877 dinner celebrating the twentieth anniversary of the *Atlantic*, "patri-archal perspectives did not completely define women's options nor their view of themselves in the world," as Susan Coultrap-McQuin puts it.[10] To support this point, Coultrap-McQuin cites "Mr. Houghton's Mistake," a newspaper account that depicts important women authors—including Stowe, Alcott, Cooke, and Dodge, who probably wrote it—declining to attend the dinner to which Houghton had surely meant to invite them and announcing their intention to start a ladies' magazine. There was a sense that anxiety and its opposite, festive celebrations, were forms of leisure in which these working women had no desire or time to indulge. Rather than worry about the slight, they just kept writing, getting a story into print almost as the dinner was being served.

My goal is not to downplay or dismiss the struggles that attend author-ship, but rather to provide a counterpoint to a dominant trajectory of unhappiness in describing it. The quotations and examples above are no more definitive of an entire career than is Ruth Hall's formulation of unhappiness, but it is the latter that is more frequently invoked. Indeed, some contemporary critics have portrayed women as internalizing the notion that writing was a form of constraint, as in Richard Brodhead's reading of Alcott as "need[ing] to *need* to write, need[ing] to think of her work as not willed but constrained." In this view, overdetermined choices both illuminate and limit authorship; we can see authors in new ways but also see them as defining themselves only through an oppositional mode that posits self-sacrifice as the primary motivation for writing. Within such a context, agency comes through what Linda Grasso has defined as an "artistry of anger," following a mode of criticism, most clearly traceable to Gilbert and Gubar's *The Madwoman in the Attic,* that views women's writing as defined by a resistance and anger toward patriarchal oppression.[11] This scholarship has been important in showing the complexity of women's writing—its ability to have subversive messages undercutting its often conventional plot lines—as well as the growing sophistication of women's self-awareness and sexual politics in the nineteenth century. Yet this scholarship has also sometimes skewed the historical record, looking for examples of unhappiness rather than satisfaction, violence rather than sociability, subversion rather than convention.

Throughout this book, and in this chapter in particular, I want to shift the focus by looking more closely at how female authorship was theorized in the nineteenth century. What we might expect to find is a kind of disciplining of unhappy female authors by male critics, a disciplining that worked to ensure their place in the domestic sphere even as it acknowledged that women did have something to offer. And indeed there is a certain amount of this, some of which inspired heated replies. In 1857, for example, the novelist Thrace Talmon (Ellen Tryphosa Harrington) used the front page of the *National Era* to take up a "crusade" against a critic in the *New York Observer* who had recommended that women should take up washing or nursing in order to stop writing the "mob of novels that have flooded the country within the last three years or so." Talmon— the author of several novels—turns the tables by advising critics to spend their time instead analyzing real "existing evils in various ranks," especially slavery. She also cautions against overgeneralizing; there are, she acknowledges, books that ought to be condemned, but there are also "highly gifted" women whose talents ought to be nurtured.[12]

Talmon's response is indicative of other nineteenth-century female authors who felt authorized to define what authorship entailed and who should be able to aspire to it. It was not that they believed that all happy women should write, or that all authors were univocally happy. But they did work to theorize the terms on which female authorship should be viewed, thereby establishing the grounds by which to judge its success. They were not uncritical in thinking about the position of the female author; the sheer number of stories and essays about writers and writings shows that there was a great deal of thought about the subject. But neither did they—like Shields's Reta Winters—engage in anxiety for its own sake. Instead, they channeled their energies toward the production of literature and the goals they set for it—goals set in part by the principles outlined in writing devoted to authorship, particularly in periodicals. In what follows, I will argue that this writing justified female authorship through three interrelated principles: first, that female authorship could be distinguished from the productions of women with a mere "writing itch," or *cacoëthes scribendi*; second, that women's "natural" powers of observation gave them particular power as authors; and third, that issues of authorial rights, including copyright, occupied a particular place within the category of female authorship.

Cacoëthes Scribendi and Authorship

One of the first things to notice about periodical essays on female authorship is the unstable taxonomy the essayists use in referring to their subjects. Such essays contain terms as various as "novel-writers," "female writers," "literary females," "literary women," "lady-novelists," "female novelists," "writing women," and "authors." Some essay writers vacillate almost in the same sentence between the terms "author" and "writer." One overview of "female authorship," for example, "recollect[s] with gratitude the authoresses who acted as pioneers" but refers to them as "women writers" when it is time to give "candid judgment." Another essayist on "female writers" talks about "authors" when women publish their work but "writers" when referring to "the purity and delicacy that characterize" that work.[13] Even within this shifting taxonomy, however, female authorship came to represent a specific category of literary production: one that was specifically distinguished from the now more common term "writer."

One of the most systematic ways in which the category of American female authorship was developed over the course of the nineteenth century was through what I will term "the *cacoëthes scribendi* plot." Taken from Juvenal's phrase meaning "writer's itch," the phrase *cacoëthes scribendi* became a stock way to talk about amateur, unrestrained writing as opposed to professionalized authorship. Its earliest iterations, interestingly enough, involve men rather than women, and they do not necessarily have negative connotations. Indeed, the earliest example I have found appears in an 1824 issue of a medical journal, the *Boston Medical Intelligencer*, in a plea to physicians to write about their medical findings. Entitled "Cacoethes Scribendi," the editorial notes the irony of encouraging more of "that rare malady, the name of which we have placed at the head of this article," when "it is our business to relieve and prevent diseases." Nor does it want to "induce every person who deals out a cathartic to become an author."[14] But the implication is that if put to productive uses, a little itch is a good thing. As numerous subsequent stories demonstrated, however, the problem occurred when the malady was not "rare" but rather ubiquitous. For men, this excess was dangerous but not ultimately debilitating. In one story "John Smith" writes verses to his beloved and ends up living in "dreary bachelorship" because the proofreader misreads his manuscript and produces a text that humiliates its intended recipient. Yet, Smith still consoles himself by "seeing [his] thoughts in print." Another story promises that a writing-obsessed young man will eventually be "purged" of his disease when he sees the reviews of his work. By the end of the century, the notion of the writing itch could be associated with particular aspects of a male authorial career: one 1904 review labels a poorly written political treatise as the work of "a gentleman who is afflicted with the *cacoethes scribendi*," while also noting that he is the "author" of other books.[15] It is a disease, but the goal is not to stop these men from getting into print as much as to suggest that there might be better uses of one's time.

Such versions of the *cacoëthes scribendi* plot remind us that nineteenth-century writers had multiple reasons for wanting to get into print, not all of which had to do with earning money within an increasingly industrialized marketplace. Amateur writing, as Ronald and Mary Zboray have recently argued, has an important place within nineteenth-century publishing history since it indicates that "a mass market for literature, served by multitudinous small operators, indeed had emerged *ahead* of extensive mass production and national distribution emanating from a few highly capitalized forms."[16] When "John Smith" writes to his beloved, even at the risk of being distorted in print, he is writing out of a social need to memorialize his love rather than from a sense of professional "calling," and such social writing registers an important counterpoint to the supposed impersonality of the marketplace.

The move to disentangle authorship from capitalism and the extensive celebrity system that accompanies it would seem, on first glance, to make it a much more capacious category: amateurs participating in social authorship coexist alongside professionals participating in a more market-driven one. Such a move is particularly helpful in bringing in minority writers whose social position did not allow them to conceive of authorship in market terms. It helps make sense, for example, of a literary career such as that of Charlotte Forten, who in her journal aspired to "write a beautiful poem of two hundred lines in my sleep as Coleridge did," but who when asked by an acquaintance about her writing replied, "No, sir, I *never* wrote any [poems]." Making occasional money from her writing, Forten occupied a "borderline," in the Zborays' terms, "between amateurism and professionalism," and between a focus on "social sense" and the marketplace respectively.[17] Yet I believe that such an emphasis on amateur writing—like the move toward the death of the author and liberation of writers—potentially devalues the work that certain nineteenth-century women did in order to establish themselves as professionals with particular talent, expertise, and discipline. Furthermore, it risks devaluing the alternate professionalisms that these authors endorsed, professionalisms that were not always synonymous with market success. Xiomara Santamarina, for example, has recently described the Cincinnati hairdresser Eliza Potter as defining her authority through her social expertise rather than through her literary abilities, but as a professional nonetheless.[18] Such a redefinition echoes what many nineteenth-century authors claimed about their own profession: that they were professionals less because of their financial compensation than because of their ability to combine innate talent with practice and self-discipline, or calling with restraint.

In *cacoëthes scribendi* stories about women, this combination justifies authorial labor on three fronts, distinguishing authors from writers by insisting that female authorship has a natural basis, a disciplinary function, and a social utility. On the flip side, female characters afflicted with the writing itch have a greater need for cure than similarly afflicted men do, particularly insofar as the affliction interferes with the possibility of marriage. (The "dreary bachelorhood" of John Smith does not convert into a comfortably dreary spinsterhood.) These stories tend to fall into two camps: women who cure their *cacoëthes scribendi* by turning from frivolous to useful subjects; and women who cure it by giving up writing altogether in order to take up the duties of being wives.

The first type is less frequent but is exemplified in an 1864 *Godey's Lady's Book* story in which a woman turns from "writing silly stories for mere amusement" to writing a story about the dangers of excessive drinking and smoking. This story is ostensibly written for a magazine, but it is really meant to reform the woman's brother, whom she asks to evaluate it for her. Also in this category is "When I Was a Man," an 1893 story about the predicament a woman finds herself in when her editor and fans want to meet the man under whose name she has been writing. The goal here is not for her to give up writing but rather to avoid the "secrecy with which I chose to conduct my cacoethes scribendi."[19] Seriousness and truth-telling here replace amusing trifles, with the implication that real authors can come before the public as long as they have a clear moral purpose.

The other, more frequent type of *cacoëthes scribendi* story imagines that the result of successful writing is not as satisfying as a happy marriage. The best-known example of this type is Catharine Maria Sedgwick's 1830 *Atlantic Souvenir* story of the writing itch that afflicts the women in a small village when they decide to contribute to a literary annual. Everything and everyone in the village becomes fair game for the ladies' writing; only the heroine of the tale, Alice, resists the urge. The narrative sides with Alice in saying that not every potential writer should actually get into print, mocking the way in which Alice's aunt feels a "call" to become an author—a "divinity stirring within her"—simply by virtue of seeing the work of some of her friends in print.[20] Alice, on the other hand, wins the hand of the most eligible (and almost the only) man in town by virtue of resisting the itch. Other stories depict women who do not share Alice's ability to withstand the itch but do succeed in overcoming it when they get married. One such woman "darned [her husband's] stockings and sewed on his shirt-buttons, and never, never wrote for the magazines any more."[21] Another woman writes for a while after she marries, but in the end, as she sees her husband "walking the grounds, and as my conscience rather smites me, I lock up the last quire of foolscap, and resolve to forget the meaning of *cacoëthes scribendi.*"[22] Only one story I have located imagines a happily married mother who continues to write. She calls herself a "young author," and if she has disappointments, they come not from her domestic life but rather from the fact that everyone she meets claims to be an author too. "Strange to say, almost everybody who spoke to me did write, . . . had written, or *could write if he chose it.*"[23] She is a happy woman who writes, and yet it is crucial to the story that she is an author—someone with particular talent and devotion—rather than someone with *cacoëthes scribendi.*

This story underscores a larger point about these stories about females with *cacoëthes scribendi,* which is that they were all written by women. When Sedgwick puts Alice's tale into print, she implicitly identifies herself as an author who, unlike the amateur annual contributors, has earned her place in print. Having already published three successful novels, Sedgwick writes a tale that valorizes her assumption of authorship even as it endorses the virtues of marriage and a domestic ideal. The women behind these stories are exerting disciplinary quality control, critiquing indiscriminate writing through stories that they themselves have succeeded in getting into print. It is true that they were submitting those stories to magazines that were, for the most part, edited and published by men, and there is a sense in which they could be said to have internalized the party line. But the frequency with which they did so reminds us of the cultural stakes at play in the adoption of the term "author" rather than "writer."

Female authors frequently extended the notion of the writing itch into their essays as well, particularly those aimed at giving advice to those thinking of joining their profession. *Godey's* staff editor Alice Neal, for example, complained about the ramifications of the "*cacoëthes scribendi,*" in which "school-girl days" are "haunted with visions of magazine covers" and "authorship is the mania of our ladies."[24] Elizabeth Stoddard similarly complained in an 1854 essay in the *Daily Alta California* that most published women follow their whims rather than striving for intellectual and artistic excellence. "The eight books in ten are written without genius; all show industry, and a few talent. Their authors are Bedouins: Hagar should be the name of some, and some should be nameless."[25] Hagar, Sarah's handmaiden, mothered a child with Abraham but was not his legitimate wife, and Stoddard's allusion suggests that not all authors are legitimately entitled to the status of "genius"—though her use of the term indicates that Stoddard is. Here the virtues of industry and talent are essential to authorship, although Stoddard subjects the category of author to even further discrimination, identifying the upper quintile as in the "genius" category. In "Collected by a Valetudinarian" (1870), Stoddard fictionalizes one of those rare geniuses, Alicia Raymond. For Raymond, however, authorship is not connected to publication; she is "perfectly obscure," except "to a few men and women of letters with whom she corresponded." Even when her cousin Helen recovers her unpublished manuscripts, she refuses to publish them, letting their "world of beauty and truth" "be lost to the world."[26] Alicia occupies a form of social authorship—one in which her work is available to only a small coterie of friends and family—but is, by Stoddard's definition, an author nonetheless.

The 1860s and 1870s, as "Collected by a Valetudinarian" suggests, witnessed increased self-consciousness on the part of successful women authors about the terms of their own labor. Despite the economic crises following the Civil War, the war had to some extent expanded opportunities for women's authorship, just as it had for other professions: as we will see, both Louisa May Alcott and Elizabeth Stuart Phelps launched their careers by writing war stories. Sarah J. Hale's final edition of her biographical compendium, the *Woman's Record* (1872), profiled ninety published women in its section on the contemporary era "of living female writers."[27] But this influx of new voices also created a new struggle for cultural legitimacy—the hierarchy of the battlefield of production, as Bourdieu terms it—that in turn led to a new need for categories of authorship. In the antebellum period it was rare even for men to claim authorship as a profession. A commentator writing about "authorship in America" in 1883 noted that the United States census "two or three decades ago, in its summary of persons engaged in various occupations included a poet. . . . He was the only poet in America to stand up boldly and be counted. The rest of us sheltered ourselves in the census behind such evasive titles as journalist, or editor, or professor, or, if especially courageous, literary man."[28] By the Reconstruction period, however, the establishment of a "culture of professionalism" had made these categories more visible.[29] Part of that visibility came through the continuing distinction between writers and authors. "It will do amateur writers good to study the habits of successful authors," Mrs. M. L. Rayne wrote in a chapter on "the profession of literature," making clear the operative distinction.[30]

The visibility of "successful authors" was increased by the fact that the figure of the celebrity author—backed by extensive publishing and promotional campaigns—had emerged in the 1860s in unprecedented ways. Female authors became household names not only through their books but also through cultural artifacts: the boat named for Fanny Fern; the clothing line named for characters from *Uncle Tom's Cabin*; the cigar line inspired by Phelps's *The Gates Ajar*. Stowe, in particular, figured during this period as the author par excellence of reform. Before serializing *Uncle Tom's Cabin* in Gamaliel Bailey's *National Era*, she had already contributed four previous domestic sketches to the paper for which she received modest payment; she was a model of "social" or amateur writing in which she could put forward what she termed her "pictures" while also taking care of her six children and entertaining her professor husband's colleagues. *Uncle Tom's Cabin*, of course, marked a watershed in her career, not only because it made her one of the most well-known authors in American history but also because it marked the moment when she began to write out of a clear sense of "call." "Up to this year I have always felt that I had no particular call to meddle with this subject," she wrote in a letter, "and I dreaded to expose even my own mind to the full force of its exciting power. But I feel now that the time is come when even a woman or a child who can speak a word for freedom and humanity is bound to speak."[31] Such speaking was not motivated by financial gain; she began serializing the novel with a $100 advance from Bailey. When she published it in book form, she left the details of her contract up to her sister (who wanted a half-profits arrangement with the publisher) and her husband (who agreed to the publisher Jewett's demand for a 10 percent royalty) and was amazed when she received royalty payments of $20,300 for the single year of 1852.[32]

After the war, however, Stowe had more fully made the transition to professional authorship. One mark of her professionalism was her expansion into coediting the weekly newspaper *Hearth and Home*, a position from which she was able to give advice to potential contributors among its primarily rural readers. An 1869 series on writing and authorship showed particularly vividly her sense of the parameters of authorship. The title of author should be reserved, she wrote, for "those who have confessedly some natural gift—or what is called, for want of a better word, genius—for writing" and who then succeed because of practice and self-discipline that teach them particular techniques, such as not using unnecessary or "hifalutin" words. Stowe reports that she frequently receives letters from women who aspire to become writers but cautions them against assuming that it is an easy way to make a living and believing that an ability to write can necessarily make one into an author. In addition to stressing the importance both of innate talent ("nature") and practice ("culture"), she establishes authorship as a form of writing that finds its own audience. The "history of the success of genius" is that of an unknown

amateur—"without patronage or means of putting himself forward"—
who eventually becomes someone "that the world [has] a call to hear."[33]
Authorship is distinguished, in Stowe's view, by a talent that is readily
discernible by others.

Rose Terry Cooke, who turned to full-time writing after working as a
teacher and governess, exemplified such a calling but, like Stowe, also
wrote a series of cautionary articles about the "ease" of authorship.
Cooke's articles, published ten years after Stowe's, were directed to a
generic woman, Mary Ann, and her "aunts, sisters, and nieces," all of
whom had written to ask her advice about "taking up literature as a profession."[34] Like Stowe, Cooke defines authorship as a specific calling that
only those with a "natural gift" or "talent" should undertake, even though
that talent must be supplemented with education (a kind of professional
training), practice, and "hard work" that is sometimes "exhausting" labor.
As an author, she also refuses to send out what she considers "trash." This
particular self-discipline distinguishes her not only from women with *cacoëthes scribendi* but also from some successful literary men: "If a man has a
reputation as a writer, it does him great service; there are a few men in
America who might write the wildest nonsense, and in their script and
under their name no editor would dare to refuse it; but it is not so with
women" (80). This sentence recasts Hawthorne's infamous private lament
that "America is now wholly given over to a damned mob of scribbling
women, and I should have no chance of success while the public taste is
so occupied with their trash."[35] Yet Cooke's critique is more layered than
Hawthorne's since it presumes that the problem is not American editors'
or readers' deformed taste but rather the way in which a kind of star system—reputation—lets some (male) writers get away with producing less
than their best work. Hawthorne adds that he "should be ashamed of
[him]self if [he] did succeed," but Cooke has no such shame; she believes
in the quality of her own writing, valuing her "own self-respect" (81).

The distinction between talented author and amateur writer articulated
by Stowe and Cooke may have been partially motivated by a fear that
greater numbers of writers would lead to fewer numbers of readers.
Nineteenth-century commentators recognized that the increase of women
readers, as well as writers, had been pivotal to the growth of the literary
market. "Now woman has become a *reader* as well as a writer," reported the
Monthly Knickerbocker, "and this has been the spring-board upon which literature has been thrown to a higher and purer level."[36] If too many readers became afflicted with *cacoëthes scribendi,* they would be so busy with
their work that they would have no time to read the work of the writers
of true merit. "So many of those who read the 'Atlantic Monthly' have
at times the impulse to write for it also," Thomas Wentworth Higginson
noted, "though Mrs. Stowe remain uncut and the Autocrat go for an

hour without readers."[37] This shift, in turn, was predicted to have a dele-
terious effect on the quality of literature. Women "have scarcely ever
written at all, except in that universal rage for Literature, which almost
always attends its decline, when all turn authors, and so many write that
none are left to read but those who cannot spell," wrote one particularly
conservative male critic.[38] Women too voiced this fear in their repeated
injunctions against *cacoëthes scribendi* and its production of a nation of
writers rather than readers. "Suppose you were a little bit of a writer—a
very little bit of one, without a reputation, without much experience, but
with the *cacoethes scribendi* strong upon you, what should you do?" wrote
a young Mary Abigail Dodge to the more established Grace Greenwood
in 1857.[39] Dodge's formulation acknowledges the problematic category
of the "itching writer," although the rest of her letter tries to move beyond
it. "I am poor enough, to be sure, and generally in debt, and would be
glad to get money for my writing; but I would rather write for a *good*
paper without pay, than a foolish one *with*," she continues. She looks to
Greenwood for advice about where to place all of her writing, much of
which has not yet found its way into print. But by emphasizing her desire
to be in a *"good* paper," she sets herself apart from the most virulent form
of *cacoëthes scribendi*.

The repeated use of this term by women suggests that the notion of the
"scribbling woman" writer, which has generally been thought to have
been imposed by male authors onto their female contemporaries, was
also imposed, in a slightly different form, by women. Thus, while it is
right to argue, as Naomi Sofer recently has, that "an ideal of a high literary art in the postbellum United States, and especially the obsession
with distinguishing high art from writing produced for the marketplace,
was driven by the figure of the scribbling woman," it is important to qual-
ify this statement in several respects.[40] First, this ideal began earlier than
we might have thought, at least as early as the 1830s. Second, it was pro-
mulgated by women as much as by their disciplining men. And third,
the division was ultimately based less on ontological difference than on
professional experience, a desire to make clear that although writing
was a "universal" middle-class act, authorship was an earned privilege.

By the end of the century, the category of female authorship had become sufficiently well developed that the review columns of high-brow
magazines regularly distinguished it from what one male critic called "literary measles." The hierarchy of artistic authorship over diseased writing meant that the goal was to move away from being a "writing woman"
toward being an "author"; women who were perceived as moving the
other way were criticized by high-brow critics for their professional "drop"
and reclassification. Indeed, the critic who invoked the problem with
"literary measles" also called for a return to the "old-fashioned Sydney

Smith standard of female authorship: 'if the stocking be blue the petti-coat should be long.'"[41] Although such a standard functions to constrain women's artistic range, its existence shows the degree to which catego-ries of literary production were becoming more codified and entrenched by the end of the century.

Further evidence of such entrenchment is seen in the retrospectives about female authorship that appeared with some regularity in Ameri-can magazines in the 1880s and 1890s. In 1889, for example, the poet Helen Gray Cone published an article in the *Century* in which she gave a history of the "'Writing Women' of America." Her use of scare quotes suggests that she knew that this term was already overdetermined, but she reappropriates it by establishing a history in which these women have moved from a dual concern with reform and with art (in which reform largely won out) to "the almost entire disappearance of the distinctively woman's novel." She prefaces this history by citing the problems with it. "In criticism a classification based upon sex is necessarily misleading and inexact," she writes, and "we cannot rear walls which shall separate lit-erature into departments, upon a principle elusive as the air."[42] On one hand, this statement confirms what I have been arguing: that the cate-gory of literature by women, and specifically by female "authors," had become a recognizable category or, in Cone's words, "department" over the course of the second half of the nineteenth century. If no such de-partment existed, there would be no need to reveal the fallacies of its principles. On the other hand, Cone suggests that the greatest indica-tion of the success of women authors would be to think about how this department no longer needs to be distinct; the women she surveys "would certainly be placed, except for the purposes of this article, among their brother authors, in classes determined by method, local back-ground, or any other basis of arrangement which is artistic rather than personal." Anticipating a move that, in the late twentieth century, would lead women's studies departments to move toward gender studies, Cone concludes with the note that by the end of the century, the "'domestic semi-pious' novels" were being written by men as much as by women and that it would be hard to distinguish the works of Henry James from those "of similar scope" produced by women. In 1894 Annie Nathan Meyer made this point even more strongly, arguing that "the very sub-jects upon which one would naturally expect women to throw a new light have really inspired the masterpieces of men."[43]

Even as female authorship came to be a category that could transcend gender restrictions, so too did the figure of the "lady journalist" emerge as a professional who could cover traditionally "male" territory. Authors and writers were still distinct categories, but the prominence of women in journalism helped convert writing from an "itch" into an important profession. As a profession, Rayne observed, it required not only "special talent of a high order" but also "the greatest amount of technical discipline, general information, adaptability, quickness of diction, and fertility of resources."[44] The viability of such a profession is seen not only in the prominence of female reporters in fiction of the period—think of Henrietta Stackpole in James's *Portrait of a Lady*, for instance—but also in discussions linking female journalists to their male colleagues. "Women in journalism today in no way differ from men in journalism," proclaimed Mary Temple Bayard in 1894; "there is no sex in brains . . . and brains and journalism are synonymous terms." In addition to intelligence, journalists were marked, in Bayard's terms, by their "sincerity," which in turn helped them, as it did authors, show effective artistic restraint.[45] Journalism had long been a common route to authorship; Lawrence Buell, for example, counts 35 percent of 276 major antebellum authors as being "engaged in it for at least a year as a primary means of livelihood."[46] In addition, in the 1890s, women such as Eliza Keith combined what one review called "sparkling" newspaper work with being "the author of many charming short stories."[47] But the key point is that journalism eventually came to make a place for professional writers roughly parallel to that of authors within literary culture. Henrietta Stackpole, the "lady correspondent," moves from writing travel sketches to owning her own newspaper, providing a fictional counterpart to well-known journalists such as Kate Field. To be sure, there was a hierarchy within journalism as within literature. Cone notes that the field of journalism is now also the home of "the irresponsible feminine free lance, with her gay dash at all subjects, and her alliterative pen name dancing in every mêlée like a brilliant pennon." This "gay dash" is reminiscent of the mania of *cacoëthes scribendi*, while specialized reporters—like authors—show strengths of "determination" and "concentration."[48] Focus and restraint continue to be key words, along with the trait that most clearly united the fields of journalism and authorship: observation.

Observation and Detail

In an 1891 retrospective assessment of nineteenth-century female authorship, Rebecca Harding Davis noted the "significant fact that so many . . . distinctively American portraits and landscapes are the work of woman. A woman's quick perception of detail, her keen sympathy with the individual man or woman rather than with the masses, fit her, if she have any power of dramatic representation, to catch the likeness of these isolated phases of our varied life."[49] In making this statement, Davis echoed nineteenth-century commentators who associated women with a "natural" attention to detail and ability to make keen observations. "Women observe and note all the varieties of the genus oddity, more readily than men, and with a certain instinctive nicety of taste and discrimination," William Alfred Jones wrote in the *United States Magazine and Democratic Review* in 1844.[50] In 1851 a critic in the *North American Review* used the figure of the daguerreotype to describe the keen observation evoked in Susan Fenimore Cooper's *Rural Hours*. The author "opens our eyes to much that escapes any less intelligent and minute observation than her own," the review states, "holding up a mirror, and daguerreotyping for our deliberate examination, [the countryside's] daily aspect."[51] A decade later a contributor to the *Knickerbocker* linked women's "natural" fertility with their powers of observation: women "evince a delicacy of perception, a fertility of resources, a power of description, and a fidelity to nature," he noted, "which prove them to be careful students and often profound thinkers." These qualities mean that "the average merit of the sexes as novel-writers is decidedly in favor of woman."[52] The same year, a critic in *The Living Age* argued that women's "keen perception" made them "most suitable for and marketable in the world of print."[53] By the beginning of the twentieth century, a male critic looking at "the feminine note in fiction" could conclude that female novelists succeed by "powers of minute observation applied to the immediate scenes around them," which are in turn enlivened by a "passion for detail."[54]

Women authors often defined their work as a kind of picture making. Stowe described her "vocation" as "simply that of a painter" whose "object," in the case of *Uncle Tom's Cabin*, was "to hold up in the most lifelike and graphic manner possible slavery, its reverses, changes, and the Negro character, which I have had ample opportunities for studying."[55] Similarly, Mary Bryan answered the question "how should women write?" by defining their "province" as being "to daguerreotype the shifting influences, feelings, and tendencies at work in the age in which [their genius] exists."[56] A phrenologist describes Fanny Fern's author double, Ruth Hall, as being "more than ordinarily observant. In passing along the street, you should see much more than people in general, and would be able to describe very accurately the style, execution and quality of whatever you saw."[57]

Even as women were constructed as having superior skills in observation, however, female authors were quick to assert that a mere recording of those observations did not necessarily make one into an author. The scribbling women in Sedgwick's "Cacoethes Scribendi" who write down every detail of village life get their work published in a literary gift book, but that publication only increases their itch. Authors are more discriminate and patient. "People in stories should talk, as much as possible, like people in real life," advised Alice Neal in *Godey's*, but such realistic dialogue, based on hearing real conversation, should not consist of "dry detail" but rather "a blending of the real with the ideal."[58] If "the easy, natural manner of female authors is a marked feature," Virginia Penny noted, that "natural" manner is actually the result of their strategic ability to "collect and arrange information obtained from books, observation, or experience, or all combined."[59] This work is, according to Penny, both healthful ("of all studies, the quiet and contemplative kind are most favorable to long life") and profitable, especially to those who have established a reputation as "women authors." Similarly, Stowe advised women to use their powers of observation to depict "simple and homely scenes of everyday life" but also noted that such a scene must be "well painted by words," a kind of painting that occurs only with "great labor, great study, and incessant practice."[60]

As Naomi Schor has argued, the "femininization" of observation has a long history in Western aesthetics. Within hierarchies of taste, visual (feminine) mimeticism occupies a lower position than does masculine mental, or "deferred," mimeticism. This higher-level representation screens out "parasitical details" in order to focus on particular impressions, valuing a masculine "great style" over a feminine "miniaturism." In the eighteenth century Sir Joshua Reynolds defined the sublime as "anti-detailism," and northern European "grand masters" were valued over Dutch still-life artists.[61] The theories of female authorship that advocated a strategic observation, then, played into two aspects of this aesthetic history, combining "natural" feminine observation with the principles of selection and restraint more normally associated with male artistic production.

Some critics used this double logic to explain why women never produce great art: even the greatest ability to isolate key details cannot make up for observations hampered by social constraints. If women's experience is "limited and monotonous," as W. L. Courtney put it, they "could not attack big canvases or create, by sheer force of imagination, new characters."[62] If women are not allowed to observe much of the world, they will not have much to write about. Instead, they are, in Frank Norris's words, "shut away from the study of, and the association with, the most important thing of all for them—real life." Since "the faculty of selection comes even to men only after many years of experience," the parameters of women's lives necessarily preclude them not only from making "real" observations but also from gaining the experience requisite to distill them.[63] Yet female authors theorized the issue differently, arguing that "real life" could be found, in Stowe's words, in modest, "every-day scenes and things." Stowe, of course, was criticized for the fact that *Uncle Tom's Cabin* was written more from "study" of a problem, as she put it, than from firsthand observation, but she insisted that authorship was less a matter of the scope of lived experience than of one's practice and discipline in describing everyday moments.

In her *Hearth and Home* essays Stowe finds a key example of such authorship in the figure of Nathaniel Hawthorne, who manages, in sketches such as "The Old Apple Dealer," to make "one of his most wonderful pieces of writing" out of "a thoughtful and careful study of apparently the most uninteresting subject in the world."[64] Her conversion of Hawthorne into a prototype for what women should aim to do works, first, to establish what she terms Hawthorne's "genius" in terms applicable to women as well as men and, second, to deflect arguments about the correlation between limited experience and bad writing.

Stowe's essay reminds us that observation was hardly an attribute limited only to women; many male authors also valorized the importance of local details. In the 1850s these details were marshaled to make a national literature out of the domestic scene; by the 1870s and 1880s they were endorsed in the name of a realist aesthetic grounded in the material conditions of everyday life. It is important to remember that *The Scarlet Letter* is prefaced by a sketch of the Salem Custom House that includes observations of Hawthorne's fellow workers, such as "one man, especially, the observation of whose character gave me a new idea of talent," and that takes Hawthorne to task for not being able to represent better the "page of life that was spread out before me." "The quest for legibility," as Michael Gilmore has recently called it, is also a quest for the observable, and the sheer number of nineteenth-century works that thematize this issue suggests its importance.[65] Poe shows the ability of Monsieur Dupin to dupe the police by observing an easily visible letter; Melville examines the process through which everyday whale watching can become monomania; Crane describes the "trance of observation" that Jimmie in *Maggie: A Girl of the Streets* has learned after standing on street corners and "watch[ing] the world go by"; and Howells and James make observation a key component of their theories of realism. Howells concluded that "the sketches and studies by the women seem faithfuler and more realistic than those of the men, in proportion to their number," particularly admiring their "honest report of observation."[66] In "The Art of Fiction" (1884), James describes novelists as those "upon whom nothing is lost," those who are hyperobservant and translate that observation into their work.

Even as he gives this advice, however, he locates his observer par excellence in the figure of an English woman novelist who reported that she had been able to capture "in one of her tales . . . the nature and way of life of the French Protestant youth" because of a "glimpse" of such a youth through a Paris doorway. "The glimpse made a picture; it lasted only a moment, but that moment was experience. She had got her direct personal impression, and she turned out her type. She knew what youth was, and what Protestantism; she also had the advantage of having seen what it was to be French, so that she converted these ideas into a concrete image and produced a reality."[67] Here a female author serves as the chief example of a general mode of "observation," or what we might term hyperobservation, that takes one fleeting moment and crystallizes it into a new "reality." Such a novelist avoids what James's Isabel Archer, describing Henrietta Stackpole, calls "reproductive instincts" in order to focus on "the inner life."[68]

Observation, then, was arguably a key word for both male and female authorship in the nineteenth century, operating in a transgendered aesthetic that made Hawthorne the locus classicus of the picture sketch and the female novelist the locus classicus of the realist novel. At the same time, as a principle of classification, observation played specific roles in defining male and female authorship. In the American male tradition, observation is often occluded, as in the tropes of blindness that characterize Emerson's later writings, or the inability of Melville's Ishmael to "strike through the mask," or the difficulty Howells's Silas Lapham has in interpreting the social masks in Boston. If observation is not occluded, it is used as a mode of emblem making in which, as Richard Brodhead puts it, "the meanings [characters] read into their chosen objects originate in an act of obsessive projection" that then "takes on an oddly objective and authoritarian status."[69] Definitions of women's authorship, on the other hand, focus on observation as its own end. These definitions avoid the problem of a dangerous proliferation of detail by arguing that authors can successfully separate "dry" details from suggestive ones and that keen observation involves astute abilities of discrimination and collection as well as of "natural" or unmediated representation. This creates a form of mimesis that leads to fresh ways of seeing the world by arranging "reality" in particular ways and exposing aspects of society that might otherwise remain hidden. Such mimesis, in turn, can lead to a profitable combination of the "real and ideal." At the same time, it is marked by the author's "sympathy" with her subject. Rather than embracing a mode of detached observation, theories of female authorship functioned, in Kristie Hamilton's words, "to redefine authority as involvement rather than detachment."[70] In the tradition of the sketch, which is Hamilton's subject, such an "emergent" theory separated itself from the masculine urbanity of eighteenth-century predecessors such as Addison and Johnson.

This view of women's authorship goes against the assumption, held by literary nationalist groups such as the transcendentalists or Young America, that the most "emergent" American literature should "fail in originality" rather than "succeed in imitation," as Melville put it.[71] Insofar as they were associated with copying through observation, women were seen by literary nationalists as promoting imitation, which was in turn associated with British and European forms rather than with a distinctive American literature. A representative articulation of this notion appeared in an essay in the first issue of the *American Review* (1845): "We take it, then, that the business of criticism, amid a young literature like ours, is, first of all, to inspire it with a manly spirit and the love of noble models, so far as models are wanted: and, secondly, to correct any casual tendency to merely imitative efforts, the chief danger of lands in close communication with others more advanced in letters."[72] With the right models, observation of American manners, landscapes, and subjects could lead to a "manly" national literature, but it could also lead to "mere" imitation of more "advanced" British literature. Many of the critics who noted women's powers of observation ascribed them to both American and British writers (and sometimes more emphatically to British ones), which itself went against the drive toward a distinct literary tradition.

In this sense, the transatlantic qualities of female authorship made them particularly suspect among certain schools of thought in the United States of the mid-nineteenth century, not only because they were allied with the market but also because they were distracting readers from more experimental American writing. Such critics did, however, admire women's writing insofar as it captured the domestic—read as "national"—scene. This national logic is seen, for example, in a review of Susan Warner's *The Wide, Wide World* as a "life-like picture" done by a "lady-novelist" possessing "keen observation, powerful satire, knowledge of the world, strong common sense, and—though last not least—democratic principles."[73]

In our own critical moment, the transnational aspects of women's authorship are as appealing as its "democratic principles" and the problem posed by women's relation to literary nationalism are not as formidable. On one hand, critics such as Amy Kaplan have convincingly demonstrated that women's writing—and cultural influence generally— was never as limited as we might have thought, extending instead to a kind of "manifest domesticity" that is itself part of the larger project of nineteenth-century imperialism and nation building. On the other hand, we can understand that nation building is not the only criterion through which to judge nineteenth-century women's writing. We might also think about how particular authors negotiated and defined their own literary goals, many of which had to do with issues of selection, discipline, and observation, or the relation between this power of observation and the gendered origins of literary realism.[74]

Privileges and Rights

If female authorship was defined in part by its relation to the more indiscriminate productions of "the writing itch" and to the "natural" strengths of female observation, it was also associated with particular legal and political principles. As Melissa Homestead has recently shown, nineteenth-century debates about international copyright presented one of the key aspects of authorship as a literary field, one that was particularly vexing for antebellum women because the law of coverture meant that intellectual property rights that women might gain from copyright often went to their husbands rather than to them. By the mid-nineteenth century the principle of coverture in the United States, which was carried over from the common law of England, was beginning to be challenged. Some states, with Mississippi being the first in 1839, adopted statutes that would give married women increased legal rights. In 1848 New York State adopted the Married Woman's Property Act, which allowed women to keep property they had acquired before marriage; coverture had effectively ended by the 1860s.[75] An international copyright act was not passed in the United States, however, until 1891. Discussions about authorship and discussions about copyright protection went hand in hand during this period. On one side were critics who believed that authors were adequately paid, particularly in relation to other professions. Such critics, reflecting a Republican ideal of literary utility, argued for the rights of consumers, or readers, over those of authors. If readers were in fact the driving force of good literature, as the *Knickerbocker* had claimed, then they deserved to be able to purchase books at a reasonable price. On the other side were critics who believed that lack of international copyright compromised free trade and hampered experimentation and ambition by native authors.[76] Both sides tended to use the term "author" rather than writer, helping to invest the term with its legal and professional connotations.

Both sides of the debate also frequently invoked the salaries of successful female authors, as well as male ones, in order to support their point. H. C. Carey, for example, argued on behalf of foreign competition by explaining that Harriet Beecher Stowe had earned much more per hour than public servants such as Lincoln, and that Alcott, having earned twelve thousand dollars from the sales of eighty thousand copies of *Little Women*, was still charging (through her publisher) proportionately more for *Little Men* than readers had paid for Charles Brockden Brown's *Ormond* a century earlier.[77] Other commentators painted a different picture, citing Catharine Maria Sedgwick's complaint that "she found it impossible to make much out of novel-writing while cheap editions of English novels filled the market" or reporting that only a handful of women make a "barely comfortable" living from writing, in some cases supplementing it with teaching and other sources of income.[78]

Even as these commentators assumed that all authors should be paid adequately for their labors (though the amount of "adequate" was under dispute), their arguments were complicated by another aspect of the debate over authorial rights, which had to do with the "privileges" of authorship. Publishers were said to compete for the "privilege" of printing works, but the greatest "privileges" were reserved for authors. For the most part, these were tied to the legal rights of the author:

What, then, —to sum up the argument, for authorship, on this point, —is the foundation of the right? Simply, justice. It is eminently just that every man should reap the rewards of his own labor and invention. It is just that another should not use his name, to his own profit, without his consent. It is expedient, too, as well as just, that an author should judge when, if ever, to publish; that he should select the manner and the extent of the publication, and the persons to whose honesty and accuracy the work shall be intrusted. In a word, it is just that each one should do with his own as he pleases.[79]

The assumption that an author should have control over "his own" was related to a possessive individualism that assumed that "great authors have, finally, a property in their own minds, which other men have not," as an earlier commentator had put it.[80] This assumption overlooked the material conditions of production and reception that helped support that "property," claiming a variety of influences, sources, and ideas that may or may not have originated with the author. Current studies of intellectual property and copyright law recognize the deep problems with this view since it effectively dismisses ideas of collaboration and cultural commons. As the legal scholar Rosemary Coombe puts it, "the Romantic author claims the expressive power to represent cultural others in the name of a heritage universalized as Culture."[81]

Female authorship, too, presented a challenge to the romantic ideal, not simply because it suggested that women as well as men should "reap the rewards" of production, but also because it represented an alternative notion of "privilege" operating in the nineteenth century. This alternative notion troubled a separate-spheres ideology that posited that it was the "privilege" of women to be "able to stand aloof from the world," inhabiting an inherently "aristocratic position" that enabled them to be "judges of a turmoil that can never reach them."[82] Transforming the notion of privileged separation to one of social privilege gave women entrance into the public sphere, including its legal rights, and also helped them redefine the romantic notion of authorship. Instead of seeing authorship as a position that required the protection of individual "genius," they returned to a model that emphasized the audience that might benefit from that social position. This model identified authorial work not as alienated or isolated but rather as a form of service that allowed them to speak on behalf of other women.[83] This position was evident as early as 1860, when Mary Bryan argued that "it is not only the privilege, but the duty of woman to aid in extending [the] influence of letters, when she has been endowed with the power" at a time when "the press is the teacher and the preacher of the world."[84] In other words, women formulated a model of authorship as "ethical technique" that understood its privileges as involving obligations as well as rights and creating opportunities for readers as much as protection for authors.[85]

When I talk about authorship as an ethical activity with certain social obligation, I have in mind Linda Kerber's forceful study of the importance of civic obligation in understanding specifically American rights from the Revolutionary period to the present. Even as women fought for their rights, they did not always demand the obligations that came with it, such as serving on a jury or in the military. By arguing that "ladies" did not need to do such things, they effectively kept themselves in a model of domestic and civic *coverture,* in which "married women's obligations to their husbands and families overrode their obligations to the state."[86] The "privileges" that seemed to result from being excluded from certain forms of obligation only served to exclude women from full citizenship.

Since nineteenth-century female authors were most admired when they were thought to be advancing a native literature, they were frequently seen as "Republican mothers" even when they had no family. Not to insist on their rights as authors would be to remain *femes covert.* From our current critical lens, women vying for authorial status and rights may seem to have been buying into a corrupt system. Yet from a historical perspective, we can see the move to identify women as authors as part of an attempt to move their obligations from the domestic to the civic realm. Their obligation was to use their authorial rights for "good" ends, which included presenting "truth" and "reality" to their readers as well as advancing the production of American literature. This position was stated most succinctly by Alice Neal, who argued that those with talent had an obligation to develop it:

For its own sake, the happiness which the power of expression confers, and for the good it may be the medium of conveying to others, real talent should never be neglected by its possessor. Not in vanity or self-seeking, but with a still thankfulness for the great gift Heaven has thought you worthy to receive, and a deep realization of the responsibility which attends it. Were talent thus regarded, and thus cultivated, we should have less flippant tales presented to our notice, and fewer poems to reject for their utter lack of novelty or thought.[87]

By emphasizing the "responsibility" and hence obligations of authorship, Neal offers an alternative to the "self-seeking" romantic author even as she asserts its political viability. To be sure, she believes that individual authors have a "claim" to their own identities and should not be hounded by the public. But these "claims" are balanced by the obligation of "good" that attends going into print. A sense of "responsibility" will lead to thoughtful and socially powerful literature.

The next chapter deals with one of the sites of such responsibility: the nineteenth-century parlor. Although the parlor has often been seen as the epitome of women's "separate sphere," my goal is to see it less as a site of constraint than as a founding site of nineteenth-century women's authorship. The magazines and periodicals that put forward the definitions traced in this chapter were frequently read and displayed in the parlor; so too were the initial publications of many women authors. To think about authorship as originating in the parlor, rather than in a secluded garret, is to think about its inherent social functions as well as the material grounding for its civic responsibilities.

Chapter 2
Writing in and out of the Home
Parlor Culture and Authorship

The mid-century daguerreotype in Figure 3 was made in the studios of Albert Sands Southworth and Josiah Johnson Hawes, who operated one of Boston's leading photographic firms. Like many early photographs, it features an occupational pose. The prop for this pose, probably an illustrated gift book or annual, is opened to a portrait of a woman. Although this daguerreotype was made in a professional studio, its setting is meant to evoke a parlor, the semipublic space in which middle-class families, especially women, both displayed and performed various artistic practices. The parlor was where one received guests who might participate in *tableaux vivants,* guessing or card games (including "Authors"), musical interludes, or communal readings; it was also the place where one could display daguerreotypes, annuals, and engravings. The parlor was an expression both of what Thorstein Veblen would call "conspicuous consumption" and of the comforts of a domestic haven. Families with less money acquired reproductions of furniture and art that would be in the finest parlors. Given the centrality of the parlor to nineteenth-century cultural life, it is no surprise that photographers such as Southworth and Hawes turned their reception rooms into commercial parlors and also used parlor furniture as part of their props.[1]

The three women looking at this portrait do not look directly at the camera but focus instead on the book. The standing woman's hand on her head suggests that she is thinking, while the woman holding the book is looking at the woman beside her, as if to gauge her reaction to the image she is viewing. In these ways the daguerreotype emphasizes self-reflection (an image of women looking at a woman) and focused concentration, a self-consciousness that points to its status as cultural emblem as well as historical artifact. As an emblem of reading, it represents a social practice that established communal bonds. As historians have shown, the bonds established by reading groups were an important aspect of women's education as well as an impetus for communal action on behalf of, among other things, abolition, suffrage, and the women's rights movements. They encouraged education and an increasing public voice by

Figure 3. Albert Sands Southworth and Josiah Johnson Hawes, "Three Ladies Reading." Whole plate daguerreotype from the Collection of Matthew R. Isenburg.

stressing writing as well as reading. Writing became a way to "reproduce" learning, in Margaret Fuller's words, rather than just to memorize or acquire it. As early as the 1760s, as Mary Kelley has shown, Milcah Martha Moore assembled more than a hundred manuscripts that had been shared in a reading group in her Delaware home, representing a practice that continued throughout the nineteenth century. In 1827 members of Philadelphia's black elite formed the Female Literary Association and began sending the essays they presented to antislavery publications. As Kelley concludes, "In nearly every town and village and in every city, women gathered to read and write together." The connection between reading circles and women's writing has also been emphasized by Elizabeth McHenry, who shows the importance of African American women's circles, such as Georgia Douglas Johnson's "Saturday Nighters" and A'lelia Walker's "Dark Tower," to the literary production of the Harlem Renaissance.[2]

Even as the Southworth and Hawes daguerreotype represents the social practice of reading, then, it also functions as an image of female writing, drawing attention to the kinds of publications (gift books, annuals, and periodicals) in which many women first found their way into print as well as to the implied audience for those publications. As was presented in the last chapter, books and magazines in the second half of the nineteenth century helped to make female authorship visible as a discrete category within the field of literary production. In this chapter I will locate this category of female authorship within the material culture of the parlor, focusing on two specific aspects of that culture: letters and portraits. On one level, both of these material objects helped to reinforce the emphasis on observation that was a hallmark of women's writing. On another level, they helped to distinguish authors from writers. The activities of the parlor authorized all middle-class women to become letter writers, but they also helped to define authors as those writers who found an audience beyond the parlor. If the parlor can on one hand be seen as the originary space for women's writing, in other words, the ability to move beyond it also stands as a measure of authorial success. This interpretation recasts the parlor not as a confining domestic sphere but rather as a kind of laboratory in which women could claim authorship in particular ways.

The Letter in the Parlor

The most immediate connection between female authorship and the parlor lies in the fact that throughout the nineteenth century, and particularly in the antebellum period, many women first gained an audience for their writing by composing letters or essays that were read aloud or silently in a parlor or other semiprivate setting. These letters, in turn, were often circulated in manuscript portfolios or newspapers or sent for publication in printed newspapers and periodicals. Margaret Fuller, for example, circulated "pacquets" of manuscript letters, poems, and journal entries within a circle of friends before publishing them in the *Dial*.[3] Other women collected their letters in printed volumes such as Mary Austin Holley's *Texas* (1833 and 1836), Sarah Rogers Haight's *Letters from the Old World* (1840), or Catharine Sedgwick's *Letters from Abroad* (1841). Harriet Jacobs published the beginnings of what would be *Incidents in the Life of a Slave Girl* as an anonymously authored "Letter from a Fugitive Slave" in the *New York Tribune*, and Harriet Beecher Stowe began her abolitionist career by writing letters to the editor of the *Cincinnati Journal* (who also happened to be her brother).[4] Noting the prevalence of such newspaper letters by women, Nina Baym argues that "the real origins of the published letter and journal lie in the form of print itself—in the 'letters to the editor' columns of newspapers and periodicals. This genre has been a public practice from its inception, and women have always made use of it."[5] Although the practice was not limited to women—these volumes of letters have their antecedents in eighteenth-century collections such as Benjamin Franklin's *Dogood Papers* (1722) and Samuel Richardson's *Familiar Letters on Important Occasions* (1741)—it was, as Baym suggests, one that offered particular opportunities for women who wanted to have their work published.[6] Letter writing allowed women to capitalize on their "natural" powers of observation without compromising their femininity, and the proliferation of newspapers increased their access into print. As a writer in *Godey's Lady's Book* observed, "In these days of thousands of newspapers, there are frequent inducements and occasions to write for the Press . . . [and] no lack of advice and suggestions upon the subject, addressed to the scribbling public."[7]

Reading letters aloud in semiprivate settings, particularly the parlor, is a practice remembered by many female authors. In the 1830s Sophia Peabody (later Hawthorne) wrote letters to her sister Elizabeth and her mother from Cuba, where she had traveled for health reasons. These letters were collected and bound by Elizabeth so that they could be read aloud at her bookstore and also by members of the Peabody family. In 1853, when Sophia wanted to read these letters aloud to her daughter Una, she realized that she did not know where they were. "They have been lent a great deal," she reported to her father, "& I do not know but some stranger has them now."[8] As a young woman in Cincinnati in the 1840s, Harriet Beecher Stowe apprenticed herself as an author by composing letters and manuscripts meant to be read aloud, both in her family's parlor back home in Hartford, Connecticut, and at meetings of the Semi-Colon Club, a salon with both male and female members who gathered to read and critique one another's writing. In 1853 Marion Harland (Virginia Hawes Terhune) read part of the manuscript of her first novel, *Alone,* to members of her Virginia family as they were "sitting in a parlor on a wild night" and "her companions had their magazines." It was, she remembered, the "'open sesame' of [her] literary life," and her family kept her "reading until nearly midnight, dipping in here for a scene, there for a character-sketch, until my voice gave out."[9] In all of these accounts parlors are clearly the founding sites of women's authorial careers.

Joan Hedrick has named such writing "parlor literature," a literature that was meant to be shared by both men and women in middle- and upper-class parlors and that was then frequently recorded in print. These parlor and club experiences, Hedrick argues, helped authors such as Stowe cross "the border between letter and epistolary novel, between the private and public realms of discourse." This discourse, steeped in observations about the quotidian details of everyday life, also "created the ground from which emerged American realism, with its attention to particular accents, local peculiarities, and regional types."[10] Parlor literature, Hedrick suggests, capitalized on prevailing notions about women's superior powers of observation in order to establish a form of writing that eventually played a significant role in the development of American realism. Even nineteenth-century critics who were wary of female authorship noted that women had a knack for what one critic termed "would-be-picturesque description," and women's journals espoused the writing of familiar letters that included "trifles" that represented "the tenor of household life."[11] A household-centered "domestic realism" rising from parlor literature succeeded, then, not only in finding women audiences but also in providing some of the key vocabulary (of observation, detail, and fact) that would eventually be integrated into the high realism of Howells and James.[12]

This genealogy provides one important way of thinking about the parlor as a transitional site between private, social writing and the public, professional writing associated with high-art realism. As appealing as Hedrick's celebration of "parlor literature" is, however, it does have drawbacks as a critical term. First, as Nan Johnson has shown, it obscures the degree to which cultural practices associated with the parlor, including letter writing and elocution, were frequently scripted to keep women in their place, "encouraged to see their rhetorical identities as a reflection of their roles as wives and mothers." If Stowe and others used parlor literature as a training ground for a successful career as public authors, they had to disregard nineteenth-century letter-writing manuals that "generally reinforced conservative definitions of female roles rather than expanded the rhetorical territory of women." Such manuals did not include advice on writing letters to editors; to the extent that they encouraged literary production, this was most often in the context of what Johnson calls a "domestic home base."[13] The internalization of such restrictive domesticity is clear, for example, in the annual reports of the Alabama Federation of Literary Clubs, which was comprised of groups that met in church parlors and homes to share papers on literary events. In the introduction to the reports, its editor criticizes the notion of the "New Woman," instead praising the fact that "these clubs afford opportunities for activity essentially adapted [*sic*] to the capacities and limitations of woman."[14] Second, a critical grounding of authorship in such a potentially restrictive or limited "home base" downplays the influences that authors such as Stowe had beyond the parlor. "Hedrick wants to keep Stowe in the parlor," as Robert Levine puts it, "when the facts suggest that Stowe by the late 1840s had left the parlor, encountering and interacting with numerous African-American people and texts."[15] In other words, a valorization of parlor literature threatens to continue the restrictive practices put forward in letter-writing manuals. At the same time, this valorization represents the transition to professional authorship as a negative "fall" rather than an enabling shift, as women had to leave the richly nurturing confines of the parlor to encounter a more hostile—and masculinized—professional world of publishing. Such an assumption, which also underlies Susan Coultrap-McQuin's *Doing Literary Business*, not only overlooks the contributions of women editors to nineteenth-century publishing but also suggests that professionalization was always a bad thing, when in fact it helped many women writers create successful and satisfying literary careers.

To me, however, the largest problem with the idea of parlor literature is that it deemphasizes the fact that its progression from private to public—what Harland would call its "open sesame" effect—was neither inevitable nor easy. Harland was nostalgically remembering her parlor moment half a century after the fact, and her account was written only after decades of work. In her essays on female authorship in *Hearth and Home*, Stowe warns against believing that good letter writers will necessarily produce successful authors. "The style of a graceful, easy, feminine letter-writer is something so different from what is necessary in newspaper or magazine articles," she writes, "that one can seldom form a judgment from a lady's letter as to what she could do."[16] Louisa May Alcott, whose first real literary success came from converting her letters written home from a Georgetown hospital into *Hospital Sketches*, similarly warned, in a letter to a prospective author, that "there is no easy road to authorship." As a young woman, Alcott admitted being surprised that anyone would want to read her letters, but as she gained more experience as an author, she came to understand that one could not simply reprint letters and expect an audience to come; indeed, she took the publisher of *Hospital Sketches* to task for not doing more to promote her book.[17]

Despite such warnings, however, the ideal of moving from parlor manuscript to published work remained an operative one throughout the second half of the nineteenth century. By 1884, for instance, Mrs. M. L. Rayne, in her book *What Can a Woman Do?*, could list "the profession of literature" as one of "several hundred different methods by which a woman can earn her own livelihood," a livelihood that does not require "the genius of a Napoleon to succeed" but rather "earnestness of purpose and power of concentration." To have a story published, Rayne advises, simply send a legible manuscript and return postage to a publisher. "If there is merit and originality in the story, and it is well told and pleasantly written, it will take."[18] Legibility here becomes as key to publishing as originality, and Rayne imagines an access to the literary field that is based not on a contested relation to the page (as it is for "tortured geniuses" such as Melville) but on following certain directions.

This ideal of universal access persisted, I would argue, because it helped reinforce definitions of female authorship that were also developed during this period. Significantly, it constructed the female author as a "natural" phenomenon. Such an author was not a social outcast but rather someone who fit into acceptable categories of womanhood: the mother or wife who was also a letter writer, or the friend who simply wanted to convey her observations to others. Such a vision was promoted by Catharine Beecher, for example, in an anecdote she wrote about her sister Harriet Beecher Stowe. In the anecdote she has come to visit Harriet in order to collect a "piece for the *Souvenir* which I promised the editor I would get . . . and send him on next week." The piece is late because Harriet's home is in disarray, with housecleaning to be done, teething babies, and an inexperienced new maid for help. Catharine saves the day by simultaneously helping Harriet organize the house and taking down her dictation for the *Souvenir* piece. "I do not know what genius is given for if it is not to help a woman out of a scrape," she writes. "Come set your wits to work and let me have my way, and you shall have all the work done, and finish the story too."[19] The point here is that writing and domestic management are not mutually exclusive, as long as one possesses a certain kind of "genius" for efficient management. Order here replaces romantic inspiration as the mark of genius in order to capture the "natural" relation between housekeeping and writing.

Such an ideal countered the notion, frequently put forward by male critics, that authorship was incompatible with femininity. In this view, writing required nothing short of a "defeminizing process," as one essay in the *Living Age* put it, that precluded "a mission quite as grand as that of literary authorship," namely that of being a wife and mother.[20] At the same time, however, representations of the trajectory from parlor to print helped to distinguish the work of authorship from the work of letter writing. Authors might begin their careers reading and writing in the parlor, but they then claimed an audience, and an expertise, that extended well beyond it. All women could be writers, in other words, but not every writer could claim to be an author.

Ironically, then, the need to distinguish authors from writers, some of which was done through letters, arose from the illusion of access generated by these very letters. Just as the advent of the ready-focus camera, and more recently the digital camera, has made it possible for anyone to be a photographer, so too did access to pen and paper make it possible for any literate woman to imagine that she could be a writer, a move that in turn led to the need for authors (like professional photographers) to lay claim to the distinctiveness of their expertise. In making such claims, they had to dispel the ease of access promoted by many of their publishers who encouraged their readers, and especially women readers, to become writers by sponsoring contests that awarded prize money for the best amateur writing. Such money was an acceptable way to earn money at home. As Rayne puts it, "There are . . . women who have time from the duties and obligations of housework to earn a little pin money, and turn an honest penny, for their own profit."[21] Susan Warner's first published piece, on "American Female Patriotism," won fifty dollars in just such a contest sponsored by Lydia Sigourney and *The Ladies' Wreath.* Harriet Beecher Stowe and Marion Harland won the same amount from the *Western Monthly Magazine* and *Southern Era* respectively. So too did Alcott win a contest early in her career; her sensational story "Pauline's Passion and Punishment" won a hundred-dollar prize from Frank Leslie's *Illustrated Newspaper.*[22]

In *A Book for the Home Circle* (1853), Caroline Kirkland points to both the naturalness of writers and the distinctiveness of authors when she satirically defends against the "threat" of women "writers" by pointing out that most women are already writers by virtue of their correspondence. In a book designed explicitly for the parlor, Kirkland wonders what, besides writing a book, might entitle a woman "to the appellation of literary": "Does writing letters make one literary? In these Californian days it is to be hoped not, lest some of our fair friends should be tempted to neglect their absent brothers rather than be liable to misconstruction, in so important a particular. Writing letters sometimes ends in writing books, as more than Madame de Sevignè can testify. How is it with keeping a journal? Does that come within the canon? Might it not be maliciously interpreted into writing a book in disguise?"[23] Kirkland's satire simultaneously embraces the trajectory from letter to print and demystifies the notion that letter writing will necessarily put one "within the canon." The cultural imperatives that encourage women to contribute to the nation's Manifest Destiny by writing to their brothers who are settling the West compete here with imperatives against having literary ambitions. Letter writing takes on particular importance, Kirkland suggests, within the context of a geographically expanding and increasingly decentralized United States; letters become a way not only to record regional differences but also of fixing moral value within a time of geographic flux and displacement. Yet if all middle-class women are to some extent called upon to be writers in their capacity as wives and mothers, the importance of this calling should not be confused with the more specific calling to be an author. "There are no more cobwebs in literary parlours than elsewhere," Kirkland concludes, but the category of the literary still connotes a cultural status beyond the parlor.[24]

In theory, then, parlor literature could mean that anyone composing letters could be engaged in "literary" activity. But as Catharine Sedgwick and the numerous other critics of *cacoëthes scribendi* made clear, such access was not necessarily a productive thing. As one critic in the *American Monthly Knickerbocker* put it, "It is now exceedingly fashionable for women to write; so much so, that those who do not wield the pen in some capacity are rather the exception than the rule."[25] John Greenleaf Whittier wrote to Dodge that "half the graduates of our high schools and female seminaries are trying to live by writing. Mrs. Stowe and Gail Hamilton, and Mrs. Spofford and Miss Alcott do it, so they don't see why they cannot. Think of the mischief you are doing to the average female mind!"[26] If writing becomes a fashion, then professional authors need to define themselves as occupying a distinct place within that fashion, as being "above average" minds that could serve as arbiters of taste, expert mentors, and artists with particular talent.

Such authors recognized the deep affinity between letters about local observations and their own character sketches, as well as the cultural benefit of aligning their own work with these unthreatening "nonliterary" productions. But they also recognized the importance within the literary field of distinguishing their work from the letters and manuscripts of social authorship. Given this recognition, their challenge was to take the letter, with its associations with proper femininity and sketches of everyday life, and suggest how it could also be used to claim authorship in particular ways. By putting authorship on a continuum with letter writing, they rejected the notion that it came only from individual inspiration or genius. But they also used that trajectory to suggest the distance that women needed to travel in order to consider themselves authors, providing advice and mentorship that helped establish certain guidelines and standards.

How specific authors did this will be presented in subsequent chapters, but here I want to suggest two general trends in female authors' use of letters. First, they introduced letter writing and parlor scenes into their own writing in order to showcase both the origins of female authorship and the distinction between themselves and their readers. Second, they used their actual correspondence with everyday writers both to consolidate their relation to their audience and to establish their own authority. In some cases these letters fit William Merrill Decker's claim that "authors by vocation" during this period employed a more "self-conscious use of language" than did "nonliterary writers of letters," seeing "the epistolary exchange as exemplary of the destiny of language in general" or of "allegories of deeper psychological and social resonance."[27] In other cases, however, they are straightforward and directive in offering advice, making sure that style does not interfere with message.

It is no surprise that some of the key texts of nineteenth-century fiction by and about women contain scenes of writing and reading letters: Hester Prynne receiving letters from Pearl in Europe; Ellen Montgomery reading letters from her mother and writing letters to John and Mr. Humphreys from Scotland; Jo March reading aloud letters from Amy in Europe as well as her own book manuscript; Isabel Archer corresponding with Henrietta Stackpole. Even Rebecca Harding Davis's "Life in the Iron Mills," heralded as a protorealist account of industrial labor, employs a frame narrator—often read as a figure of the female professional artist—who sits writing in what she describes as a library. Using a narrative technique that Robyn Warhol terms the feminine "engaging narrator," she directly addresses the reader in a pseudoepistolary form, encouraging her reader to observe what she does: to "see how foggy the day is" and to have "eyes as free as mine are to look deeper" than the surface.[28] On one level, such scenes use the medium of the letter to justify female writing, appeasing conservative male critics who could conclude, as one contributor to the *North American Review* did, that the female author writes not for fame but rather with the hope of addressing "partial friends." This *Review* essay is explicit in drawing a connection between writing letters and novels: the female author "writes her book as she writes a letter, and expects a response in the spirit of it."[29] Yet these letters also help demonstrate the distance between letter writers and authors. In Fanny Fern's *Ruth Hall*, for example, the fan mail that Ruth receives underscores the distinction between the projections that readers put onto implied authors (in this case "Floy") and the actual life and work of a flesh-and-blood author (Ruth).

The readers who write to "Floy" not only interfere with Ruth's writing time but also burden her with nonliterary concerns, such as marriage and paying off debts. By including copies of such letters, Fern creates a behind-the-scenes intimacy that encourages her own readers to keep turning the pages of her book. In one letter a male fan, Reginald Danby, writes about his grandmother—an unpublished poet who could also recite *A Midsummer Night's Dream* by memory—and his desire to get his family history published in order to fund his own college education. In this history his "grandmother's poetry would probably read to advantage; if so, it would be a great saving, as her writings are voluminous. Your book would be sure to have a large sale, and the profits would pay my expenses at College."[30] Danby writes to Ruth not only because of her literary talents but also because of her business acumen; as a successful author, she knows the world of publishing in a way that his grandmother, an amateur writer, never could. The irony, of course, is that Reginald is enlisting the literary labor of the grandmother and of Ruth to support a higher education that was available to neither of them. Yet Fern's satire does not undermine her basic point, which is that readers, as literary protégés, were attracted to an illusion of easy entrance into authorship that their more seasoned mentors had to refute.

As noted in the last chapter, Ruth's declaration that "no happy woman ever writes" has become a watchword for the obstacles and anxiety that women faced getting into print. But Fern's use of letters also suggests that this phrase can be read as a move to demystify the ideals of parlor literature as much as a statement of aesthetic angst. As a girl, Ruth has been drawn to literary pursuits and to this ideal: she steals into her brother Hyacinth's room to "'right' his papers," and in boarding school she shows a facility in composition that prompts her classmates to ask her to write their essays for them (6). Her own compositions, moreover, are put into print with almost no effort: "an editor of a paper in the same town used often to come in and take down her compositions in shorthand as she read them aloud, and transfer them to the columns of his paper" (145). This easy movement from manuscript to performance to print becomes the founding moment of authorship for Ruth Hall: when she decides, as a widow desperate for money, to turn to writing, she remembers these early compositions and reasons that she will write even better than she did as an "inexperienced girl" (146). Yet even as *Ruth Hall* invokes the ideal of parlor literature, with amateur compositions leading to a professional literary career, it also reveals the ways in which such a trajectory can interfere with individual rights. The plagiarizing of Ruth's classmates and the local newspaper editor are initially portrayed as innocuous enough. As a widow trying to support her children, however, such a system of reprinting or exchange publication keeps Ruth in poverty while her (male) editors and publishers get her profits. In Fern's case, as Melissa Homestead has pointed out, such exchanges gave her a reputation as a "woman of easy virtue" who could make herself a "hot commodity" largely by pointing to how often others are poaching her work.[31]

Although Ruth, at least initially, is not as savvy about using exchange publication to her advantage as Fern is, Fern does gesture toward Ruth's
"easy" reputation by describing her, when she begins to write, as living
across the street from a brothel. By the end of *Ruth Hall*, however, Ruth
has, with the help of a male mentor, negotiated an exclusive contract with
one newspaper and published a book whose profits enable her to purchase stock. This plot not only reinscribes a Franklinian rags-to-riches
success story but also demonstrates the importance of receiving fair compensation for one's literary labors.

It is not strictly true in *Ruth Hall*, then, that no happy woman writes.
As a newly married woman, Ruth has continued her facility in composition; her mother-in-law Mrs. Hall, snooping in her house, finds not only
annotated books but poetry "in Ruth's own hand-writing" (29). She is
happy in this writing in just the way that Reginald Danby's grandmother
delighted in writing her poetry or that Gilbert Osmond's mother, in *Portrait of a Lady*, enjoys writing poetry that dubs her the title, among her
friends, of "the American Corinne." What leads to unhappiness is the
plagiarism of such manuscripts—and the reprinting of work that does
not support the author—or the inability of such manuscripts to find an
audience when one is needed. Ruth's friend Mary Leon writes a letter
from the insane asylum, where her husband has left her, that never makes
it beyond the pocket of the matron of the establishment, Mrs. Bunce
(141). Similarly, her neighbor Mrs. Waters has done experiments that
she wants to publish in a medical journal but that never appear, "owing,
probably, to the editor being out of town" (143). The move from private
manuscript to public print is complicated by a sexist system of publishing that Ruth Hall must learn to negotiate successfully. Women might
happily write in private or happily publish with equitable contracts; the
unhappiness comes in trying to negotiate the middle ground between
the two. Fern analogizes this middle ground, represented in editorial and
publishing offices, to the position of outsiders trying to penetrate "'know-
nothing' hieroglyphics" (155). The Know-Nothing Party, which in the
1850s tried to stem the tide of immigration by calling for a twenty-one-
year residency requirement for citizenship and for voting and elected
offices to be restricted to American-born men, becomes aligned with the
efforts of the male literary establishment to restrict access to women. The
issue, as Fern's analogy makes clear, was knowledge and access. The move
from parlor writer to published author was not as easy as sending out a
manuscript, but neither was it an impossible task if one had knowledge
of the system as well as great personal discipline.

Fern's newspaper columns also reveal this dual concern with both the
attractions and difficulties of writing. "[A] woman who wrote, used to be
considered a sort of monster," she commented in 1867. But all of that had

now changed: "At this day it is difficult to find one who does not write, or has not written, or who has not, at least, a strong desire to do so. Grid-irons and darning-needles are getting monotonous. A part of their time the women of to-day are content to devote to their consideration when necessary; but you will rarely find one—at least among women who *think*—who does not silently rebel against allowing them a monopoly."[32] Although she applauds the notion that thinking women such as Ruth Hall can find time to write while maintaining their domestic duties, she also warns against thinking that "successful literary ladies *always* pen their contributions with a golden nib, in a damask chair, on a tapestry carpet, inhaling the luxurious aroma of hot-house plants, clad in purple and fine linen, and faring sumptuously every day." Fern here reveals that the organic ease with which women are supposed to write is in fact as unnat-ural as a hothouse plant. "No, no, no," she goes on to say. "I tell you, with a dark picture of suffering indelibly daguerreotyped on my memory—*no!*" Responding directly to a *New York Times* editorial that posited that "sympathy, admiration, praise" create a "fragrant atmosphere" and "float around the plant of [woman's] genius," Fern posits the facts of her own experience—observations significantly "daguerreotyped" in her mem-ory—against the romantic illusion of ease and prosperity.[33] That romantic illusion, in turn, is connected not only to an organic flowering of iso-lated genius but also to a parlor culture that reifies the transition from manuscript to print as being natural and inevitable.[34]

Even as a work such as *Ruth Hall* distinguishes the pleasures of private writing from the challenges of moving that writing into print, other female authors made similar distinctions by printing open letters of advice to their protégées. As seen in the last chapter, Stowe and Cooke issued advice that sympathized with their readers but warned against assuming that authorship was an easy thing. If letters did not always lead to print, print often generated letters. The letters that female authors received from readers suggest the intensity of their personal identification. "I think you have preached many sermons, and done much good for the world," wrote Ella Blake to Susan Warner. "I feel as if I knew you and you were my personal friend."[35] A generation later another young reader used similar language in a letter to Alcott. "We have all been reading 'Little Women,'" she wrote, "and we liked it so much I could not help wanting to write to you. We think *you* are perfectly splendid. We were all so dis-appointed over your not marrying Laurie; I cried over that part,—I could not help it. We all liked Laurie . . . ever so much, and almost killed our-selves laughing over the funny things you and he said."[36] For this reader, Alcott *is* Jo; there is no distinction between author and character.

The intensity of the reading experience, these examples suggest, led readers to want to create written responses in the form of letters. This writing, in turn, could also result in a letter writer wanting to become an author herself. "I have aspirations, but they are to occupy such a position as yours," Eugenia Sadler wrote from Kentucky to Susan Warner.[37] The authors serving as mentors to such protégées took their role seriously, even when they found it physically and mentally draining. As Lydia Sigourney reported in 1866, "My epistolary intercourse is extensive, frequent, and exceeds a yearly exchange of two thousand letters. It includes many from strangers, who are often disposed to be tenacious of replies, and to construe omission as rude neglect." Sigourney takes solace in the fact that her requests from strangers are balanced by "the epistles of long-tried friendship." She also recognizes the irony inherent in her success. Having developed "habits of writing that were deepened by the solitary lot of an only child," she now wishes that she were solitary more often.[38] Writing her memoirs three decades later, Elizabeth Stuart Phelps makes a similar point when she describes the "storm" of letters that she received after publishing *The Gates Ajar* (1868). One of these was from a "distinguished writer" who wanted to "encourage a beginner in his own art." Phelps's joy on receiving this affirmation prompted her to "make it a rule to answer every civil answer that I received," even as she was "snowed under" by the letters.[39] Her experience as a protégée helped maintain her resolve to uphold her responsibilities as a mentor.

As Phelps's experience suggests, authors also wrote each other fan mail, supporting each other and also, at times, complaining about writers who did not fit their own critical judgments of taste. The most famous examples of such literary correspondence in American literary history tend to be those between men: the heated letters between Herman Melville and Nathaniel Hawthorne, for instance; or those between Ralph Waldo Emerson and Walt Whitman (Whitman published a congratulatory letter from Emerson in his second edition of *Leaves of Grass*); or between Henry James and William Dean Howells.[40] Yet women also engaged in productive literary correspondence with fellow authors.[41] As we will see, Alcott had an important correspondence with Caroline Dall, Dodge with Sophia Hawthorne, and Phelps with Stowe and George Eliot. Marion Harland reported in her autobiography how much she appreciated the letters of support from Grace Greenwood and Lydia Sigourney that greeted her first novel, *Alone*. Sigourney, a generation older, sent "three or four letters of motherly counsel, one of which advised me to take certain epochs of American history as foundation-stones for any novels."[42] Sigourney continued such "motherly counsel" in 1863, when she wrote to Dodge in order to welcome her "into our fraternity of Authors" and praise her for "that quiet and delightful humor, which with the exception of our lamented Washington Irving, and a few other instances, is almost a deficient department in American literature."[43]

This epistolary "fraternity of Authors" was not without its competition and infighting. Cooke, for instance, complained to Dodge about Phelps's overblown style. "I feel as if the language was really 'going to the dogs' as well as the people," she wrote, "and I lay a great deal of it to the mighty example of Mrs. Browning whose genius itself scarcely excused her assiduous absurdity. Miss Phelps has no such excuse; yet she has talent and goodness enough to write very excellent stories if she would not speak in unknown tongues."[44] Elizabeth Barrett Browning was a significant influence on Phelps, who read *Aurora Leigh* at the age of twelve. What is interesting about Cooke's comments, however, is not only that she links Browning and Phelps (and thus British and American traditions) but also that she resents the fact that she cannot better control the stylistic productions of the "fraternity of Authors." Cooke concludes her letter by telling Dodge that she "ought to have the Victoria Cross, if we had any such decoration to bestow; but it is one among many traits of our wretched form of government that merit is literally its own reward. I sigh for a good healthy despotism!" Even as Cooke here distinguishes between American and British governments, she also claims for herself and her literary compatriots a policing role that, if decidedly undemocratic, is also based on professional affiliation. She wanted the "fraternity of Authors" to have a role as an arbiter of taste, and if that role required a certain hierarchical control, then she was prepared to exercise it. The epistolary bonds among women authors were supportive but also discriminating, as they extolled, for instance, those with a particular use of humor (as Sigourney did) or with a particular style (as Cooke did).[45]

Letters and letter writing, then, played an important role both in providing literary access and in helping to categorize the terms of that access. The women who began their authorial careers by reading aloud letters provided a model for authorship that was social rather than professional. Yet, as these women became successful professionals—with large circulations, fixed contracts, specific editorial and aesthetic expertise, and professional affiliations ("fraternities of authorship")—they used the form of the letter both as a figure in their writing and as an actual practice to help describe the various steps necessary in moving from manuscript to print. Far from an easy "eureka" moment, these steps were at the same time much more transparent than the romantic ideal of inspired genius. The authors accounting for these states were, for the most part, genial and direct, providing a model that others might emulate while also militating against an easy adoption of that model.

If letters both endorsed and demystified the ideals of parlor literature, they were reinforced by another aspect of parlor culture: visual and biographical portraits. As will be seen in the next section, images of female authors downplayed the economic and material aspects of authorship even as they helped to promote the works of the authors (and sell the periodicals and books in which they appeared). Letters called on women to channel their natural observations into a domestic sketch, but portraits of female authors provided models through which their protégées and fans could observe particular traits of character. These character traits, in turn, tended to reinforce the ideals of parlor literature, putting women into domestic settings and emphasizing their personal character above their artistic talent.

The Portrait in the Parlor

The parlor culture that supported letter writing in both private and public forms also vested material objects—such as locks of hair and photographs—with sentimental value. Almost as soon as the daguerreotype was invented in 1839, people began sending photographs to one another in the mail, but this became an even more common occurrence as technologies gave rise to the tintype and paper *cartes de visite*. Given such exchanges, it is not surprising that early forms of celebrity portraits of authors often took an epistolary form, signed, with an inscription, by the author. Such images gestured toward the intimacy of a letter while also protecting authors from direct contact with their fans.

Sarah J. Hale, for example, printed a portrait of herself in the magazine she edited, *Godey's Lady's Book*, that included her signature with the phrase "Truly yr. Friend" (see Figure 4). Since she could not send an individual autograph to every reader who might want one, she did the next best thing by providing a facsimile. Such a practice transferred into print one of the key features of the manuscript—a gracious closing and personal signature. By the end of the century this sentimental practice had been adopted more generally in the circulation of portraits, crossing race and gender lines. Frederick Douglass, for example, circulated a *carte-de-visite* photograph to his admirers with his autograph and the inscription "With sentiments of highest regard, Very truly yours."[46] The poet Walt Whitman included a reproduction of his autograph on all editions of his writings published after 1888.

For Hale and other antebellum authors, however, this form of personalized iconography served a particular purpose, allowing women's images to circulate in public while at the same time protecting their socially constructed need for privacy.[47] These images, in turn, put forward an idealized vision that downplayed the individual achievements of specific authors. Even as women were claiming authorship in the 1850s, then, they were doing so in the context of a print iconography that deemphasized their individual accomplishments by stressing their continuity with domestic pursuits. The iconography of female authors, in other words, continued

Figure 4. Sarah J. Hale. Engraving from *Godey's Lady's Book* (1850). Courtesy American Antiquarian Society.

to ally them with parlor literature well after they had moved into print. When women authors were pictured in books and magazines, they were presented in demure, nonthreatening poses, such as that in the book illustration used as a prop in the daguerreotype shown in Figure 3.

Consider, for example, the portrait of Sigourney that was included in John Hart's *The Female Prose Writers of America* (1852) (see Figure 5). Sigourney published under her own name, but her pose in this portrait is diffident and modest. The light and clothing emphasize her bust and the head, symbolically the heart and the mind. The inscription, "I am ever your friend," links the portrait with a personal letter and also underscores Sigourney's sincerity. Her appearance is a transparent reflection of her inner character and faithfulness.[48] The essay about her in *The Female Prose Writers of America* expands on this idea, praising her ability to shape "the American mind and heart."[49] In another essay written about Sigourney in 1869, the Reverend E. B. Huntington similarly praises her ability to write "what her kind heart prompted, that she might please or aid those who seemed to her to have just claims upon her." This sense of duty prevents her from "using the precious moments on the mere style of her expression." In this way Sigourney avoids what Huntington deems a self-centered focus on production, or "style." Indeed, "she could not stop to think of her literary reputation when some dear friend was pleading at her heart, or some sorrowing soul needed to be comforted. More than almost any other writer of the day, she wrote not for herself, but for others."[50] Like Hart, Huntington justifies Sigourney's literary production by depicting her as an altruistic true woman rather than an author concerned with her reputation, despite the fact that Sigourney identified herself as a member of a "fraternity of Authors."

These depictions of Sigourney pay less attention to her individual characteristics than to her general traits; there is little distinction between the individual authorial "self" and her "type" as a woman writer.[51] This merging of self and type was exacerbated by the fact that many readers assumed that they could know an author through reading her characters. There was little narrative distance between the author and the fictional world she created. The assumption that an author was just like her characters, in turn, increased the sense of friendship and intimacy between the author and her readers.

The title plate of *The Female Prose Writers of America* (see Figure 6) is telling in its use of the term "writers" rather than "authors." In his introduction, Hart switches terms, noting that "it seems to be an instinctive desire of the human heart, on becoming acquainted with any work of genius, to know something of its author." Hart allies authorship and genius, and yet the overall force of the book is to downplay genius and create a generalized portrait of the female writer. "Women," says Hart, "far more than men, write from the heart. Their own likes and dislikes, their feelings, opinions, tastes, and sympathies are so mixed up with those of their subject, that the interest of the reader is often enlisted quite as much for the writer, as for the hero, of a tale."[52] Such disciplinary pronouncements at once homogenize women into a single group and assume that their lives are as important as, if not more so than, their works—a trend that has continued in much work on women authors throughout the twentieth century.[53]

The frontispiece to Hart's book (see Figure 7) also contributes to this iconography of the woman writer. This image channels the emotional appeal of these writers into a particular patriotic response. A woman, holding a bouquet of flowers rather than a pen, leans on the United States flag. There are books at her feet—demonstrating the foundational aspects of reading—but they are less obvious than the lyre beside her and the pomegranates above her. The lyre associates her with the Greek Muses, while the pomegranates associate her with Persephone, the Greek goddess of fertility and eternity; she is part of a mid-century nostalgia for classical forms. At the same time the natural background, picturing a

Figure 5. Portrait of Lydia Sigourney, from John Hart, *The Female Prose Writers of America* (1852).

tranquil and almost sublime landscape of mountains and streams, suggests that women writers are natural as well as unabashedly American. Women who are artists for their own sake might be unnatural, but women who are true to what they observe in nature and to their country can become patriotic emblems.

The nationalistic iconography evident on Hart's frontispiece was supported by a sense that women had a particular contribution to make to American literary nationalism. As Mrs. A. J. Graves put it in 1847, "in our national female character there is a rich mine for our writers as yet unexplored, which will amply reward all who seek for its virgin ore" and will produce "beautiful revelations of character, more full of originality and deep interest than are to be found in the creations of the most gifted genius."[54] Graves takes some key terms of literary nationalism—originality and national character—and shows how applicable they are to women's sphere. The domestic, in short, becomes equivalent to the national. In the process Graves also disentangles writing and genius; women are not romantic authors, or geniuses, but that makes them more valuable to the project of literary nationalism.

Figure 6. Title page from John Hart, *The Female Prose Writers of America* (1852).

If we link this overall project to the parallel interest in American Manifest Destiny, we can also think of the domestic as bridging separate spheres, uniting, as Amy Kaplan puts it, "men and women in a national domain and [generating] notions of the foreign against which the nation can be imagined as home."[55] In the context of such a "manifest domesticity," depictions of women authors in biographies and portraits become part of a larger national project of defining and civilizing the new nation, especially through normative depictions of white womanhood. It is less important what an author is really like than that she fulfill certain ideals about what she should be like. Consider, for example, an 1843 *Graham's Magazine* engraving entitled "Our Lady Contributors" (see Figure 8). The engraving contains framed portraits of Lydia Sigourney, Catharine Sedgwick, Frances Osgood, Elizabeth Oakes Smith, and Emma C. Embury. But their individual traits are subsumed into the nationalistic iconography of the whole, with the eagle at the top sitting on an emblem of the stars and stripes. Like the Hart frontispiece, this engraving also contains allusions to Greek poetry, with the Muses in the center and the lyre at the bottom. It is thus an image both of national solidarity and of particular

Figure 7. Frontispiece to
The Female Prose Writers of America (1852).

Figure 8. "Our Lady Contributors." Engraving from *Graham's Magazine* (1843).
Courtesy American Antiquarian Society.

cultural origins. The new country is not associated with England and its long literary traditions but rather with classical Greek paradigms.

Although each of the women pictured in *Graham's* holds an individual place in the engraving, the curtain framing the portraits suggests that they could quickly be hidden from view and thereby maintain privacy. The captions on the frames identify the authors, but the overall structure of the image tends to erase individual difference. In this way the image is in line with Hart's unnamed generic writer and also with the "Anonymous Contributor" included in a plate in an 1846 issue of *Godey's Lady's Book* (see Figure 9). Partially framed by lace and by a stylized landscape, this writer merges culture and nature without exposing anything about her private life. The text that accompanies this portrait suggests that her friends will readily identify her. In this sense, it anticipates Walt Whitman's notion, in identifying himself in the 1855 *Leaves of Grass* only by an engraving of his daguerreotype, that those in the know—or perhaps those who should know—will expose the anonymity.

The tradition of publicizing female writers in stylized and idealized

ONE OF OUR ANONYMOUS CONTRIBUTORS.

Engraved by Dick for Godey's Magazine

Figure 9. "Our Anonymous Contributor." Engraving from *Godey's Lady's Book* (1846).

images continued throughout the nineteenth century. Portrayals of the black female body were especially carefully orchestrated. Like Walt Whitman, the evangelist Jarena Lee included her portrait as the frontispiece to her spiritual autobiography, *Religious Experience and Journal of Mrs. Jarena Lee* (1849) (see Figure 10). Her white hat and garment associate her with simple Quaker clothing and lead our eyes to the light on her eyes and on the books at her right arm. Like most portraits of women during this period, she does not look directly at the viewer but rather at a distant place. This pose is echoed in several of the photographs that Sojourner Truth distributed after her lectures in the 1860s and in the well-known 1894 photograph of Harriet Jacobs. This image associates Jacobs more with the genteel character of the grandmother in *Incidents in the Life of a Slave Girl* than with Jacobs's fictional double, Linda Brent, creating an image of the author as wise and upright elder stateswoman rather than sexually violated slave.[56]

Such idealized images persisted after the Civil War. In the late 1860s and 1870s, for instance, the publisher Daniel Lothrop sponsored a five-hundred-dollar prize series and a one-thousand-dollar prize series for aspiring writers—largely women—who presented the best manuscripts on certain subjects. Significantly, the title page for the five-hundred-dollar series features a portrait of a woman reading (presumably in her parlor), while that for the one-thousand-dollar series features a woman sitting at a writing desk (see Figure 11). Good readers can become good writers, the implication seems to be, and good writing can have substantial monetary rewards. The binding on the thousand-dollar series features a gold-embossed check; quality—represented by the gold—does not come without a price.[57] However, by focusing on the writing woman as a particular type (here, the amateur writer who can earn some "pin money," in Rayne's phrase, by entering a contest), Lothrop continues to emphasize a genteel parlor literature more than financially successful professionalism.

In *What Can a Woman Do?*, Rayne further undergirds the domestic nature of such success by describing the homes of two successful female authors. One of them, Mrs. A. D. T. Whitney, lives in a perfectly "home-like place" in which "everything shows the work of hands at home, from the pretty parlor curtains of an unbleached muslin" to "the combination of the shades of brown in the furniture covering." The parlor also contains "photographs which bring to mind 'Sights and Insights'" (one of Mrs. Whitney's books) as well as European engravings "and some pretty little chromos."[58] It is not clear from this description whether the photographs inspired the writing or the writing inspired the photographs, but the title suggests that the visual culture of the parlor ("sights") can lead to observations that in turn produce deeper "insights." As Whitney

From life by A.Hoffy.   Printed by P.S.Duval.

MRS JARENA LEE.

Preacher of the A. M. E. Church.

Aged 60 years on the 11th day of the 2nd month 1844.

Philada 1844

Figure 10. Portrait of Jarena Lee, from *Religious Experience and Journal of Mrs. Jarena Lee* (1849). Courtesy American Antiquarian Society.

Figure 11. "The Thousand Dollar Prize Series." Plate from Julia A. Eastman, *Striking for the Right* (1872). Courtesy American Antiquarian Society.

puts it in the preface to *Sights and Insights,* a book is "a mere medium; a battery of type plates, which you hold by its covers, to receive a magnetic current. And the little black characters upon which you fix your eyes are hypnotizers. The book tells you nothing. You simply perceive. The places, persons, occurrences, are or have been, and you come into intuitive relations with them."[59] Whitney locates the book as an object akin to the other objects that Rayne lists: curtains, furniture, photographs, engravings, chromos. But she also understands that those objects' significance derives from one's "perceptions" about them, perceptions that lead to "intuitive relations" such as those entered into by readers with their authors. The description of Whitney in Rayne's book also emphasizes the idea that being a writer, and even an author, does not interfere with domestic duties. Whitney's writing, which she does on a lap desk wherever it is convenient, does not preclude her maintaining a perfectly "homelike" space.

Even as the Lothrop prize series and books such as Rayne's continued to emphasize women writers in idealized domestic settings, some postbellum portraits did move toward giving more realistic, and individual, portraits of female authors at home or at work in their studies. This was part of a larger move to picture authors in general in private spaces, indicating a shift from focusing on them exclusively through their texts to seeing them as people whose individual lives were interesting in their own right. As Constance Fenimore Woolson put it in 1885, "there is a fancy at present for bringing out 'series' of 'authors' likenesses;' & a photograph of some sort is sure to be obtained of everybody, somewhere; & the thing done whether the victim likes it or not. Therefore how much better to have a good likeness brought out in the proper place."[60] As the term "proper place" suggests, such depictions were still gendered in particular ways. Richard Stoddard's *Poets' Homes* (1879), for example, included a detailed engraving of the novelist Elizabeth Stuart Phelps at work in her study (see Figure 12). Phelps is barely pictured; sitting at the far left of the image, she reveals only her back and part of her silhouette, her body almost lost in an overstuffed chair and behind a large, solid writing desk. The accompanying biographical sketch similarly draws attention to all of the objects in the room rather than to the author: "All the day the sun shines in as cheerfully as it can, struggling through those little windows and those little panes. There are subdued green curtains at these windows; and about the room are books, pictures, a few easy chairs, tables, and many of the nothings which make a study pleasant."[61] Rather than calling attention to Phelps, this sketch emphasizes the "nothings" that make up her domestic surroundings, suggesting that she is both a woman of taste and a woman who shares the desires of her readers to maintain home as a "pleasant" space. If the sun can only partially penetrate this private space, so too do the readers receive only a carefully constructed glimpse of the private life of the woman whose writings had set sales records through highly successful marketing campaigns.

Phelps's case is typical of other nineteenth-century women authors whose books garnered large sales. The more successful the author, the more the surrounding publicity worked to show her to be a "normal" woman working quietly at home. Alcott's success with *Little Women* and its sequels helped her become one of the most famous novelists in the nineteenth century, with readers making pilgrimages to Concord to catch glimpses of her. Her association with other Concord authors is clear in a full-page illustration in an 1880 issue of *Frank Leslie's Illustrated Newspaper*, entitled "Four Luminaries of American Letters" (see Figure 13). The top of this engraving groups Alcott with Emerson, Whittier, and her father, Bronson Alcott. The fact that she is on the same level with these authors (her portrait being merged with theirs and being the same size) suggests, on the one hand, that women were not necessarily seen as inhabiting a separate literary sphere, especially in the second half of the century. Yet of the four authors, only the home of "Miss Alcott" is pictured, as if it is especially important to picture the domestic space in which she lives. At the bottom her father is pictured lecturing in the public hall of the Concord School of Philosophy, which ironically began in his study at Orchard House. There are a few women in the audience but none on the stage. Female authors can be luminaries, the illustration seems to suggest, but that celebrity status needs to be balanced by a close tie to the

Figure 12. Portrait of Elizabeth Stuart Phelps, from Richard Stoddard, *Poets' Homes* (1879).

home rather than the lecture hall. When Louisa May Alcott is pictured addressing a crowd, as in the frontispiece to Ednah D. Cheney's *Louisa May Alcott: The Children's Friend* (1888), it is still in a generic domestic setting rather than a lecture hall. In this image (see Figure 14), Alcott sits in a chair reading to a throng of rather etherealized children, as if Jo March herself were reading to her boys. Again the author is seen only from the side, and the emphasis is not on her individual visage but rather on her relation to a group of children.

A year after publishing *The Children's Friend*, Cheney released a compilation of Alcott's private journals and letters. On one hand, this release was emblematic of a larger trend toward publishing such volumes. The 1880s also marked the publication of Julian Hawthorne's account of his father and the beginning of Horace Traubel's visits with Whitman that would result in *With Walt Whitman in Camden.* All of these volumes were biased toward celebrating the author, but they also indicate the extent to which the lives of American authors had now become subjects in and of themselves. On the other hand, Cheney justifies publishing her volume by returning to the long-standing and familiar notion that works reveal what we need to know about female authors. "Of no author can it be more truly said than of Louisa Alcott that her works are a revelation of herself," Cheney writes. "It is therefore impossible to understand Miss Alcott's works fully without a knowledge of her own life and experiences."[62] The logic here is tautological; the works reveal the author, but it is important to know something about the personal life of the author in order to fully understand the works. To put it another way, the primary reason we become interested in literary biography is because we have read authors' works, but we also read their works primarily to find out something about their lives.

Such thinking is the result of shifting ideas of authorship in the late nineteenth century. Vestigial notions about the privacy of true womanhood and the private sanctity of the romantic author merge with public demands to know more about authors' lives, with the compromise being that biography will enhance understanding of the work. Alcott probably would not have supported publication of such a volume. Cheney acknowledges that Alcott wished to have most of her letters destroyed, and she quotes an 1885 letter to Alcott's publisher Niles in which she declines giving information for another biographical sketch: "I don't like these everlasting notices; one is enough, else we poor people feel like squeezed oranges, and nothing is left sacred."[63]

Alcott's comment suggests that in broad terms, structures of publicity shifted between the antebellum and postbellum periods, from an emphasis on generalized domestic ideals to one on what we might term a cult of personality, an interest in authors' private and nonliterary lives as well

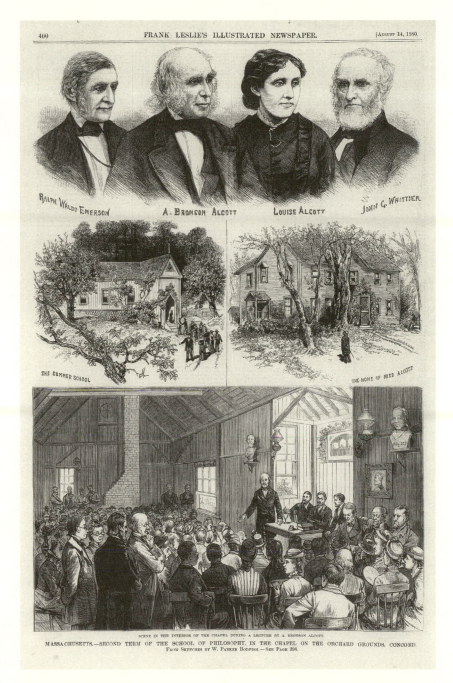

RALPH WALDO EMERSON   A. BRONSON ALCOTT   LOUISE ALCOTT   JOHN G. WHITTIER

THE SUMMER SCHOOL

THE HOME OF MISS ALCOTT

SCENE IN THE INTERIOR OF THE CHAPEL DURING A LECTURE BY A. BRONSON ALCOTT.

MASSACHUSETTS.—SECOND TERM OF THE SCHOOL OF PHILOSOPHY, IN THE CHAPEL ON THE ORCHARD GROUNDS, CONCORD.
FROM SKETCHES BY W. PARKER BODFISH.—SEE PAGE 398.

Figure 13. "Ralph Waldo Emerson, A. Bronson Alcott, Louise Alcott, and John G. Whittier." From *Frank Leslie's Illustrated Newspaper*, August 14, 1880. Courtesy General Research Division, The New York Public Library, Astor, Lenox and Tilden Foundations.

as in their literary lives. At the beginning of this period, biographical sketches of authors frequently refer back to their works: to know the work is to know the author. By its end, however, readers wanted to know details about the authors' lives that are not revealed in their writings.[64] They also increasingly appreciated authors as commodities apart from their works, a shift seen in the large numbers of portraits of authors circulating in magazines, photographic studios, and even card games. At the same time, the increasingly large numbers of illustrations in magazines and annuals, along with the photographs, engravings, and lithographs that were staples of the middle-class parlor, challenged viewers to develop a visual literacy that could create, in Whitney's words, "insights" from "sights." Paradoxically, such visual literacy, combined with the claims to innate powers of observation that undergirded discussions of female authorship, created opportunities for women to lay claim to "realistic" portrayals of everyday life. In other words, they encouraged them to be writers. The authors they studied embraced such writing while also emphasizing the distance between social parlor writing and print. Their images similarly evoked a universal exceptionalism that simultaneously encouraged writing and defined the structures of legitimacy within the literary field.

Figure 14. Frontispiece to Ednah Cheney's *Louisa May Alcott: The Children's Friend* (1888), with engraving by Lizbeth Comins. Courtesy American Antiquarian Society.

In this chapter I have argued that a related set of parlor activities—the reading and writing of letters; the reading of magazines and books that represented female authors both as "friends" and as professionals with a particular expertise; and the prevalence of photographs and engravings as parlor ornaments—worked together to create a particular view of female authorship. In this view, female authorship was grounded in letter-writing practices accessible to all middle-class women. Such writing honed innate skills of observation and ensured that writing did not defeminize the author, who, like the images that surrounded her, was "daguerreotyping" particular scenes and memories. Yet these letters and portraits also helped to distinguish authors from writers, establishing authors as individuals with particular expertise, experience, and character. By the end of the century, the authors singled out for celebrity portraits may still have looked much like everyday women—sitting at desks, talking to children, posing in parlor rooms of commercial studios—but they did not occupy the same position with the field of literary production. Instead of being the women who wrote letters to friends and sent in entries to writing contests, these authors were women who negotiated contracts and wrote to protégées whom they could not always encourage to continue to write.

The next chapter will focus on Maria Cummins, who exemplifies particularly well the transition from parlor writing to authorship. As an author who began by writing private stories for her nieces and ultimately published one of the nineteenth century's best-selling novels, Cummins helps illuminate the trajectory from parlor writing to international celebrity. In Cummins's case, domestic writing is inextricably related to an exploration of authorship, an exploration that, on one hand, deepens and expands the connection between observation and literary authority by focusing on inner as well as external perception while, on the other hand, foregrounding the importance of reception in forging that authority.

Chapter 3

Authorizing Reception
Maria Cummins and The Lamplighter

In 1854, at the age of twenty-seven, Maria Susanna Cummins published her first novel, *The Lamplighter*. She had attended a boarding school run by Catharine Sedgwick's sister-in-law, and Sedgwick may have encouraged the young woman's literary pursuits. A contemporary newspaper account reported that when Cummins left school, Sedgwick told her father, "You must encourage Maria in composition; she has a remarkable talent for it."[1] As we have seen, Sedgwick had parodied the ease of amateur writing in "Cacoethes Scribendi," but like other female authors of her generation, she also saw herself as a literary mentor to women with "remarkable talent." By making this connection between Sedgwick and Cummins, then, the newspaper account draws on a definition of female authorship that involves both professional expertise (the ability of a mentor to identify talent) and an origin in amateur writing. Like Ruth Hall, Cummins initially shows her talent through manuscript compositions written in school. Another newspaper account of Cummins's career ties this amateur writing directly to the parlor culture examined in the last chapter: "She was not aware of the gift she had in authorship. 'The Lamplighter' was not even written with a view to publication. It was composed to entertain Miss Cummins' nieces, and was read to them in installments."[2]

Cummins's practice in composition and her oral reading to her nieces are, in these two accounts, portrayed as reciprocal activities, with reading providing training for writing that then gives another occasion for reading. Yet these two anecdotes also give very different accounts of female authorship, with one emphasizing the expertise of an established mentor and the other emphasizing the author's initial lack of ambition. One places emphasis on a structured practice (encouraging composition), while the other sees success as stemming from an innate "gift." Both of these ideals, as we have seen, were present in periodical accounts of female authorship. This interplay between studied practice and unself-conscious literary production presents Cummins as a successful author while still reassuring readers that she is a properly domestic woman, one who writes to family members as much as to an anonymous audience through print.

Early reviews of *The Lamplighter* similarly employed many of the terms most associated with female authorship in the second half of the nineteenth century: they focused particularly on its author's realism ("word pictures," "scenes in lowly life"), keen observations, and careful attention to language.[3] The *Knickerbocker*, for example, called it "one of the most original and natural narratives we have encountered in many a year" and promised that "you will rise from its perusal with a purer and more elevated idea of human nature."[4] The *Boston Daily Atlas* concluded (with emphasis added by Cummins's publisher) that its author "has evidently a highly *cultivated* and *refined* as well as an *original* and *imaginative mind*, and writes with the ease, the *classical correction of diction*, and that choice selection of terms which indicate the *good English scholar*. In this respect, the 'Lamplighter' is *much superior to 'Uncle Tom's Cabin,' whose inelegancies meet us at every turn*."[5] Stowe would go on to describe attention to diction as one of the key distinctions between an author and a writer, but in 1854 Cummins was praised as the "author" in part through a comparison to the less-studied writing of Stowe.

Since *The Lamplighter* was published anonymously, such initial praise was based on reading knowledge of *The Lamplighter* rather than on individual knowledge of Cummins. As such, it supports Foucault's notion that the author is a function that goes far beyond "the simple attribution of a discourse to an individual," with many of the qualities of that authorship being "projections" proceeding from "our way of handling texts." The initial reviews made assumptions about *The Lamplighter*'s author, but they were based on the text. At the same time, the early publication history of *The Lamplighter* also supports Foucault's notion that "literary anonymity was of interest only as a puzzle to be solved."[6] Readers immediately began to speculate about the identity of its author. Asabel Huntington reported from Cummins's native Salem, Massachusetts, that "the great question in the literary circles of the city" has become "who is the author of 'The Lamplighter'?"[7] The press capitalized on this public curiosity, with several Massachusetts papers reporting that the work was rumored to be by a Boston-area lady. Within a month of the novel's publication, Boston's *Universalist Quarterly and General Review* had connected this rumor to a particular name: "The author is said to be a young lady by the name of Cummings, who resides in Dorchester."[8] With the secret out, editors from the *Boston Evening Gazette*, the *American Union*, and *Waverly Magazine* wrote to Cummins to invite her to contribute a story to their pages. The open secret of Cummins's identity underscores Mary Kelley's assertion that "the paradox of literary domesticity was that secret writers were not so secret."[9]

Even as Cummins's name was quickly identified, however, her authorship remained connected more to *The Lamplighter* than to any individual facts of her biography, both in her own time and in subsequent literary history. In 1857, for example, Cummins's publisher John P. Jewett released her second novel, *Mabel Vaughan*, with no other attribution on its title page than "By the Author of 'The Lamplighter,'" and in 1860 Ticknor and Fields released another novel, *El Fureidîs*, with no other attribution than "By the Author of 'The Lamplighter' and 'Mabel Vaughan.'" The author serves here as a unifying function that connects these texts but has no identity external to those texts. Although Cummins's name did eventually appear in subsequent editions, she was still known largely through an authorial tag line. Even as late as 1922, when James Joyce rewrote Gerty Flint as Gerty MacDowell, she appears in Gerty's mind as "Miss Cummins, author of *Mabel Vaughan* and other tales."[10]

In our own critical moment, studies of *The Lamplighter* have focused less on her authorial biography or attributes than on cultural work. The impetus for such readings is usually Hawthorne's question, in a letter to William Ticknor, about "the mystery of these innumerable editions of *The Lamplighter*, and other books neither better nor worse," a question that follows his infamous complaint about the "d——d mob of scribbling women."[11] It is likely, as Nina Baym has persuasively argued, that Hawthorne never even read *The Lamplighter*, probably assuming that it was a sensational novel about "low life." His anxiety was as much about his own publisher's marketing strategies as it was about the success of women in the literary marketplace.[12] Yet his letter is still *The Lamplighter*'s primary claim to fame.

In this chapter I want to put pressure on Hawthorne's comment by thinking about the publication and reception history of *The Lamplighter*: a history that suggests that its "innumerable" sales were directly related to Jewett's vigorous promotional campaign. As I have already suggested, in the 1850s Hawthorne was anomalous in associating *The Lamplighter* with the production of "scribbling women" or, in the terms I have been using, writers. Instead, most reviews of *The Lamplighter*—many of which were quoted by Jewett in his advertisements for the book—referred to an "author," even when that authorship was not directly linked to Cummins. It is important, I think, to pay attention to this nomenclature and to see the ways in which Jewett's promotion of *The Lamplighter* capitalized on notions of American authorship, and of female authorship in particular, that were being developed in periodicals and other print sources at this time. Despite the fact that Cummins was not well known and that the book was published anonymously, Jewett still used authorship as a means to appeal to his book-buying public. This use, in turn, suggests the important distinction between legal, personal, and discursive conceptions of the author.

After examining Jewett's promotional campaign, I will turn to a reading of *The Lamplighter* and the ways in which it theorizes issues of authorship. While rooting the novel in many aspects of the parlor culture discussed in the last chapter, Cummins also defines successful authorship as decentered rather than unified, focusing on reception, rather than composition, as a point of production. Although *The Lamplighter* may have originally been written as a parlor entertainment, in other words, it ultimately demystifies the idea of amateur writing—particularly in the form of the personal letter—as the originary point of female authorship. Instead, it suggests that the greatest value of writing comes from its ability to move beyond its own origins: to go from manuscript to print to the individual mind of the reader. Such a formulation, while drawing on romantic conceptions of the immediacy of print, also suggests the ways in which authorship can operate as a conceptual category apart from any one historical person.

John P. Jewett and the Promotion of *The Lamplighter*

Nineteenth-century accounts of Cummins's decision to write *The Lamplighter* tended to emphasize her literary mentorship or her connection to a parlor literature that linked literary production to family entertainments. These same accounts also frequently credited Cummins's Boston publisher, John P. Jewett, for the successful promotion of the book (although at least one found his "pre-announcements" to be "injudicious" and to arouse suspicion rather than confidence, suggesting the ways in which such an advertising campaign could lead to misconceptions, as they may have in Hawthorne's case).[13] The book was, as one early review put it, "unheralded except by the publisher's advertisement, without the prestige of a name, without pretension of any sort, without a dedication or even a preface."[14] Its "prestige" came from its publisher's advertisements rather than from an author's name. And indeed, in 1854 Jewett was enjoying considerable fame. Having entered the publishing business producing textbooks, Jewett did not take up fiction until 1851, when he published Elizabeth Stuart Phelps's *The Sunny Side, or the Country Minister's Wife*. By establishing a branch in Cleveland under the name Jewett, Proctor, and Worthington, he positioned himself to distribute his books both to the East Coast and to the growing western market. In 1852 Jewett acquired the rights to Stowe's *Uncle Tom's Cabin*, which by the end of the year had sold 305,000 copies. The same commentator who speaks of Cummins writing to "entertain her nieces" also recognizes the importance of Jewett's connection to Stowe, noting that "the prestige that Mr. Jewett had attained in 'Uncle Tom's Cabin' doubtless aided it, and advertising's artful aid was fully called into requisition to promote its sale." Such a comment effectively leaves Cummins in the parlor, as distant from promotional activities as she is from authorial ambition.

In fact, however, Cummins signed a contract with Jewett that stipulated that he would "keep the market constantly supplied" with her book and "use all reasonable efforts to promote an extensive sale."[15] In return, she would receive a royalty of 10 percent of the retail price of each copy of the book sold, the most common percentage at that time.[16] Stowe, like Cummins, received a 10 percent royalty on *Uncle Tom's Cabin*, having turned down Jewett's offer of a half-profit agreement, in which she would have had an equal share in both the costs and the profits.[17] Cummins's contractual agreement with Jewett established her legal rights to financial compensation, although Jewett retained the copyright. The fact that *The Lamplighter* appeared anonymously did not preclude her having financial benefit as an author; as an unmarried woman, she retained the money that she earned.

At the same time, Cummins's contract with Jewett did not prevent others from reprinting and adapting the book. Almost immediately after *The Lamplighter*'s publication, Boston's Theater Company produced a stage version of the book. The company's manager offered Cummins a free ticket to see the show but no other rights, either artistic or financial. In fact, the playwright, John Durivage, made egregious changes to the plot, adding an attempted robbery and murder on the Boston Common; a scene in which a physician (presumably Dr. Jeremy) stops in front of the Revere House to sing "The Old Folks at Home"; and a love scene in which a gentleman addresses the Frog Pond, "Farewell, thou mimic ocean, where oft in childhood I have sailed my mimic barque."[18] Cummins appears to have let this farcical adaptation go unchallenged, letting it serve in tandem with Jewett's promotional campaign to create interest in the novel. Similarly, when Cummins received a letter from the German publisher Bernhard Tauchnitz requesting permission to reprint the novel, she granted permission based on the rights of her publisher rather than her rights as an author. Since his foreign reprinting would "never interfere with the rights of [her] American publisher," she wrote, she was happy and indeed "flattered" to gain "admission to a place in [his] list."[19]

Legal status, however, is not the only way in which authorship was deployed as a conceptual category in Cummins's case. Since the book was published anonymously, Cummins's own proprietary interest in the book was initially obscured. Even the printer's proofreader did not know her name, writing "to the author (whoever she may be)" and hoping that his "verbal alterations . . . will meet the author's sanction."[20] Such proprietary interest or "sanction" has often been invoked and debated as a founding component of professional authorship, as authors struggle to protect their property within an increasingly commodified literary market. In the nineteenth century in particular, the legal status of the proprietary author and the persona of the romantic author combined (perhaps only circumstantially) to posit the importance of the author as an individual subject. Yet, as Robert J. Griffin points out, "the history of publication shows unequivocally that there is no cause-and-effect relation between the ownership of literary property, or the lack of it, and the presence or absence of the name of the author." Indeed, "a book can have several of the characteristics of the author-function as Foucault defines it— status, copyright, relation to other books by the same author, and so on— and yet not have a named author."[21] To publish anonymously, in other words, does not necessarily mean relinquishing an authorial identity.

The relation between anonymity and legal contract was particularly complex for women, even if they were unmarried. Rebecca Harding Davis, for example, published anonymously in the 1860s in both the *Atlantic Monthly* and *Peterson's Magazine*, enjoying the cultural prestige of the former and the higher payment (and circulation) of the latter. Yet after *Peterson's* began using the byline "by the author of Margret Howth" (a Ticknor and Fields publication) and after Davis published a story called "Ellen" in both magazines, James T. Fields removed Davis from his list of contributors to the *Atlantic*. Although Davis was publishing anonymously in both cases, then, she was also writing with particular agreements about her pay and attribution, and her failure to meet those agreements led Fields to distance himself from her.[22] Cummins's case was not quite as complicated as was Davis's; she moved progressively from one publisher to another without running into problems of dual submission or attribution. But like Davis, she established her agreements with publishers under her own name while appearing in print anonymously (if not entirely secretly). The fact that her authorship was so often invoked without her name helps us to see the ways that authorship was used as much to designate a conceptual category as to refer to an individual biography.

Jewett began such invocations even before the book was published, when he aroused interest in it by running advertisements in periodicals and trade publications predicting it not only to be another best-seller ("great curiosity has already been excited," his awkwardly passive formulation put it) but also to be "a work of extraordinary power and ability, one which will rank among the very best productions of American or Foreign Genius."[23] "Genius" becomes a synonym for "author," here defined as an autonomous and transcendent (and transnational) creator who, in the tradition of the medieval *auctor*, breaks down "the reciprocal relationship between the author and the rest of culture," as Donald Pease puts it.[24] Other advertisements that Jewett used more specifically associated this "genius" with a restrained use of language and keen observation, traits frequently identified with female authorship in particular. But the key point is that Jewett's prepublication promotional campaign consistently invoked an author without using a specific name, thereby claiming the expertise, talent, and status of the author without drawing on the name of the person who had a legal interest in that status.

As soon as the book was published, Jewett began a two-pronged promotion of the book that linked sales to quality. He provided frequent (and probably not wholly reliable) updates on its sales, announcing on April 1, 1854, that sales of the book totaled "20,000 COPIES IN TWENTY DAYS" and a month later, "40,000 COPIES IN EIGHT WEEKS!!," with "the immense demand continuing without abatement." By October 16 Jewett could boast the publication of 65,000 copies of "the most charming of American romances."[25] He sold the book for $.75, helping to stimulate sales (his editions of *Uncle Tom's Cabin* had been priced between $1.50 and $3.00), but he had also given it attractive packaging, issuing it in cloth instead of paper and including a picture of the lamplighter stamped in gold on the spine.

His advertisements emphasized its quality by quoting reviews that noted its textual sophistication. One advertisement, for example, identifies it as "one of the most fascinating and elegantly written volumes ever issued from the American Press," a volume that "stands out above and superior to all other emanations of the American and European Press, as the Great Book of the year 1854."[26] In order to support these claims, Jewett quoted reviews praising *The Lamplighter*'s originality, cultivation, and refinement, and calling it as "affecting" as the "best sketches of Dickens." In this way the reviews associate the author of *The Lamplighter* with the culturally prestigious name of Dickens without having to make a personal connection.

In an effort to enhance further the literary prestige of *The Lamplighter*, Jewett followed the initial edition of the novel with a deluxe illustrated edition. This edition, published in 1855 to mark the sale of 73,000 copies of the book, sold for twice as much as the original ($1.50) and was meant to last. It was, as one review described it, "published on fine white paper, with clear type, and bound in the very finest style." This quality, moreover, reflected that of the text: "it is a story of great merit," the review continued, "and the deep, benevolent, and moral tone it breathes inspires a kindred principle in the heart of the reader."[27]

Jewett then capitalized on the engravings used in the deluxe edition to create an inexpensive picture book for children. *The Lamplighter Picture Book, or the Story of Uncle True and Little Gerty, Written for the Little Folks* (1856) abbreviated the story, ending with the death of Trueman Flint, but continued to promote its excellence. The book ends with an advertisement directed to parents: "If the reader would learn more of Gerty's after life, he will find what he wishes in perusing 'The Lamplighter,' a most excellent book, which all should read; published by JOHN P. JEWETT AND CO., BOSTON."[28]

This children's edition glossed the book as an abolitionist tract, inspiring reform by drawing analogies between Gerty's story and the horrors of slavery. The reader pitying Gerty is encouraged to extend that compassion to enslaved people in the South:

Ye who weep o'er little Gerty,
Squalid, ragged, friendless, poor,
Weep the more for slaves now mourning,
Oft with tyrant's lashes sore.

Similarly, the kitten that Trueman Flint gives Gerty becomes a metaphor for the fugitive slave, and the plaster cast of a bowing Samuel stands for "one in chains, with upraised hands."[29]

Jewett probably initiated the plan to recast one version of *The Lamplighter* as an abolitionist allegory. Although *The Bibliography of American Literature* attributes the verse condensation to Cummins, albeit with some reservations, she most likely would have written it at his direction.[30] Even before he published *Uncle Tom's Cabin*, Jewett had gained a reputation for publishing abolitionist writing, and Stowe's success strengthened that reputation. Furthermore, Jewett had already issued *Pictures and Stories from Uncle Tom's Cabin* (1853), which similarly combined verse and illustrations with a heavily abridged plot. Its purpose was "to adapt Mrs. Stowe's touching narrative to the understanding of the youngest readers, and to foster in their hearts a generous sympathy to the wronged Negro race of America."[31] Living in Boston, Jewett would have been especially aware of the appeal of such sympathy; in the mid-1850s Boston was a center of abolitionist reform, with the offices of the Massachusetts Anti-Slavery Society, the American Anti-Slavery Society, and the *Liberator* all located close to the city's printer's row.[32] *The Lamplighter Picture Book* catered to this abolitionist market by giving the novel a more explicitly political agenda that would appeal to parents as well as children.

The effectiveness of Jewett's campaign can be seen not only in the successful sales of *The Lamplighter* but also in the number of early readers who sent him letters to the "author" of the book even when they did not know her name. As was the case with other popular female authors of the period who wrote under pseudonyms, such as Susan Warner and Fanny Fern, readers did not focus on the author's actual identity and personality. Instead, they wrote to the author of the book, projecting onto her the qualities they assumed such an author should have. Paul Swanwick, for example, wrote from Boston requesting Cummins's autograph. "I have smiled and wept, over your story," he wrote. "I have felt that it could come, only from a mind of the most exalted order, —only from a heart, full of the best traits with which humanity is blessed." He thinks of her, furthermore, as "one who writes, not merely to please and amuse, but to learn your readers ever to turn a trustful eye Heavenward."[33] A year before Hawthorne wrote to Ticknor complaining about *The Lamplighter*'s innumerable editions, then, another Massachusetts man was writing to the author in order to distinguish her mind, heart, and morality from other writers.

To be sure, some of Cummins's fans were overly intrusive, making demands on her similar to those that Fern parodies in *Ruth Hall*. Jewett reported to Cummins that he was "frequently importuned by Gentlemen from various sections of the country, to give them an introduction to you," but he reported having "positively refused all such applications, deeming it not only improper, but decidedly annoying."[34] One of Jewett's jobs was to discriminate between inappropriate advances and ones that he should pass on to Cummins, and he based these discriminations on letters that addressed the author rather than the individual behind that author.

The fact that Jewett had to make such judgments suggests that authorship, as a discursive category, was in the 1850s still intimately connected to parlor culture. A book that may have begun as an entertainment for Cummins's nieces led readers to want to share their own stories with Cummins, in letters that she could read (if Jewett passed them on) at the same desk where she had written the manuscript. Even as Jewett promoted the book as the work of a transnational "genius," then, readers assumed (and then read in the press) that it was the work of an American woman, and they projected those domestic traits onto her as well. The very speculation about her identity constituted a kind of parlor game, a form of gossip that helped promote interest in the book.

Yet for Cummins, as for Stowe, writing for the parlor was only a key first step in the movement from manuscript to print. "Miss Cummings [*sic*] has the true satisfaction of having seen a production which she commenced for the entertainment of a private circle, welcomed throughout the land as a pleasant and gracious benefaction, and taking an honorable place in our distinctively American literature," one review concluded in 1854.[35] This review—written at the height of Jewett's promotional campaign—presents an alternate authorial construction to Jewett's. Whereas Jewett focused on sales figures and transnational success (the reviews quoted in his advertisements tend to emphasize the author's connection to Dickens and European authors), this review focuses on Jewett as a domestic author, in the sense both of writing from the home and of writing a distinctively American literature.[36] While Jewett's sales campaign did much to promote its author as a genius, in other words, other reviews and everyday readers were constructing her authorship differently: as domestic, American, and intimately moral.

None of this, significantly, depended on the actual facts of Cummins's life, except the vague—and often repeated—idea of the manuscript having started in the "private circle." Yet current scholars trying to determine some of these actual facts have corroborated the importance of this "private circle" to her authorship. For example, Heidi Jacobs has shown that when Cummins read the proofs for the English edition of her third book, *El Fureidîs* (1860), she did so from the homes of her London hosts, one of whom was the publisher Sampson Low. In a letter to her mother from the Lows' home, she reports testing some of her language by sharing it with Low's daughters, re-creating the scene of reading that is implicit in the newspaper anecdote about entertaining her nieces. Yet, in this case she shares her work not to hide her ambition but rather to foster it; the Low daughters become a focus group through which she can test the success of her writing in communicating with its readers. If her editorial work, or what she termed "business," continued in the same parlor setting in which she was said to have originally begun writing, it also complicated the notion of the parlor as a private social space separate from business concerns. Even as she engaged in such literary business, however, she continued to write letters home to her mother that contained, in her words, "observations" about London life framed into what she terms "my long stories."[37] Even after her work had moved from the parlor to being an international best-seller, then, she continued the practice of writing letters that were themselves conceived as stories to be read by her mother.

This international parlor scene presents important nuances to the idea of parlor culture put forward by Joan Hedrick and others: while still rooted in the reading practices of the "private circle," it also fosters transnational business. These nuances, in turn, help connect Jewett's market promotion of *The Lamplighter* to the parlor culture that supported Cummins's initial composition of the book. Jewett supported the parlor culture by deciding which mail would be appropriate for Cummins to read in her home and by producing editions of the book that could be displayed as well as read in the parlor. Yet, he also promoted the book as a national and international event, comparing it to British and European productions and "ensuring its extensive sale."

Jewett's various editions, and the sales they generated, turned out to be a mixed blessing. In order to accommodate the continuing demand for *Uncle Tom's Cabin* and *The Lamplighter,* he had to intensify his capital investment, and he declared bankruptcy in the wake of the Panic of 1857.[38] He had just published Cummins's second novel, *Mabel Vaughan,* on the same terms as publication of *The Lamplighter*; after the bankruptcy he signed over his rights to Crosby, Nichols and Company. Cummins, in the meantime, continued to use Boston publishers until her death in 1866, contracting with Ticknor and Fields to publish *El Fureidîs* and with

J. E. Tilton to publish *Haunted Hearts* (1864). Ticknor and Fields agreed to pay her "fifteen percent of the retail price" of all copies sold, while Tilton moved to thirty cents per copy, up to a maximum sum of five thousand dollars.[39] As we will see in Chapter 5, the move to paying a fixed price rather than a percentage was a common one among publishers in the 1860s, and one that Mary Abigail Dodge, among others, believed was inherently unfair. Nevertheless, the publishers did appear to honor them. Her brother and literary executor, Thomas Kittredge Cummins, was still receiving royalties as late as 1898.[40]

These continuing revenues corresponded to the continued publication of her books, and of *The Lamplighter* in particular, throughout the nineteenth century. The novel was reprinted by American publishers at least thirteen times after Jewett's bankruptcy.[41] The book also had British and foreign editions for which Cummins would have received no compensation. In 1854, the year *The Lamplighter* first appeared, the British House of Lords had decided in *Jeffreys v. Boosey* to deny British copyright to foreign authors unless they were in residence in Britain when their work was published.[42] Since Cummins was not, she did not retain copyright over any of numerous British editions of *The Lamplighter*, including six separate editions in 1854 alone and subsequent editions in 1856, 1862, 1864, 1867, 1875, 1888, 1889, and 1893.[43] (Her residence in London at the time of publication of the British edition of *El Fureidîs* suggests that this situation changed with her later publications.) The first British edition of *The Lamplighter*, published in April 1854, was a joint imprint of Clarke, Beeton and John Cassell that was first issued in the Penny Weekly Numbers. George Routledge soon added another edition to his Railway Library, selling more than one hundred thousand copies in two months. As in America, there was also a farcical play produced in tandem with the book, complete with an added tableau set in a California mining camp and a climactic appearance of "a flying figure with extended wings" who is "surrounded with a blaze of light."[44]

The popularity of *The Lamplighter* was not confined to Britain. It also attracted English readers on the Continent. In 1854 the German publisher Bernhard Tauchnitz published it as part of his Collection of British Authors series (an ironic rubric, given, on the one hand, American reviewers' celebration of Cummins's native genius and, on the other, the anti-American slant of the British stage version). Tauchnitz had gained fame not only for publishing affordable, reliable editions but also, in the era before international copyright, for obtaining permission to do so from the authors he reprinted—editions he labeled "copyright editions."

The Lamplighter was translated into French, German, Danish, Italian, Dutch, and Czech, also often with free adaptations. Dutch publishers, for instance, abridged the novel to focus on Gerty's story exclusively, reducing character description and development in order to create an easily grasped, edifying tale particularly appropriate for children.⁴⁵ These translations and abridgment again suggest the ways in which parlor literature and market production could go hand in hand: the international distribution of *The Lamplighter* created new sites in which the book could again be an entertainment for the "private circle," with that circle now expanded to encompass not only Cummins's nieces but also Dutch children.

Authorship in *The Lamplighter*

This abridgment, while gesturing back to the book's idealized status as parlor literature, also indicates a more profound shift in the reception of *The Lamplighter*. By the early twentieth century it was beginning to be viewed as children's literature rather than as an adult novel. Although Jewett had promoted it as a great American novel and an international publishing event, it eventually assumed a different marketing niche. A 1901 article in the *Pall Mall Magazine* on the success of the Tauchnitz editions reported that *The Lamplighter* "continues to fascinate young readers—and certainly no one can be sorry for that."⁴⁶ If Cummins was mentored by Catharine Sedgwick, *The Lamplighter* later came to influence other authors who read it as children. Henry James, for example, remembered it as a book "over which [he] fondly hung" but refused to recognize as a "truly grown-up" novel, reserving that title instead for works of "ranker actuality" and "impropriety."⁴⁷ James Joyce alluded to it in similar ways in *Ulysses*, using it as a sign of the innocence and sentimentality that attract Bloom to Gerty MacDowell.

Joyce's views of *The Lamplighter*—and Hawthorne's—remained the dominant ones throughout the twentieth century. Even after the revival of interest in women's writing, there has, until recently, been a remarkable sameness about criticism of *The Lamplighter*. Such criticism has tended to focus either on its status as popular fiction and as a market phenomenon—usually only in passing—or its articulation of sentimental ideology, often in a continuum with Susan Warner's *The Wide, Wide World* (a move that reviewers noted almost as soon as the book was published).⁴⁸ Nina Baym, for example, describes it as a "rewriting of Warner's story in a more benevolent and rationalist mode."⁴⁹ This particular line of succession has in turn been put to some provocative uses: Orm Øverland, for example, shows how Warner and Cummins contributed to a Norwegian-American literary tradition; Lawrence Buell places *The Lamplighter*, as a popular novel, in a continuum with the "high art" of Hawthorne and Emerson in terms of its concern with questions of "literary and moral authority"; and Alfred Habegger uses it to think about the construction of masculine anxiety and that anxiety's relation to realism.⁵⁰

These readings, however, tend to assume that Cummins's writing, while influential, lacks what Buell terms "ironic self-consciousness" and "self awareness" about the issues that it presents. This assumption, in turn, posits authors, particularly "high-art" ones, as bringing to their writing a high level of self-reflexivity about the goals and status of authorship. Yet, *The Lamplighter*, I will argue, does present a significant commentary on the transition from parlor writing to print. Although it is difficult to nail down exactly how aware Cummins was of these issues, *The Lamplighter* provides a significant case study of the way in which assumptions about authorship can operate within a text. If Jewett used particular ideals of authorship to help promote the book—ideals that may or may not have intersected with the facts of Cummins's life—so too *The Lamplighter* engages with many of these ideals. In the rest of this chapter I want to unpack some of these ideals in order to examine the ways in which we can see *The Lamplighter* as enacting the trajectory from parlor culture to print and the related trajectory (in nineteenth-century terms) from writer to author. Cummins's portrayal of these issues is less antagonistic than reciprocal, showing the ways in which letter writing, reading, and story-telling are interrelated activities.

Although most of *The Lamplighter* is presented in third-person narra-tion, Cummins sometimes highlights the telling of the story by creating an "engaging" first-person narrator. In the second sentence of the open-ing chapter, for example, this narrator describes the "close streets where my story leads me" (1).[51] Story here is prior to the storyteller, or the orig-inating consciousness of the author; the primary author is suggested in the first epigraph in the novel, which invokes a "Good God." By referring to God and "my story" within two sentences of each other, the narrator simultaneously deflects and asserts her own agency. Just as the promotion of the book distinguished its "author" from the legal identity of Maria Cummins, so too the opening distinguishes the authority of God and story from the voice of the narrator. But by inserting a first-person nar-rative intrusion so immediately, she also compels the reader to be aware of her presence as a narrator. The narrative intrusions in the rest of the novel—though rare—continue this dialectical approach, establishing her authorial persona as beneficent but restricted by her class status. "We have often pitied such little drudges," she says later in the first chapter (8). Even as she shows pity for laboring children, however, she claims that she has even more sympathy for her heroine Gerty Flint, who is poor but also bored. If Gerty's problem is that she has leisure but not the middle-class status to support it, the narrator's articulation of this prob-lem marks her as someone who is removed from the everyday life of "drudges" but has converted her leisure into something productive: writ-ing in order to instill sympathy for others.

The relation between sympathy and sentiment is further invoked in another narrative intrusion soon after, when the reader is, for the first and only time, invoked directly: "Reader! Do *you wonder* who they are, the girl and the old man? or, have you already conjectured that they are no other than Gerty and Trueman Flint?" (87). Time has passed, and Gerty has been adopted by the lamplighter, Trueman Flint, who has in turn suffered a paralytic stroke. However, as the interjection suggests, these changes have not rendered Gerty and True unrecognizable to the reader, who is adept at "conjecture" and has also been given various narrative clues. By appealing to readers' ability to make observations and conjectures, the narrator distinguishes them from the less observant townspeople about whom they are reading. This direct address comes after a description of "Miss Peekout" and "Miss Grumble" looking out their windows at the unlikely pair, along with Belle and Kitty Clinton. The Clinton sisters will eventually become Gerty's social rivals as well as members of her extended family; their aunt marries Mr. Graham, father of Gerty's adopted mother Emily. But the point here is that Cummins's implied reader has a more intimate understanding of characters than do the middle-class women who stare out of their windows all day while gossiping. Like these gossips, the readers "peek" at the story passing by, probably as a way to pass leisure time. However, unlike the gossips, the readers learn to be sympathetic and discerning observers. Gerty and True remain in a different social category than that of either the reader or the narrator (although we are told early on that Gerty has "good taste . . . inborn" [47], which is confirmed in the revelation of her true parentage), but the reader and the narrator become intimate with one another through their engagement with the characters.

Such beneficent connection between reader and narrator is a key feature of parlor literature since it assumes a personal conversation between the two that is more akin to a conversation or letter between friends than to gossip about strangers. By appealing to keen observation, Cummins also identifies her readers more with the author-narrator than with the characters. The Clintons and the Misses Peekout and Grumble are in their parlors, idly watching the activities on the street, while the reader is in the narrator's metaphorical parlor, sharing her story and her superior ability to observe character traits.

Given this connection to parlor culture, it is not surprising that the first thing that Gerty does after her adoption by Trueman Flint is to learn to clean his room and make tea, making it a lower-class approximation of an ideal parlor. Her neighbor Willie Sullivan even brings her a plaster figurine of Samuel praying, which he puts "in the middle of the table for a centre ornament" (33), making it proper parlor furniture. She also learns to read aloud to Emily Graham, who is blind, and to write letters to Willie, who soon goes to India to work as a merchant. Although the reader is early established as already inhabiting this parlor, Gerty has to learn its proper functions.

Gerty's first letters to Willie show this education in process, as Gerty uses the letters as exercises in describing the details of everyday life. "You made me promise, Willie, to write about myself," she writes in one, "so, if my letter is more tedious than usual, it is your own fault" (109). In this particular letter she focuses on the Clintons' country house, which she is visiting with Emily. Acknowledging that she "talked enough about my first visit here to excuse you for being quite tired of the subject," she goes on to describe the narrowness of the entry and piazzas and the lowness of the rooms. Even as she does so, she foregrounds Willie as the reader of these descriptions: "I think I hear you say, when you have read so far, 'O dear! now Gerty is going to give me a description of Mr. Graham's country-house!'—but you need not be afraid; I have not forgotten how, the last time I undertook to do so, you placed your hand over my mouth to stop me, and assured me you knew the place as well as if you had lived there all of your life, for I had described it to [you] as often as once a week ever since I was eight years old" (109). This extraordinary passage simultaneously invokes and critiques the practice of letter writing as parlor entertainment. On one hand, it suggests the routinized nature of descriptions in letter writing; if observation is one of the hallmarks of women's writing, it is an art that is learned rather than innate, taking weekly practice over years. On the other hand, it suggests the disciplinary nature of such learning; Willie's hand over Gerty's mouth is an emblem not only of the self-control that Gerty must learn but also specifically of a male editorial function that both demands and controls the terms of women's observational powers. The fact that she imagines Willie making such a move even from Calcutta links her domestic writing with Willie's nascent imperialism: her letters support him in his work as a mercantile clerk, in which he teaches the Indian workers to internalize his words as much as Gerty has. The complication, of course, is that Cummins—although just writing her first novel and envisioning it above all as a parlor entertainment—is also setting herself up in this disciplinary function, becoming the author who has moved beyond set description.

Once Gerty has mastered these skills, however, not only does she learn how to read and police her own letters, internalizing the critique that she can imagine receiving, but she also increasingly becomes the recipient or copyist of others' letters. Having established that private writing is learned, not innate, Gerty models another aspect of parlor culture: learning to be a consumer as well as a producer by reading letters aloud. Gerty writes letters to Willie, but she also takes dictation for Mrs. Sullivan and for Emily. At the end of *The Lamplighter*, as the plot continues to thicken, so too do the letters, many of which are reprinted in their entirety. These letters represent a different kind of narrative intrusion, in this case by a different narrative voice altogether, but they also continue to anatomize authorship as letter writing made public.

The first interpolated letters are a series that Gerty receives, in one envelope, from Mrs. Ellis (the Grahams' housekeeper, who is upper class but reduced to work), Emily, and Mr. Graham. Their collective purpose is to inform Gerty of Mr. Graham's marriage to Mrs. Clinton, which has occurred in New Orleans after an initial courtship in Cuba. Of the three letters, Mrs. Ellis's is the most like parlor conversation, full of personal asides and circuitous in getting to "the principal thing," which she finally reveals to be the fact that the Clintons would like Gerty to join them in Europe. She combines a report of the Clintons' complicated travel schedule with psychological studies of the people she describes: Mrs. Clinton's posturing, Mr. Graham's weakness ("he didn't really mean to have her," but "she carried her point"), and Emily's fortitude (181). Emily's note, short and sweet, also displays this fortitude, encouraging Gerty to come by telling her how much she misses her. Mr. Clinton's has all the markings of a business letter, getting straight to the point and talking about how she might get the money she would need to travel. Taken together, they indicate how letters reveal as much about the writer as they do about their apparent subjects.

The next letter we see is from Gerty, who has also moved away from descriptions of country houses to an interest in character. She reports to a neighbor, Mrs. Jeremy, that she has met up with the wedding party but that Mr. Clinton's illness has caused them to cancel their European trip. The striking thing about this letter is that she has become a character in the drama about which she had previously only read. Telling Mrs. Jeremy that "we" will soon return to the country house, she notes that "I say we, for neither Mr. Graham nor Emily will hear of my leaving them again" (187). Just as Cummins's narrator becomes a "we" with the reader, so too does Gerty (becoming increasingly middle class) become a character as well as a reporter. And this participation enables her to write different kinds of letters, ones that go beyond stock descriptions in order to include character judgments. She has moved beyond the conventions of the familiar letter to create what one 1856 article on letter writing called the "best" letter, one that "comes close home to the heart."[52] In such a candid "heart" letter, Gerty is willing to admit that she and Emily both have "a degree of selfish satisfaction" that they are returning home since they did not want to travel in the first place. She realizes that such satisfaction is inappropriate, given the fact that illness causes the cancellation, but her willingness to give it a name suggests that she is aware of the importance of self-satisfaction as well as of self-control. It also suggests that having learned to record everyday details, she is now able to move to identifying character traits in herself and others, an observational expertise often associated with female authors.

After writing this letter, Gerty continues to practice her powers of observation by functioning as eyes to the blind Emily, giving "glowing description[s] of nature" (196) as well as verbal tours of art museums. But as she does so, Gerty becomes increasingly aware of the "self" producing what she describes, whether it is God (in the case of nature) or the artist (in the case of the paintings). In the galleries of a museum, "Emily listened while Gertrude, with glowing eyes and a face radiant with enthusiasm, described with minuteness and accuracy the subject of the pieces, the manner in which the artist had expressed in his work the original conception of his mind" (253). As an eight-year-old tutored by Willie, Gerty learned to describe external appearances, but as an adopted member of the Clinton family, she has learned to think about the production of what she sees. Her descriptions of art take her beyond being a copyist—or a woman writer—to internalizing the "original conceptions" of artists—or authors. Her abilities in this score ironically anticipate those of Hilda in Hawthorne's *The Marble Faun*, whose copies are better than the originals they imitate. Just as Gerty learns to combine selfhood and selflessness, so too she demonstrates an artistry of observation that is not incompatible with the idea of originality and the organizing consciousness of an author. Cummins emphasizes the importance of this moment by distancing her readers from the immediate scene, remarking that Gerty and Emily were "a study, if not for the artist, for the observer of human nature, as manifested in novel forms and free from affectation and worldliness" (253). She has made a book ostensibly written for her nieces into a "novel form" of the novel, one that pushes observation beyond surface detail to glean something about "human nature."

The trajectory of Gerty's development, then, has her learning the conventions of parlor culture, particularly its emphasis on observation and reporting everyday details, and then moving out of the parlor to nature, museums, and various travel sites in which she can learn to apply these observations to inner as well as outer life. This trajectory, which mimics the movement from writer to author, is complicated, however, by two other aspects of Cummins's plot: first, its treatment of the writing of the two central male characters, Willie Sullivan and Philip Amory (Gerty's future husband and rediscovered father, respectively); and second, its final location of authorship in the practice of reading rather than writing.

In a key scene near the end of *The Lamplighter*, Willie and Philip—both world travelers who have returned to the United States after significant absences—meet "in a well-furnished private parlor of one of those first-class hotels in which New York city abounds" (340). The casual allusion to "one of those first-class hotels" suggests the middle-class status of Cummins's intended audience, but it also suggests the centrality of the parlor to the reintegration of these travelers into the domestic (national) sphere. As Katherine Grier points out, "the public rooms of city hotels were perhaps the most influential form of commercial parlor between 1830 and 1860," creating model spaces that individual families could replicate at home.[53] The "private" space of the parlor was, in this sense, constructed by a public consumer culture that was embraced by men as well as women. Rehearsing their stories in this space, Willie and Philip in turn become the producers of a certain kind of parlor literature. In this case, the parlor is not a site of restriction but rather of reintegration, not a place of idle watching out the window but rather of recounting international travels. Yet, as they sit in the parlor, they also again replicate many of the features ascribed to women's writing. Philip identifies himself as "a mere spectator of Saratoga life," who implores Willie not "to be blinded to the opportunity" he has (344, 346). Willie, for his part, admits that he is "not blind to the advantages of wealth" but that he now looks forward above all "to a *home*" (347). Although these men in many ways demonstrate the logic of separate spheres, in which the home is available to men as a retreat from the vagaries of public life, it is crucial, I would argue, that their retreat into a hotel parlor is associated with certain characteristics of women's writing, particularly observation and the ability to channel that observation into a realization of inner desires and virtues.

Having being reintegrated into the domestic sphere through their meeting in the hotel parlor, Willie and Philip are ready to reintroduce themselves to Gerty. Philip, not surprisingly, decides to make the key revelation of the book—that he is Gerty's long-lost father as well as the man who accidentally blinded his beloved Emily—in a letter. In this letter, which is reprinted in its entirety, Philip assumes many of the attributes ascribed to female authorship in the nineteenth century: concealing his identity; utilizing keen powers of observation ("I stood at the window of Mr. Graham's library; saw the contented, happy countenance of Emily" is a typical position [385]); assuming the voice of an "engaging narrator" by making numerous asides to the intended audience for his letter, Gerty. At the end of the letter, this engagement moves beyond the page as he writes that he will be waiting for Gerty outside the door as soon as she has finished reading his words.

This final move in many ways encapsulates the fantasy of parlor literature, which assumes that entrance into print can come from the transition from private letter to public performance. Not only is his long letter printed, verbatim, in the text—a fantasy of ease of publication just as strong as that in Sedgwick's "Cacoethes Scribendi"—but it also leads Gerty, who has read the letter while "hid[ing] herself in her own room"

(369), to run out of the house to join him outside. The reading, in other words, prompts action in both the reader and the writer while also offering a public revelation (through its reprinting in *The Lamplighter*) of all of the secrets that had accumulated in the novel.

As the scene between Gerty and Emily in the museum suggests, however, there is another model of authorship that *The Lamplighter* ultimately validates more: that of the author who can produce visions from within rather than observations from without. If Philip's writing promotes action, Gerty's verbal descriptions to Emily promote an inner vision that is even more foundational. Both kinds of writing promote action on the part of their readers, but Gerty's "reading" to Emily allows Emily to "speak out . . . truths of the inner life" (253). The "inner life" is not dependent on physical vision but rather on interpretive abilities. These abilities, in turn, allow the reader (or hearer) to become producers of an inner message. Here, ideas of women's authorship as being exceptional in detail and observation merge with ideas of the author as prophet of invisible insights. Yet, the fact that the author here is Emily, not Gerty, locates such prophecy not in exceptional geniuses but in attentive readers. This is less a hierarchical field of cultural production than a reciprocal one, in which readers can become authors not only by rehearsing details but also by attending to inner truths.

As we saw earlier, there are two stories undergirding Cummins's own entrance into authorship. The first, circulated widely in newspapers and magazines, claimed that she wrote the novel with no ambition except to entertain her nieces, thereby aligning the work within the tradition of parlor literature. The second, gleaned by looking at the historical archive, positions her as someone who, having been encouraged by a professional author, Sedgwick, contracted with Jewett to "ensure an extensive sale" of *The Lamplighter*. Jewett ensured this sale, in turn, by promoting the book both on its own terms—without any attribution or discussion of its author—and as the emanation of an abstract "genius." Readers of the actual book, in turn, could find depicted in it a range of authorial personae, including the detailed nation-building writing and original observations of Gerty, the revelatory agency of Philip Amory, and the prophetic insights of Emily Graham. The existence of these various depictions, in turn, suggests the structural openness of the novel. Although it has often been read as a didactic novel of class and gender consolidation, its depictions of writing, reading, and authorship suggest the ways in which it is also a remarkably open text.

Michael Davitt Bell has noted this openness in terms of *The Lamplighter*'s generic instabilities, reading it as a "hodgepodge" of literary forms competing for prominence in the 1850s. Some of the most recent readings of the novel support Bell's notion. These readings, which have had

the salutary function of moving beyond the domestic-sentimental para-
digm in which *The Lamplighter* has most often been read, discuss the book
variously as a female Gothic, a work of realism articulating the syntax of
class, and as a fictionalized exploration of the contractual law of adoption.[54] The latter reading, by Cindy Weinstein, is particularly important
not only for its insight about the enabling relation between multiple adoption and self-possession but also for its placement of the novel within
the historical development of "the legal category of domestic relations."
It also signals a key shift in the construction of authorship in the novel
since it suggests that contract, rather than letter writing, can be identified as an entrance point into print—a shift that I will examine in some
detail in Chapter 5. In Weinstein's interpretation, the prime model for
writing becomes Patty Pace, the single woman who frequently appears
"incognito" and writes her own legal will (77). The fact that this will is
disregarded—she has given her money to Willie, who promptly gives it
to the nephews she was trying to disinherit—complicates this model but
does not, as Weinstein says, "take away from the significance of the act."[55]

If it does not take away its significance, however, there is an aspect of
that significance that Weinstein does not mention: namely, the importance of reception in fulfilling the "will" of the author. Although Pace is
less of an "author" than Philip, Emily, or even Gerty is, she does suggest
the problems of a writing, legal or textual, that is flagrantly discounted,
even in the name of benevolence. Willie may think he is doing the right
thing, but he bases his actions on his belief in the unreliability of Pace's
writing: "Notwithstanding the protestations of several respectable individuals who were present at the attestation of the document, all of whom
pronounced Miss Patty sane and collected to her last moments, he never
would believe that a sound mind could have made so wild and erratic a
disposal of the hardly-earned and carefully-preserved savings of years"
(363). In Willie's view, Pace has given the money to him only because of
her sentimental valorization of one heroic act (he helps her up from a
fall early in the novel) and the disorder it has caused in her mind, and
he sets himself up as the proper interpreter of her words.

This scenario presents the flip side of the reader as producer para-
digm that we saw earlier in the museum scene between Emily and Gerty.
There, surface detail leads to inner truths. But in the case of Patty Pace's
will, the (false) assumption about those inner truths of character leads
to a disregard for Patty's actual words. The reader continues to be a producer of meaning, but in ways that distort the actual text. Such misreadings, in turn, have had an important role in interpretations of *The
Lamplighter*, beginning with that of Nathaniel Hawthorne and continuing to the present day. Weinstein, for example, claims that Amy Kaplan
has "misread the novel" in her "effort to make the case against the text

as exemplifying the imperialist logic of antebellum sentimentalism." Kaplan, according to Weinstein, describes Gerty's trajectory as becoming "her own first colonial subject" by "purg[ing] herself of her origin in a diseased uncivilized terrain," a purging that is evidenced by the fact that "she was born in Brazil to the daughter of a sea captain, who was killed by malaria." This is a misreading, Weinstein says, because in the book's conclusion, "we learn that Gerty's father didn't die but rather 'after an almost interminable illness . . . made [his] way, destitute, ragged, and emaciated, back to Rio'" (384). But I believe that Weinstein may in turn be misreading Kaplan, who has made claims about Gerty's mother and grandfather rather than about her father.[56]

The larger question here is What produces this cycle of misreadings? One answer may lie in the "extensive sale" that Cummins contracted for Jewett to promote. Those sales, which eventually included various adaptations, translations, and abridgments, helped ensure the book's success, but they also continually rewrote the book, changing Cummins's manuscript—like Patty Pace's will—to fit particular agendas. In the nineteenth century these included making the book into an abolitionist tract, an anti-American farce, a traveling companion, and a novel appropriate for young readers, as well, of course, as a marker of the "damned mob of scribbling women." Another answer may lie in the fact that *The Lamplighter* is a generically and thematically open text. In the twentieth century this openness has allowed critics to have radically diverse readings of it, working variously to show the book as a sign of the feminization of America (in both negative and positive ways) and, more recently, as a marker of the complex relation of American literature to the history of the law and imperialism.

Significantly, the text foregrounds its own interpretive openness, as well as the problems of misreading that come from such openness. Take, for example, Patty Pace's discussion of the portrait of the second Mrs. Graham (Philip's mother). Having come to call on the new (and third) Mrs. Graham, Patty takes a careful survey of the "large parlor" of the Grahams' house. As we have seen, parlor culture frequently includes portraits and photographs, and Patty's survey notices one of these missing. "Gertrude, my dear, what have they done with the second wife?" she asks. Seeing Gerty's confusion, Patty "correct[s]" her remark to "O, it is the counterfeit that I have reference to; the original, I am aware, departed long since but where is the counterfeit of the second Mistress Graham? It always hung there, if my memory serves me" (208). Patty comes to this space with preconceived notions of how it will look, expecting to see the portrait of the second wife even as she welcomes the third. It is typical of Patty that she does not understand the social rudeness of such a remark (one thinks of Browning's "My Last Duchess") and does not even take the hint when Gerty "whisper[s]" a reply to her question. "The gar-ret! well, 't is the course of nature; what is new obliterates *the recollection, even,* of the old," she says in a "soliloquy" (209).

This comment fits entirely with Patty Pace's general character, which claims to love the "modern" while also tenaciously holding on to the old. Her own parlor, for instance, is made up "of the gleanings of every age and fashion, from chairs that undoubtedly came over in the May-flower, to feeble attempts at modern pincushions, and imitations of crys-tallized grass, that were a complete failure" (115). However, her comment here suggests the "course of nature" underlying the interpretive field of *The Lamplighter,* in which the old and new cannot coexist but rather in which the "new obliterates *the recollection, even,* of the old." The book as a whole holds together different stories, narrative threads, and charac-ters, but—like Mrs. Graham's portrait—these tend to supplant each other depending on one's critical point of view. What Pace objects to—but what happens repeatedly throughout the book—is the obliteration of one story (the old) as it is succeeded by the new. By the end of the book, the lamplighter's story has been almost completely forgotten, as gaslights have replaced his work. The church that is important early in the book (the site of the first meeting of Emily and Gerty) is replaced by an urban housing project by the end. Philip and Emily have retreated to Philip's ancestral home, which has been "judiciously modernize[d]" (419).[57] Gerty's foreign origins are, as Kaplan suggests, "purged" in her forma-tion as an American citizen and wife. Patty Pace's will is effectively invali-dated by Willie (making the pun between "will" and "Willie" all the more ironic). And so on. Even the name of the central character changes; while at the beginning she is the orphan Gerty, and eventually the adopted daughter Gerty Flint, she becomes by its end Gertrude Sullivan. A selec-tive reading of these transformations, or, as Patty suggests, our almost "natural" amnesia about them, could and has produced radically differ-ent interpretations of the text as the text itself works to render recol-lection difficult.

It is important, of course, that Patty's discussion of the now-absent por-trait occurs in the "large parlor" of the Grahams' house and is about a parlor ornament now consigned to the attic. Putting such a pivotal scene in a parlor underscores the "recollection" of the book's origins—whether apocryphal or not—as parlor literature meant to be read aloud to Cum-mins's nieces. But it is the nature of most parlors, with the possible excep-tion of Miss Pace's, to shift with different visitors, occupants, and tastes, which is precisely what has happened to *The Lamplighter* itself.

Yet there is one major recollection that the novel insists on preserv-ing: the story of Emily's blinding. Its full telling is withheld until Philip's letter, but the blindness is a theme throughout, extending beyond Emily to Gerty, who is blinded by tears when she first sees Willie again and during the boat fire (297, 331). Then, after Philip's telling, the story is rehearsed again to Emily and to Mr. Graham. Just as Emily turns out to be a kind of author figure for Gerty, adding "genius" to the external descriptions she provides, so too she turns out to be a model reader, one who recollects the past even in the face of the "new." Her blindness is central to this in that she cannot see external details. As a result, she does not read nature (through Gerty's oral descriptions) with preconceived notions; rather, "as she listen[s] to the glowing description of nature, as she unfold[s] herself," she experiences "a participation in Gertrude's enjoyment" (196). This particular scene of reading occurs not in the parlor but rather above it, in a "quiet room" where one can hear only the muted laughter of the "company from the city" in the parlor below. Just as Emily suggests a mode of female authorship that extends beyond the parlor, and beyond an emphasis on observations about everyday life, so too she models a new reader: one who is open to "participate" in whatever the text has to offer while in the privacy of a secluded room.

A later scene in a "rustic arbor" at West Point provides the apotheosis of this new model. Again, Emily reads the scene by hearing Gerty's words as she "pours" into Emily's "ear the holy and elevated sentiments to which the time and the place gave birth. To pour out her thoughts to Emily was like whispering to her own heart, and the response to these thoughts was as sure and certain" (265). This moment is so intense that by the next day Emily must take refuge in a ship's cabin. The intensity comes not only from the romantic identification with the landscape but also from the fact that such identification merges Emily and Gerty into a single heart. Gerty provides the eyes, but Emily provides Gerty with access to "her own heart." Reading promotes sympathy and also a knowledge that goes beyond quotidian detail. Given the rhetoric of reading and writing that pervades the novel, we can also see this scene as a final piece of the novel's allegory of its own reception. This allegory understands that reading is selective and forgetful—that as one person or scene replaces another, the previous one falls into oblivion. But it also understands that reading is as much subject formation as parlor activity.

The connection between literacy and selfhood is nothing new, but it is new, I think, in readings of *The Lamplighter*. Just as I think that Weinstein is right to say that Gerty's selfhood is enhanced, not erased, by her various legal and quasi-legal domestic arrangements and adoptions, so too I think that it is ultimately enhanced, not erased, by her various misreadings, and I mean by this both her own reading practices as a character and the various critical readings that have emerged about her character. Over the course of the novel she moves from being an author

(of letters, of vindictive actions against Nan Grant, of romantic attachments to Willie Sullivan) to being a reader—for Emily, primarily, but also
of letters from Mr. Graham, Willie, and Philip. Along the way she also
misreads Willie, whom she falsely supposes is in love with Belle Clinton
rather than herself; and her father, whom she—and the reader—is led
to believe is a potential suitor, not a father. However, by learning to read
in a way that whispers the truths of her heart, she ends this cycle. She
joins her reading with her previous activities as a writer, since that reading frequently takes place through her observations and descriptions to
Emily. In this way Gerty emblemizes not only the connection of reading
and writing—a central component of parlor literature, particularly for
women—but also the trajectory from writing to authorship. Just as the
depictions of Cummins in contemporary reviews described an author
who joined realistic detail with original "genius," so do her depictions of
Gerty combine innate powers of observation with the depth suggested by
"whispers to her own heart."

In this respect, *The Lamplighter* presents a clear case of the "author function" being more important than the flesh-and-blood author. The initial
readers of *The Lamplighter* did not know who the author was (though
they made speculating about it into a pastime), and Jewett, in promoting
the book, described its author only in general terms. The fans who wrote
letters to Cummins in turn constructed their own idealizations of her
that were largely extrapolated from the text. Jewett and other adapters
of the book alternately imagined an author producing an abolitionist
text, or a children's book, or a farce, all in concert with their own interests. Hawthorne, writing in a moment of private pique, made *The Lamplighter* into an emblem of his own authorial frustration and in turn
inspired generations of critics to read (or not read) the book in "purely"
sentimental terms. More-recent critics have found in the book an elucida-
tion of critical social issues, including class, empire, and changing notions
of the family. All of this would suggest that Cummins's status as a historical author or as an authorial presence in the text is overridden by the
openness of the text to a range of reader responses.

In the end, studying authorship in and around *The Lamplighter* both
exposes and authorizes the history of misreading and appropriation that
has characterized this text. Rather than complain about misreadings,
I would rather understand them as a sign of the success of the text in
fulfilling its own terms. When Cummins signed a contract ensuring an
"extensive sale," she did not give up her authorial rights, but she did
agree to let her novel enter a diverse market. At the same time, she constructed a text that, despite its subsequent reputation for didacticism,
anatomized reading as both open-ended and cumulative, with earlier rec-
ollections—like the portrait of the second Mrs. Graham—often being lost

to new insights. Given this construction, it is hardly surprising that *The Lamplighter* has had so many readings and also so many of the same ones; although there are a variety of possibilities, we tend to lose them in historical retrospect, so that the difference is collapsed into a single story.

At the same time, the example of *The Lamplighter* provides a different way of thinking about authorship, one that focuses on being heard rather than on original production. The novel ends with the "still, small voice within" that speaks to Mr. Graham's "awakened soul" and two paragraphs of quotations attributed to that voice. The voice, of course, invokes the biblical idea that God speaks to those who are quiet enough to listen. This ending certainly reflects the Protestant culture in which Cummins wrote, but it also provides a fitting frame to the opening scene, in which no one notices Gerty sitting on a step outside of Nan Grant's house. Through Gerty's readings to Emily, the book teaches readers to be observant, but it ends by extolling openness to an inner voice. Cummins is following certain conventions in quoting an oracular voice at the end of her novel; the graven rocks at the end of *The Narrative of Arthur Gordon Pym*, the heraldic emblem at the conclusion of *The Scarlet Letter*, and the quotation from Job in the epilogue of *Moby-Dick* suggest the prevalence, in this period, of ending with a voice from beyond the text. Cummins's deployment of this convention not only highlights her own position as an author but also suggests that authorship need not be possessive in order to be effective. Cummins signed a contract to publish *The Lamplighter*, but textual evidence and the history of its reception suggest the degree to which authorship was, in this case, a category that went well beyond proprietary interests. In this sense, the challenge for readers of *The Lamplighter* is now not to condemn its past readings—its "recollection of the old"—but rather to continue to be open to new readings that both respect and expand the novel's literary authority.

Chapter 4

Revising Romance
Louisa May Alcott, Hawthorne, and the Civil War

If Maria Cummins is now known almost exclusively as the author of *The Lamplighter*, Louisa May Alcott's current claim to fame is her authorial versatility. Indeed, since the republication of her "unknown thrillers" in the 1970s, it has become a critical commonplace to talk about the double life that she lived as an author. On the one hand, she was the "children's friend" and the celebrity author of *Little Women* and its sequels; on the other, she was the epitome of the veiled lady "behind a mask," publishing Gothic thrillers under an assumed name. To return to the terms I have been tracing, she has been portrayed as both an author and a writer, a respected friend of Hawthorne and Thoreau as well as a "scribbling woman." It is significant, in her case, that she could fulfill both of these roles at once. In this way she was unlike Jo March, who in *Little Women* famously relinquishes her story-paper writing in order to move, first, to a "healthier" writing and then to a full-time role as wife, mother, and teacher.

Despite the contemporary interest in Alcott's double life, we could also easily locate her within the trajectory from social writing to professional authorship that I have been tracing. Like Stowe and Cummins, she began her writing as a kind of parlor entertainment; her father reported in his journal that "her culture has come from the writing of letters and the keeping of a diary, chiefly."[1] She wrote plays that she and her sisters could perform as parlor theatricals at home and then included scenes of such theatricals in "Behind a Mask" (1866), *Little Women* (1868), and the revised edition of *Moods* (1888).[2] Her first publication, *Flower Fables* (1854), was written for Emerson's daughter Ellen. Her first critical and popular acclaim, moreover, came from *Hospital Sketches* (1863), an account of her experiences as a Union nurse during the Civil War that was based on letters she had written to her family from the Georgetown hospital in which she worked. First published serially in the *Commonwealth*, a Boston newspaper, *Hospital Sketches* was published in book form by James Redpath. Alcott saw its publication largely as a way to help raise money for her family, while Redpath, an ardent abolitionist and supporter of John Brown, promised to donate to war orphans five cents of each copy sold. In both cases the movement from manuscript to print was conceived as a form of charity work, a conception that links its production as much to social reform as to professional authorship.

Within *Hospital Sketches,* the letters home that Alcott's narrator, Tribulation Periwinkle, transcribes for wounded soldiers put forward a particular vision of the social efficacy of such letters; they not only describe the details of the war but also often capture a soldier's emotional state. Indeed, the emotional climax of *Hospital Sketches* involves the death of a Virginia blacksmith named John, who dictates a letter to his brother with words that are "sadder for their simplicity."[3] Tribulation places the reply to this letter, which arrives after John's death, in his hands during his viewing, an emblem of the intimate emotional power invested in the letter. The final chapter of *Hospital Sketches* builds on this intimacy by being framed as a collective answer to letters that Alcott had received after serializing her sketches in the *Commonwealth*: "My dear S.: —As inquiries like your own have come to me from various friendly readers of the Sketches, I will answer them *en masse*, and in printed form, as a sort of postscript to what has gone before."[4]

On a variety of levels, then, we can see *Hospital Sketches* as belonging to the tradition of parlor literature that provided a point of origin for many women writers. Yet after the war, as we saw in Chapter 2, Alcott became a literary celebrity who continued to receive large amounts of fan mail and whose image circulated in engravings and even the "Authors" card game. At this point her deployment of parlor writing shifted. Instead of positing letters and parlor performances as an initial step toward print, she began, first, to emphasize the distance between amateur and professional authorship and, second, to describe parlor culture as an end rather than a beginning. Her distancing as an author is evident, for example, in a letter she wrote to a Miss Churchill—one of "the many young writers who ask for advice"—in which she claims that "there is no *easy* road to successful authorship." She does not enjoy authorship, she says, except in its tangible benefits ("taking care of my family"), but she is clear about the distance between her work writing "Hospital Sketches by the beds of my soldier boys in the shape of letters home" and the authorial work she is now doing.[5] Those sketches may have occasioned her initial critical success, but they were also something of an anomaly. The ease of moving from letter to sketch was, indeed, too good to be true. Its success, she wrote at the time, was "a great joke to me, & a sort of perpetual surprise-party, for to this day I cannot see why people like a few extracts from topsey turvey letters."[6]

By the late 1860s Alcott had moved from seeing letters as a "surprise" access into print to seeing parlor culture as being useful only after a great deal of lived experience. In "Happy Women" (1868), the author "A" has compiled "an usually varied experience" before deciding to make literature her "fond and faithful spouse"; experience precedes the settled state that accompanies authorship.[7] In *Work* (1872), the orphan Christie Devon leaves the home of her aunt and uncle at the age of twenty-one to support herself and obtain work experience. At the end of the book, two decades later, she has accumulated a great deal of such experience by working as a domestic servant, an actress, a governess, a caregiver to a suicidal madwoman, and a seamstress. Having gained such experience, she is able, at age forty, to sit alone in her "flowery parlor," with its "letters and papers on her table," and advocate a different kind of intellectual work than the writing of sketches for pin money. Instead of aiming to write for a periodical or annual, she gives stirring speeches to working-women that are effective because of her own work experience. Whereas other reform-minded society women speak too abstractly or abstrusely, Christie speaks as an "interpreter between the two classes." Her words come "faster than she could utter them," but they come so effortlessly because of the experiences she has accrued. *Work* ends with Christie encouraging her friend Bella, who has remained single in order to avoid her family's hereditary propensity toward insanity, to establish a new kind of parlor culture in which all callers are "to come as intelligent men and women, not as pleasure-hunting beaux and belles." In this way Bella will be able to devote herself "to quietly insinuating a better state of things into one little circle."[8]

If Maria Cummins's authorship exemplifies the trajectory from parlor writing to a mass audience and from production to reception, then Alcott's authorship could be said to exemplify the trajectory from experience to parlor writing. *Hospital Sketches* was the result of letters, but they were letters written from a Civil War hospital, not from a parlor. *Work* ends with a view of the parlor or home "circle" as a site of intellectual and social reform, but it does so only after depicting the main proponent of that reform as having experienced manual and physical labor, withstood abuse from her employer, and observed suicide, insanity, and sexual seduction in others. While critics such as Frank Norris assumed that women could not be great novelists because of their limited life experiences, Alcott posited the opposite: that women's experiences could in turn put them in a position to become not only accomplished authors but also advocates of social change.

Yet, Alcott's inversion of parlor culture, as compelling as it is, is only one trajectory through which we can understand her authorship. As I have already hinted, her "double life" as an author also invites us to think about her as collapsing distinctions between Gothic and high-art writing or between sensational and sentimental writing.[9] In this scenario, the

movement from amateur manuscript writing to public print (or performance) is not so much reversed as attenuated, as Alcott simultaneously
writes the passionate thrillers she finds privately cathartic and the genteel children's and adult fiction that her publishers and her audience
demand. Elaine Showalter points out that Alcott taught herself, near the
end of her career, to write with her right and left hands and sees her
ambidexterity both as a sign of her status as "a doubly efficient writing
machine" and as a "striking physical metaphor for her creativity."[10] This
creativity, as Showalter notes, has in turn often been described in terms
of conflict. More specifically, critics have often used the Civil War—the
occasion of Alcott's first critically successful book as well as the setting for
Little Women—as an analogy for Alcott's divided life. In 1979, for example, Judith Fetterley argued that "the Civil War is an obvious metaphor
for internal conflict and its invocation as background to *Little Women* suggests the presence in the story of such conflict." More recently Elizabeth
Young has argued that "in Alcott's internal 'civil wars,' the Civil War
functions symbolically to reveal and realign the faultlines of femininity
in Victorian America," while Lora Romero has claimed that Alcott relo-
cates within the home the heroism traditionally associated with the battlefield. *Little Women* uses "the backdrop of the Civil War to create a value
system that gives priority not just to women but to women as the representatives of the interior life."[11]

In this chapter I want to put pressure on this analogy in two ways: first,
by thinking about the war as a historical and political as well as symbolic
event; and second, by questioning just how different Alcott's domestic
writing is from her sensational writing—and hence just how much of a
conflict there really was. Focusing on three texts from the 1860s—"Pauline's Passion and Punishment," *Moods,* and *Little Women*—I will show the
ways in which Alcott presents and resolves issues of rebellion and conflict.
I chose these works because they represent the three main categories of
Alcott's fiction: anonymous sensational tale, feminist novel, and domestic children's book; because they are directly or indirectly engaged with
the connection between the Civil War and authorship; and because they
all respond to the model of authorship put forward by Alcott's Concord
neighbor Nathaniel Hawthorne. *Hospital Sketches* is, as Elizabeth Young
and Alice Fahs have pointed out, the book most directly grounded in
Alcott's experiences as a Civil War nurse.[12] But as I have suggested above,
it links Alcott's authorship more directly to the tradition of parlor literature than do these other works; it is also more directly indebted to the
sketches of Dickens than to Hawthorne. In what follows, I want to see
what happens when Alcott moves beyond the parlor. Specifically, I will
examine how these three works of the 1860s use the war to provide historical and material grounding for Alcott's authorship. This grounding,

in turn, leads to an emphasis on issues of realism and truth telling, most frequently by juxtaposing them against the tradition of Hawthornean romance. By adopting a form of domestic realism, Alcott separates herself from this romance tradition while still acknowledging her debt to it, defining authorship less as oppositional than as a form of reconciliation.[13]

"Pauline's Passion and Punishment"

One feature of parlor literature, as noted in Chapter 2, is the fact that it can be produced in the private sphere while also giving leisured women pin money that enables them to engage in commercial exchange. The promise of such money was embodied in the prizes frequently offered by magazines and book publishers. One such publisher was Frank Leslie, who offered a hundred-dollar prize in his *Illustrated Newspaper*, which Alcott won for "Pauline's Passion and Punishment." Alcott's financial precariousness meant that she needed more than just pin money, however. She learned that she had won the prize while serving as a nurse at a Union hospital in December 1862. The assistant editor who informed her of the award anticipated that her check would be on hand in time "for those little Christmas purchases," but she reported in her journal that it did not arrive until the new year, at which time she used it to repay debts.[14]

Although "Pauline's Passion" won a prize in what was essentially an amateur writing contest, it is very far removed from a parlor writing steeped in everyday observation. Published in a "story paper" similar to those that Professor Bhaer would later excoriate in *Little Women*, the *Illustrated Newspaper* targeted an urban audience by featuring crime fiction, gossip, and heavily illustrated sensational stories. Madeleine Stern has argued that the success of Leslie's newspaper also sprang from its escapist appeal to "soldiers in camp" who "could while away tedious hours between battles by escaping to an ancestral estate in Britain or a tropical paradise in Cuba."[15] Yet, a close reading of "Pauline's Passion" reveals that it could be read as a commentary on the war as well as escapist fiction. Although on the surface it is about a woman's revenge through socially acceptable means (subterfuge, romance, and charm), its concerns with issues of slavery, rebellion, wounds, and conflict would have resonated with readers used to daily accounts of battle. In this sense, its escapism was only a kind of Gothic veil for war commentary that was the staple of newspapers at the time.

The political allegory of "Pauline's Passion" is evident from its opening scene in Cuba, a setting that would likely have been glossed by Frank Leslie's readers less as a tropical paradise than as a potential slave state. Throughout much of the antebellum period, the United States had sought to purchase Cuba from Spain. As early as 1823 Thomas Jefferson had written to President Monroe, "I candidly confess that I have ever looked on Cuba as the most interesting addition which could be made to our system of States." In 1848 the United States under President Polk offered Spain more than one hundred million dollars for Cuba (an offer soundly rejected by Spain). For three years following Polk's offer, groups of "Filibusters" made four invasions from the United States attempting to establish a Cuban republic. In 1854 President Franklin Pierce made another attempt to acquire Cuba. The Ostend Manifesto, which he drafted in conjunction with the United States ministers in London, Paris, and Madrid, argued that the United States ought to purchase (or even seize) Cuba as soon as possible. President Buchanan continued this policy, and the Breckinridge and Douglas 1860 presidential platforms contained planks in favor of the annexation of Cuba. Had it been annexed, it would have been a slave state, and debates about Cuba became inextricably linked to debates about emancipation and the abolition of slave states.[16]

Alcott and her family were ardent abolitionists who had particularly supported John Brown's raid on the arsenal at Harper's Ferry. Although some of their Concord neighbors might have viewed Cuba as a tropical paradise (Mary and Sophia Peabody [Hawthorne] traveled there for health reasons in the 1830s), it seems more likely that Alcott would have viewed it as a would-be slave state, a stand-in for the Confederacy. In "Pauline's Passion," she hints at her attitude toward the acquisition of Cuba in a scene in which Manuel Laroche, who is Cuban, overhears the gossip about his marriage to the white Northerner Pauline. Manuel surveys "a brace of dandies"—the gossipers—"with an air that augured ill for the patronage of Young America."[17] Young America was the New York-centered nationalist group that competed with the Massachusetts-based Transcendentalists for control of the northeastern, and by extension United States, literary market. It also had connections to the radical branch of the Democratic Party of the same name, which manifested its nationalism by advocating that the United States acquire Cuba. This allusion to Young America, then, could be a commentary on its dandified weakness, particularly as in relation to imperialist expansion in Cuba. Young America will not patronize Manuel because he—who is, as we will see, coded black—has a white, Northern woman on his arm. Manuel's rebellion does not fit with the distant nationalism of Young America.[18]

In the story, Pauline marries Manuel after learning that her true love, Gilbert Redmond, has married another woman. Orphaned five years earlier, Pauline has gone to serve as a companion to an island girl in Cuba, where she meets Gilbert. Her anger over being jilted by Gilbert leads her not only to marry Manuel but also to follow Gilbert and his new wife,

Babie, on their travels. Manuel lures Gilbert to gamble with him and Babie to fall in love with him; when Gilbert realizes that he has been duped, he murders Manuel by pushing him off a cliff, with Babie jumping closely behind Manuel.

If this story is, on one hand, what Sarah Elbert terms "race melodrama," it also, on the other hand, articulates a particular relation to Alcott's Concord neighbor Nathaniel Hawthorne.[19] Gilbert's murder of Manuel at the cliff echoes Donatello's murder of the mysterious model at the end of *The Marble Faun* (1860). In addition, Pauline functions as a Hester Prynne in reverse. When she feels that she has triumphed over Gilbert by telling him that she now loves Manuel rather than him, she tears away the "scarlet nosegay" that Gilbert had just given her. Having done so, she "set her foot upon it, as if it were the scarlet badge of her subjection to the evil spirit which had haunted her so long, now cast out and crushed forever" (150). Gilbert has, as his last name Redmond suggests, given her a scarlet badge, but unlike Hester with her scarlet "A," Pauline refuses to wear it or internalize its disciplinary power.

In one way, then, the story recasts melodrama as Hawthornean romance, suggesting that the terms are not diametrically opposed but rather firmly embedded within each other. Its generic conflicts, in other words, eventually give way to a hybrid form that resolves the conflict. The same impulse occurs in the story's treatment of sectional conflict, although here it is in the service of showing the ravages of war on both North and South. At first the story seems to reinscribe sectional divisions: Pauline, a Northerner, marries a Southern man (Manuel), only to have him killed off by her Northern lover. Marriage here does not mitigate sectional conflict; rather, the ending banishes the Southern rebel. Yet, the racial politics of the story complicate such a sectional reading. Although Manuel is repeatedly referred to as a Southerner ("The savage element that lurks in southern blood leaped up in the boy's heart" is a representative description [113]), his physical darkness associates him with black slavery. He is frequently in an attitude of servitude. When he dresses Pauline, he "hover[s] about his stately wife as no assiduous maid had ever done" (118), and when she embraces him, her "white arms took him captive" (135). She constantly tells him not to rebel, keeping him perpetually childlike, "half boy, half man, possessing the simplicity of the one, the fervor of the other" (115). Given his childlike state, it is not hard to believe that he is able to seduce Gilbert's wife, appropriately named "Babie." Although Gilbert also claims to be a slave to Pauline's will, and Babie has a "spaniel-like" submission that allows her to return to Gilbert even after he has physically assaulted her, Pauline's cautions to Manuel are akin to those trying to curb a slave rebellion. He is called a "rebel," but his rebellion ultimately is linked not to that of the Confederacy but rather to that of the slave—the kind of rebellion that the Alcotts had supported in the case of John Brown.

If Manuel becomes associated with the black slave, Pauline ultimately becomes his white mistress. The beginning of the narrative carefully separates her from her Cuban surroundings, securing her as a Northerner: "There was no southern languor in the figure, stately and erect; no southern swarthiness on fairest cheek and arm; no southern darkness in the shadowy gold of the neglected hair; the light frost of northern snows lurked in the features, delicately cut, yet vividly alive" (109). But once she marries Manuel, the couple is generically referred to as "the Cubans," with Pauline extending a "truly Spanish foot" (118). One of the engravings commissioned to illustrate the story (see Figure 15) pictures Pauline lying in a hammock, "indolently swinging . . . as she had been wont to do in Cuba." A dark-skinned Manuel looks out at the garden, expecting to see Gilbert looking back in, while Pauline's white body is submerged under a fan and the drapery of her dress, which falls on a pillow stacked with books. Too indolent even to read, Pauline is the picture of the Southern belle, reminiscent of Harriet Beecher Stowe's Marie St. Clare or Harriet Jacobs's Mrs. Flint. In a different context she could be a convalescent, but she is not physically sick, making her lack of self-discipline and control all the more pronounced. Following a familiar abolitionist argument, Alcott suggests that Southern indolence and its institution of slavery can infect the national body as a whole, stripping women of the discipline that makes them suitable mothers, writers, nurses, and healers of the nation. The fact that Pauline is a Northerner, and that she is staging this scene in order to hurt her ex-lover (she hopes that Gilbert will see her and become jealous), makes the moral all the more clear: sectional distinctions ultimately do not hold.

In the final scene of the story, Gilbert reveals that he has for some months been carrying a glove that Pauline had earlier stripped off her hand when he touched it at a ball. At the time he had called it a "gage," his chivalric image of an object thrown down as a challenge to fight. Taking it out during the murder scene, he admits to wearing "this since the night you began the conflict, which has ended in defeat to me, as it shall to you. I do not war with women, but you shall have one man's blood upon your soul, for I will goad that tame boy to rebellion by flinging this in his face and taunting him with a perfidy blacker than my own" (152). As if on cue, Manuel's "brown hand" appears to snatch the glove away, at which point Gilbert pushes him off of the cliff.

This complicated scene shifts the terms of civil conflict in several respects. First, it suggests that such conflict never leads to victory. Pauline and Gilbert, though alive, have "ended in defeat," and their remorse over what has happened will constitute, according to the final sentence

Figure 15. Illustration from "Pauline's Passion and Punishment," *Frank Leslie's Illustrated Newspaper*, January 3, 1863. Courtesy General Research Division, The New York Public Library, Astor, Lenox and Tilden Foundations.

of the story, a "long punishment" (152). No matter the outcome of the war, this ending suggests, reconstruction will involve punishment and suffering for all. Second, it suggests that Northerners are the true rebels, as Gilbert has "goad[ed] that tame boy to rebellion." This civil conflict knows no defenders of a union, but rather varying degrees of rebellion. Third, Gilbert's "blackness" is darker than Manuel's "brown hand." The provoking Northerner has become more savage than the dark Southerner, just as Pauline, the traveling Northerner, has become a Southerner by virtue of her association with Manuel. By collapsing racial and sectional categories, the story effectively undoes civil conflict. It is not a celebratory collapse, but one that nonetheless serves as a critique of civil war by showing the basic similarities between the conflicting parties.

Alcott's collapse of racial and sectional difference in "Pauline's Passion" continues through her thematic treatment of wounding in the story. This treatment is evident from the start, when Pauline reads a letter from Gilbert (printed verbatim in the text) announcing his marriage to Babie, and she is immediately "conscious only of the wound that bled in that high heart of hers" (109). This wound instills in her a need for revenge, though by the end of the scene she also foresees her own cure. She imagines that she might learn to love Manuel, though he must wait until time "has healed my wound" (116). In the rest of the story her healing takes the form of wounding Gilbert: she taunts him and exults "to see his self-love bleed, and pride vainly struggle to conceal the stab" (124), and at the end tells him she loves Manuel in words more shocking than "if she had lifted her white hand and stabbed him" (150).[20] Most disturbingly, she uses Babie (her old school friend) as a pawn against Gilbert. When Gilbert realizes that Babie is falling in love with Manuel, he beats her, and she runs to Pauline and Manuel to show them "the red outline of a heavy hand" on her arm. In turn, Gilbert realizes that claiming to love Babie will allow him to "deal a double blow by wounding Pauline through her husband" (142–43).

We might read these images as stock conventions of sensational fiction or historically as one of the first explicit scenes of domestic violence in American fiction. But they also show the influence of Hawthorne: the imprint of the red hand is an enlarged version of the "pygmy" red handprint that leads to Georgiana's demise in "The Birthmark" (1844). Given the fact that "Pauline's Passion" was written and published during the Civil War, the metaphoric allusion to the violence of civil conflict seems unmistakable. As Elizabeth Young has argued, the representation of wounding is an important site for thinking about the gender politics at work in women's writing about the Civil War. Young reads *Hospital Sketches* as using the metaphor of wounding to create a "productive cultural fantasy" in which women (whether nurses or authors) posit "female self-mastery as a metaphorical model for male development" and, by extension, as an allegory for how to "reconstruct the warring nation."[21] By giving the nurses masculine power while reducing male patients to a weakened, feminized state, Alcott suggests a new, "carnivalesque" model of gender relations that also frees (or "transforms") her as an author.

Young does not mention "Pauline's Passion," but her understanding of the paradoxical empowerment of wounding can shed light on that story as well. Even before Alcott went to Washington, this is to suggest, she was already thinking in these terms. Here too there are certain gender inversions at work: Pauline inflicts wounds rather than allowing her inner wound to torment her, and Babie, though "spaniel like" in her devotion to both of her men, displays physical violence against women that is usually kept hidden. Babie reveals her "battle scars" to Pauline, who herself wounds others because of the scars in her own heart. The gender constructions at work here, however, are ultimately quite familiar; Pauline lives for love and, once scorned, uses her passion to bring revenge on those who have hurt her. Pauline does not nurse "convalescent veterans," in Young's term, but rather makes herself into a convalescent— an indolent woman swinging in a hammock—in order to wound Gilbert's pride.

Given Alcott's emphasis in "Pauline's Passion" on the act of wounding rather than on the process of recovery, it is difficult to see it enacting the valorization of female authorship that Young sees at work in *Hospital Sketches*. There, according to Young, "female authorship is newly validated as political duty and battle legacy," a means of reframing "female inadequacy" as "male wounding."[22] In "Pauline's Passion," the unopened books beside Pauline's hammock are a stark reminder of the contingent nature of that political duty. The indolence that is part of civil conflict—recall that Pauline reclines in the hope that Gilbert will see her and be jealous—can also leave books and magazines, even *Frank Leslie's Illustrated Newspaper*, untouched. Yet, the fact that the books are in the picture at all suggests their importance to helping articulate the experience of the war. As we will see in the next section, Alcott continued this articulation in *Moods*, a novel that also responds to the crisis of the Civil War.

Revising Romance in *Moods*

"Pauline's Passion" and the hundred dollars it earned her inaugurated Alcott's turn to sensational fiction. About the time she began to write it, she wrote to her friend Alfred Whitman that she intended to write a "blood and thunder tale as they are easy to 'compoze' and are better paid than moral and elaborate works of Shakespeare."[23] Yet even as she entered this prize contest, she was completing *Moods*, her first and arguably most complex novel. *Moods* was written primarily between 1860 and 1861, but Alcott had trouble placing it with a publisher. Most prospective publishers, including Redpath, wanted her to shorten it, and she made revisions to the book throughout the early years of the Civil War. It was finally published in 1864. "In trying to suit various people I've damaged my book," she wrote to family friend Caroline Dall. "I've come to the conclusion that as I've got to bear the praise or blame I'd better hold fast to my own idea, work it out in my own fashion, & take the consequence."[24] Her sense that the book was produced (and wounded) through conflict and division is echoed in the text's treatment of Cuba—as we have seen, a potential Southern state during the 1850s—as well as its discussion of wounds, slavery, and manhood. When the book is seen in this way, we can locate Alcott's simultaneous writing of sensational and "high" fiction not as divergent activities but rather as related modes of responding to Civil War conflict.

High art comes to Alcott through the Concord literary community of which she and especially her father were active parts. The novel rewrites Thoreau's *Week on the Concord and Merrimack River* (1848) as well as Hawthorne's *The Scarlet Letter* (1850). These revisions show the direct lines of literary influence in Alcott's work, lines that were complicated by her own complicated relationship with her father. Yet, *Moods* also constitutes a rethinking of genre and specifically of romance. Alcott's ambition is not to reproduce the high-art form of romance as practiced by Hawthorne and promoted by his publishers Ticknor and Fields. Instead, she adopts a form of realism that posits the romance as sentimental and outdated. In the world of *Moods,* the most sentimental art is practiced not by women but rather by men unprepared to confront realities such as war. Realism becomes a specifically feminine response to civil violence, one that does not appropriate a distant war as a symbol of gender conflict or inversion but rather demonstrates the power of female observation, and hence the female author, to engage the realities of war. At the same time, the practice of realism is ultimately not discontinuous with romance but rather is a rewriting of it. Although romance is presented as outmoded, in other words, that does not mean that it is not useful. Just as "Pauline's Passion" combines sensation fiction with Hawthornean romance in order to create a hybrid genre that resolves conflict, so too does *Moods* combine romance and realism. If *Moods* in one way gives credence to the well-worn truism that the Civil War "produced" realism, then, it also complicates that truism, first by defining realistic observation as a particularly feminine trait and, second, by showing generic continuities between romance and realism.

At the level of plot, Alcott sets up this combination in the opening chapter, when Adam Warwick, a white Northerner, admits to his Cuban love, Ottila, that he has made a mistake in becoming engaged to her. The romance world that would unite this white Northerner with a "passionate yet haughty" and "dark" Cuban woman gives way to what the narrator terms a "bitter truth" or "tardy candor" about their differences.[25] As Isabel Archer and Casper Goodwood will later do in James's *Portrait of a Lady*, Adam and Ottila resolve their differences by agreeing to give themselves a year, during which they will go their separate ways but not become engaged to anyone else. At a metaphorical level, however, what is striking is the way in which Ottila's and Adam's differences correspond to those (from a Northern perspective) between the Union and the Confederacy. Adam sees Ottila as "rebellious" and as in need of subduing. "Ottila, I have no faith in you, feel no respect for the passion you inspire, own no allegiance to the dominion you assert," he tells her (9). At the same time, he feels that his association with her has degraded him through a "spiritual slavery" that has left him weak and indolent (8). "This luxurious life enervates me; the pestilence of slavery lurks in the air and infects me; I must build myself up anew and find again the man I was," he says (12). This building, in turn, takes the form of "hard battle." Adam realizes that he has "fallen into an ambuscade and must cut [his] way out as [he] can" (10). Although he does not observe the "dominion" that Ottila represents, he realizes that his battle with that dominion—the South— is essential to preventing him from becoming a victim of slavery as well. To escape such dominion, he returns to Massachusetts. The fact that he returns still betrothed to Ottila, however, shows that he cannot really escape her influence; the South and the North are joined even when they battle against each other.

When Alcott revised *Moods* in 1882, she cut the Ottila subplot, creating what Elbert calls a "tidier, more formulaic work" that removes "Gothic touches" that are "out-of-date and distracting."[26] Yet, these "Gothic touches," centered most prominently in the Ottila subplot, are also the most clearly related to the Civil War, showing Adam's attempts to distance himself from Southern slavery. If they are out-of-date, in other words, it is less because they are merely "touches" than because the country had now moved through Reconstruction. Elbert asserts that "*Moods* is about the other civil war, in which the conflicts were the inner struggle for modern individuality and the simultaneous battle to win for woman the rights of man."[27] To make it about the "other" war, however, is to distance it from its engagement with issues of sectional conflict and slavery. Although *Moods* does consider women's rights, particularly in relation to marriage, its understanding of those rights, and of possessive individualism more generally, is (in its original version) inextricably linked to its representation of actual civil violence.

Although the wages of sectional conflict are laid bare in the "bitter truth" of the opening Cuban scene, much of the rest of the book shows the problem of trying to escape that truth through what Alcott terms "honeyed falsehood" (8). This is nowhere more evident than in Adam's brand of heroism, which turns out not to be in a real ambuscade but rather in what one might term "picturesque heroism." This heroism begins when Adam returns from Cuba to visit his childhood friend Geoffrey Moor, whose next-door neighbor is Sylvia Yule. Although Adam and Sylvia are clearly attracted to each other, it is Geoffrey whom Sylvia eventually marries. Adam extricates himself from his attachment to Ottila but is still unable to act on his love for Sylvia.

Soon after Adam arrives in Massachusetts, he and Geoffrey go on a week-long camping trip and river expedition with Sylvia and her brother Mark. During the expedition, Adam is burned while trying to save a man from what Sylvia views as a "grand" forest fire, and Sylvia, who admits to having "some experience in wounds," insists on dressing the heroic Adam's burns (51, 53, 56). Later the group joins a wedding-anniversary celebration in progress at a country house, and Adam, having no appropriate clothes, dresses up "in an old uniform, in which he looked like a volunteer from 1812" (64). In 1864 such play acting would have placed Adam in an elegiac world in which veterans of the War of 1812 have sentimental value. Yet it would also have marked him as out of step with the current conflict. Although Civil War rhetoric in the North and especially the South frequently returned to prior wars, especially the Revolution, to inspire soldiers, Adam's "old uniform" marks him as an anachronism. Retreating eventually even from this imaginary world, he returns to Ottila and Cuba, where he immediately sickens with a fever and has to be nursed for weeks in Havana.

Adam's wounds come not from Civil War valor but from an outmoded form of chivalric romance in which he fights fires, dresses in old uniforms, and plays the role of unrequited lover. Reporting to Sylvia about his illness in Havana, he uses a Haitian proverb "which must comfort you if I am a gaunt ghost of my former self: 'A lean freeman is better than a fat slave'" (127–28). Given that the novel was published during the Civil War, such a proverb has an ironic resonance: at the end of his illness, he has been freed from his "slavish" love and commitment to Ottila, but he has done so not by fighting (as he promises in the opening scene) but rather by becoming sick. This ironic construction of Adam— a representation of Henry David Thoreau—reveals him to be hopelessly removed from the realities of the 1860s United States. Like the soldiers in *Hospital Sketches*, he is nursed by strong women: Sylvia, who dresses like a boy, as well as a Cuban Sister of the "Sacred Heart." But here his wounding and nursing are not in the service of national healing but rather in the healing of his own quixotic visions.

Adam undergoes a more genuine test of valor at the end of the novel, when he goes with Geoffrey (now married to Sylvia) to fight with Garibaldi in the Italian revolution of 1848–49. Like Margaret Fuller, Adam and Geoffrey believe in Garibaldi's republican cause. But to Alcott's readers, their fighting spirit might have seemed misplaced, given the Civil War battles at home. The revolutionary setting indicates, I believe, Alcott's ongoing interest in the memory and metaphor of revolution, although the timing of the book's publication would have muted the strength of the metaphor.

Adam is wounded in the chest while involved in a cannon fight in Rome, but the wound is only superficial because he has been saved by a miniature portrait of his mother that he carries over his chest. He is even well enough to receive an encouraging visit from Garibaldi in his hospital room. In using a maternal portrait to save Adam, Alcott gestures toward a long-standing tradition of portraits and miniatures as talismatic icons that save lives. Antebellum tales, for example, frequently used daguerreotype miniatures as similarly protective objects.[28] In Adam's case, the fact that he is saved by an image of his mother identifies him as one of Alcott's many "little men" and calls into question his ability to act on his revolutionary fantasies. In the end he dies, like Fuller, in a ship wreck en route back to the United States. Before he dies, he manages to save Geoffrey, to whom his dying words are "wife" and "home."

At the level of plot, these words inspire Geoffrey to return to his rightful place with his wife Sylvia, who has written to him, "Geoffrey, come home" (202). But these words also idealize the power of the domestic sphere. They echo the end of Melville's *Typee* (1846), where the native father Marheyo encourages Tommo to leave the island of Typee by using "the only two English words [Tommo] had taught him—'Home' and 'Mother.'"[29] Geoffrey needs the encouragement of returning to his wife, and Adam dies with the miniature of his mother, a portable image of his emotional home. In *Typee*, Marheyo's words indicate the influx of "civilized" ideas about domesticity that Tommo had introduced onto this "savage" island, and they leave open to question whether these domestic values are ultimately superior to those of the native culture. In *Moods*, however, these words again evoke a nostalgic vision of antebellum domestic ideals. Adam and Geoffrey are not fighting for their home, as Civil War soldiers were, but rather see home as a stable locus of domestic value to which they can return. They are the sentimental heroes of the novel.

Given such domestic ideology, it is not surprising that Alcott gave one of the first copies of *Moods* to her mother as a Christmas present, writing of her hope that "Success will sweeten me and make me what I long to become more than a great writer—a good daughter."[30] This letter continued the acknowledgment of her mother that she had begun in creating the pen name A. M. Barnard, with the initials echoing those of her mother, Abigail May, and that would continue in her celebration of Marmee in *Little Women*. (In fact, Mrs. Alcott was known for her gossipy exaggerations and sensationalism as much as for her maternal stability.)

The miniature that saves Adam in Italy is an image that he has drawn himself. It is "rudely drawn in sepia; the brown tints bringing out the marked features as no softer hue could have done, and giving to each line a depth of expression that made the serious countenance singularly lifelike and attractive" (200). The "lifelike" countenance suggests that Adam's fidelity to and observations of his mother have enabled him to draw a realistic miniature that reveals both external similitude and internal "depth of expression." These qualities are exactly the ones that Henry James used as critical standards in his 1865 review of *Moods* in the *North American Review*, although he used them to argue that Alcott had failed to be realistic. "Her play is not a real play, nor her actors real actors," he concluded. She had not made "lifelike" characters, instead using her imagination and the "depths of her moral consciousness" to inspire them. James predicted, however, that Alcott would someday write a very good novel, "provided she will be satisfied to describe only that which she has seen."[31]

In advising Alcott to write what she has seen, James is echoing his earlier pronouncements about the particular affinities between women writers and realism, given their superior powers of observation. But he is also anticipating his famous dictum, in "The Art of Fiction," to "be one of those on whom nothing is lost" and "write what you know." In describing the novel to Caroline Dall before its publication, Alcott adopted a similar view, justifying her negative depiction of marriage (to which Dall objected) on the grounds that "I've seen a good deal of married life" and "hav[e] had my own experiences, so I do not speak of love & friendship from mere hear say."[32] Capitalizing on the keen observation associated throughout the nineteenth century with women's writing, she justifies her authorial independence by linking the mature author—the one who has stopped trying to please each critic—to the author of experience.

Moods foregrounds "the art of fiction" by including several characters who are artists. Adam paints the "lifelike" miniature of his mother, but he also writes and publishes *Alpen Rosen*, a collaborative work written with Geoffrey. In *Alpen Rosen*, Adam's essays alternate with poems taken from Geoffrey's diary. The work is primarily a private tribute to Sylvia, but it appears on "many study tables, where real work was done," if not in "fashionable libraries" (194). Earlier in the novel, after Geoffrey departs for Italy, Sylvia reads the diary from which his part is taken and finds "her husband's heart laid bare before her" (175). She immediately recognizes the "genuine" quality of his "genius and affection" (176) and

regrets that she had not known about it, regret that she adds to the
material book in the form of tears that signal her "involuntary comment
on some poem or passage made pathetic by the present" (176). There
are literary precedents for such private male writing—one thinks of
Pleyel's journal in Charles Brockden Brown's *Wieland* or Aylmer's in
Hawthorne's "The Birthmark," and Alcott's father kept a journal throughout his life, as did Hawthorne, Emerson, and Thoreau. But it is striking
that the person who would most seem to need the outlet of a diary—
Sylvia—becomes the sympathetic reader of her husband's diary rather
than the writer of her own, and furthermore that Geoffrey uses this private writing to get himself into print. Nineteenth-century conceptions
of female authorship often assumed, in W. L. Courtney's words, that
"the beginning of a woman's work [of writing] is generally the writing
of a personal diary."[33] However, here such a "feminine note" is represented by a man. Sylvia does write to Geoffrey to "come home" but in
the most telegraphic means possible, and her letter is inspired by her
reading of Geoffrey's and Adam's book.

Adam's maternal miniature is paralleled by the domestic genre scenes
painted by Mark, Sylvia's brother. He sketches scenes of real life that he
encounters, so often using his family as models for his art that Sylvia
complains about seeing her "eyes, arms, or hair in all his pictures" (16).
Although Mark is sometimes "tempted by more ambitious designs" (103),
his "true branch of the art" lies in sketching domestic scenes such as the
golden-anniversary celebration that is part of his river journey. His
"Golden Wedding" sketch is given an enthusiastic review in an art exhibition by "the best Art critic in the country," while his rendition of
Clytemnestra is roundly ignored. His success with the former painting
inspires him to propose to his true love, Jessie; his art is not for its own
sake but rather in the service of a larger domestic order. On the one
hand, he stands in as a prototype for the American artist, who is better
at sketching the scenes around him than reaching to outmoded classical and European sources. This explains Alcott's nationalistic emphasis
on "the best Art critic in the country," although ironically the actual
anniversary scene that the painting represents may have been inspired
by Alcott's reading of the biography of the German novelist Jean Paul
Richter.[34] On the other hand, it is significant that this model is coded
feminine. The golden-wedding scene that he describes is a prototype of
the regionalist women's writing of the later nineteenth century (such as
the Bowden family reunion in Jewett's *The Country of the Pointed Firs*) and
also of a domestic realism that privileges the quotidian and everyday
rather than the classical and philosophical. On her deathbed, Sylvia
gazes at another of Mark's sketches, a "lovely picture" of "the moonlight
voyage down the river," which Mark had given her the very day of the

voyage (216). Hastily sketched and commemorating a private boating party, the painting stands as a model of restorative art.

Throughout *Moods*, art that does not fit this model is criticized for its exaggeration and excess. A picture of the Fates in Geoffrey's library, for example, is of no comfort to Sylvia; they merely look "back at her inexorably dumb" (171). Only paintings that have some correspondence to real characters are seen as worthy: a portrait of Milton that has "curling locks" just like Geoffrey's (163); or Correggio's Mary, whom Sylvia resembles as she reads Moor's diary, "with the book, the lamp, the melancholy eyes, the golden hair that painters love" (176).[35] To love these qualities for purely aesthetic ends would, in the economy of this novel, be frivolous, but the fact that they refer to Sylvia's actual features renders them credible. Given this aesthetic economy, it is ironic that James's review of *Moods* complains about its lack of realism. This may identify James as a weak reader of Alcott; did he not see that her narrative endorses the same aesthetic qualities as his review? At the same time, it underscores the extent to which we can see Alcott as grappling with the promise of realism long before James started writing his great realist novels—novels that, like *Moods*, are deeply invested in showing the reality behind the "honeyed falsehood" of appearances.

In the revision of *Moods*, Sylvia looks at the moonlit river portrait not on her deathbed (she lives in this version) but rather in a scene of reconciliation with Geoffrey. Looking at the picture, her mind turns from "the painted romance to the more beautiful reality" of a "long and happy life . . . [in which] love and duty go hand in hand" (280). This ending, while obviously catering to readers of *Little Women* and its sequels, nonetheless puts the greatest reality in the lived life of an individual character. In this version the novel becomes more realistic than the painting, which remains a "romance" while her marriage is a "beautiful reality." The plot of *Moods* makes it difficult to believe that this reality will be as "long and happy" as the narrative would like us to believe, but this too underscores its reality: it is more realistic to have Sylvia live, even in an unhappy marriage, than to die as a sentimental heroine. In this way, Alcott claims a privileged position for writing, one that allows for more depth than painting or sculpture while also allowing for the verity of the lifelike sketch.

If *Moods* privileges realism as the preferred American art, it does so by showing realism's ability to transcend gender distinctions (men can be keen observers too), on the one hand, and to replace sentimentalism, on the other. The sentimental ideal implicit in "The Golden Wedding," Adam's War of 1812 costume, and the revolution in Italy is rendered archaic and old-fashioned, particularly in the context of the Civil War. If *Moods* replaces sentimentalism, however, it ultimately has a more complex relation to romance, especially since Alcott's narrator characterizes Sylvia as part of the "sad sisterhood called disappointed women" and compares her to Hawthorne's Hester: "As Hester Prynne seemed to see some trace of her own sin in every bosom, by the glare of the Scarlet Letter burning on her own; so Sylvia, living in the shadow of a household grief, found herself detecting various phases of her own experience in others" (190). Even in her pain, Sylvia rejoices that she, unlike Hester, has "no child to reproach me hereafter" (179). Adam, like Chillingworth, has had "a sojourn among the Indians" (48); the meeting of Adam and Sylvia in the woods echoes the meeting of Dimmesdale and Hester; and throughout, Alcott reanimates the complications of the romantic love triangle represented by Adam, Geoffrey, and Sylvia. After Adam's death, Sylvia dreams that she sees "the pale outlines of a word stretching from horizon to horizon . . . burning with a ruddy glory" (210). This word turns out to be "Amen," rather than the scarlet *A* that burns in "The Minister's Vigil" chapter of *The Scarlet Letter*. Alcott's version is less ambiguous (and allegorical), giving closure either to Sylvia's own life (in the 1864 version) or to Adam's (in the 1882 one), but the rewriting of Hawthorne is unmistakable.

Alcott was quite familiar with Hawthorne's work. Her journals report her reading *The Scarlet Letter* at least three times, and Hawthorne was her neighbor in Concord from 1860 until his death in 1864. In late 1862 she wrote a verse tribute to the Hawthorne family acknowledging that she was grateful for their recognition of her thirtieth birthday and concluding that the Hawthorne tree, "with Emerson's pine and Thoreau's oak / Will . . . be loved and honored still."[36] The Alcotts and the Hawthornes had a falling out sometime in early 1864, possibly over their different takes on the Civil War or over the Hawthornes' increasing frustration with the gossip and exaggerations told by Abigail Alcott.[37] Nevertheless, Hawthorne remained an undeniable literary influence.

Like Melville, Howells, and James, Alcott was an energetic reader of Hawthorne and transformer of his works. As such, she belongs to what Richard Brodhead has termed "the school of Hawthorne." Focusing on Hawthorne's influence on Howells and James, Brodhead identifies him as "the concatenator, the author who pulls disparate writing into a coherent and continuous line" and whom writers "organized *as* a literary past, then reactivated *from* the past."[38] As we have already seen, Alcott reactivated Hawthorne even in sensational tales such as "Pauline's Passion," referring to scarlet badges and birthmarks. In *Moods* she undertakes to reactivate his work at a more generic level, showing the link between the Hawthornean romance of Hester Prynne and her own domestic realism. Indeed, in 1882, in the introduction to the revised edition of *Moods*, she calls it her "little romance," adopting Hawthorne's preferred term for his own work. Even in the first edition, however, Alcott's readers were quick to seize on this comparison. An anonymous reviewer in *Harper's Weekly* noted that "after Hawthorne we recall no American love-story of equal power," and Bronson Alcott identified "her predecessors in fiction" as "Hawthorne, Judd, and Mrs. Stowe."[39] When Henry James grouped her with the country's "two or three celebrated names . . . to whom, in this country . . . we are to look for a novel above the average," he also was no doubt placing her with Hawthorne.[40]

Yet, when Alcott and others alluded to Hawthornean romance, which version of that term did they mean? The essay title "The Custom House," which prefaces *The Scarlet Letter*, famously defines romance as a "neutral territory" between the real and the imaginary, analogous to the uncanny effect of moonlight on a familiar room. Hawthorne's other prefaces, particularly in *The House of the Seven Gables*, make a stronger distinction between the "real" world of the novel and the "world elsewhere" of romance. However, it is the romance of "The Custom House" that Alcott engages most directly in *Moods*. "The Custom House" emphasizes the interdependence of the novel and romance, not only in the image of the moonlit room but also in that of a mirror that takes images of the "fancy . . . one remove farther from the actual." The mirror here is not an image of transparent mimesis or imitation but rather of a deepening of the imagination.

Alcott, too, rejects a realism linked to strict imitation or copying, a realism that *Moods* associates with Adam's "lifelike" miniature of his mother or Mark's domestic sketches. Mark is too literal a realist, copying the body parts of his models in a way that can never be fully assimilated into a picture. Geoffrey writes simply by reprinting parts of his journals, laying his heart bare. Although Alcott consistently describes *Moods* in her letters and journals as "founded upon fact," with "characters drawn from life" and out of her own "observation and experience," she does not explicitly equate this foundation with realism.[41] Observation and copying, she knows, do not themselves lead to successful—or even realistic—art.[42]

Alcott points to the key to a deeper realism in her epigraph to the 1864 edition of *Moods*. Taken from Emerson's "Experience," this quotation compares life's moods to a "string of beads" that "prove to be many colored lenses, which paint the world their own hue, and each shows us only what lies in its own focus" (1). Experience is "colored" by moods that make it impossible to observe the world whole and analytically.[43] Observation is not a scientific or "objective" skill but rather—like Hawthorne's mirror—a faculty that "colors" the actual through sympathetic engagement, an engagement that sometimes involves fancy as much as truth.

Moods comes closest to embodying what Hawthorne in "The Custom House" calls "a different order of composition," the kind of color sketch that he prefers not to write (despite the admiration of Stowe for pieces such as "The Old Apple Dealer"):

I might, for instance, have contented myself with writing out the narratives of a veteran shipmaster, one of the Inspectors, whom I should be most ungrateful not to mention; since scarcely a day passed that he did not stir me to laughter and admiration by his marvellous gifts as a story-teller. Could I have preserved the picturesque force of his style, and the humorous coloring which nature taught him how to throw over his descriptions, the result, I honestly believe, would have been something new in literature.[44]

The "coloring" here echoes Emerson's colored beads, suggesting a mode of writing that is founded on fact ("the narratives of a veteran shipmaster") but warmed by "picturesque style" and humor. Hawthorne's sense that this writing is something he could "have contented" himself with suggests that it does not fit the bill for his particular artistic ambitions, but his description of it as "something new" suggests that he does recognize it as a mode that might offer opportunities to others. In Alcott's hands this mode of composition is not so much a counter to romance— the road not taken—as an adaptation of it. In other words, although Hawthorne distances himself from this "picturesque style," Alcott sees it as integral to a new kind of writing that combines romance with realism.

One emblem of this "new writing" is in the *tableaux vivants* that Sylvia acts out in the revised edition of the novel. She emerges first as Ophelia, then as Lady Macbeth, and then as Rosalind, and she then ends with an encore in which she plays Juliet on the balcony. The material circumstances of the performance—her hard work, her desire "to do her best" for her brother and his friends (her love interests), and her love of the play—combine with the actual moonlight of the evening to allow her to "act the impassioned Juliet to the life" (245). She uses her own mood, in other words, to strengthen her performance, and she uses her natural surroundings to gain "an enchantment no stage moon" could give. Following the performance, she and her fellow travelers stay up all night talking about Shakespeare's characters, "which will always be full of intense interest to those who love to study human nature as painted by the Master who seemed to have found the key to all the passions" (246).

Here, Shakespeare—and by extension Sylvia—becomes the painter of nature, adding color and "hue," in Emerson's terms, that give it a greater mimetic power. Sylvia's art here is not "mere" copying but rather a reanimation that leads to a new understanding of character. She bases her art not on artifice (an enchanted stage moon) but rather on her ability to absorb the reality of her actual surroundings into a performance that is not "lifelike" but "life" itself. "Realism" in this case incorporates romance—moonlight, mood, hue, fancy—but renders it more strongly actual. Alcott's use of the term "Master" reminds us of the historical importance of such an insistence on the actual. Mastery here is a matter not only of influence (Sylvia rewriting Shakespeare or Alcott rewriting Hawthorne) but also of slavery. Sylvia's performance and the ensuing late-night conversation inspire—or liberate—her and her friends to engaged conversation in which they do not imitate or follow a Master as much as build on his ideas. In 1882 the immediate connotation of the word with slavery may have subsided, but Alcott's use of it suggests the importance of art in working through the legacy of the master-slave relationship. The 1882 edition of *Moods* drops the Ottila plot, with its emphasis on mastery and subjection, and adds a scene in which realistic performance leads to an appreciative engagement with a "Master." Realism—not as mere copying but as an engaged, sympathetic encounter with some form of actuality—becomes a way to continue the work of moving beyond slavery.

"Don't ascend into the air like a young balloon, child, but hear the conditions upon which you go," Mark tells Sylvia when she convinces him to let her participate in the river trip (30). Alcott's vision here is to have a balloon of imagination and feeling tethered by certain material and real conditions. In the Shakespeare example above, this means that one can encourage an expansive imagination and reception while still keeping in mind the "conditions upon which you go," conditions that in the 1860s necessarily included the fracture of war. That war did not serve merely as a metaphor but rather as the main "condition" upon which metaphorical expression could be built.

Alcott's image of the balloon held by material realities anticipates one of James's most famous descriptions of romance, from the preface to *The American*: "The balloon of experience is in fact of course tied to the earth, and under that necessity we swing, thanks to a rope of remarkable length, in the more or less commodious car of the imagination; but it is by the rope we know where we are, and from the moment that cable is cut we are at large and unrelated: we only swing apart from the globe—though remaining as exhilarated, naturally, as we like, especially when all goes well. The art of the romancer is, 'for the fun of it,' insidiously to cut the cable, to cut it without our detecting him."[45] James, writing retrospectively, wants to distinguish the romance (with which he identifies *The American*) from realism, implying, as Brodhead puts it, that "Hawthornesque romance . . . is at best an immature or imperfectly developed form of realism."[46] In doing so, James overstates Hawthorne's own separation from "the earth," but he also reveals how well Alcott anticipated and instantiated his own move toward realism. Although James dismisses *Moods* as insufficiently real, in fact its own aesthetic visions are remarkably similar to James's own. For him, as for Alcott, realism involves an "analytic consideration of appearances" that sees "the connection between feelings and external conditions."[47] In this respect, *Moods* is an important link between the romance of Hawthorne and the realism of James, a link that was itself conditioned by the material realities of the Civil War.

Realism in *Little Women*

Little Women, the best-known of Alcott's novels, has often been seen as Alcott's "turn" to realism. As I hope I have made clear, I believe that Alcott was engaged with issues of realism well before *Little Women,* thinking both about the material and historical conditions of her writing as well as about the properties of realism. If anything, it might be more appropriate to term *Little Women* a condensation of some of her previous ideas: a children's book that, while using simple language, crystallized her aesthetic credo.[48]

The story of the writing of *Little Women* is now well known. Alcott, having enjoyed a great success with *Hospital Sketches,* did not have as great a success with her subsequent works and was having trouble completing *Work,* which she had begun in 1861. She and her family continued to need money, and so when Thomas Niles approached her about writing a "girls' book," she complied. She noted in her journals and letters that she did not know anything about girls except through her sisters. As she wrote to Thomas Wentworth Higginson's wife Mary, "I find it impossible to invent anything half so true or touching as the simple facts which every day life supplies me."[49] "Simple facts" remain at the heart of her writing, but they must be "touching," conveying the mood that makes possible an analysis of their conditions. At the same time, Alcott's endorsement of such facts comes from her willingness to work with her publisher in fulfilling a particular sales niche.

Critics have disagreed about the extent to which Niles, not Alcott, should be credited with the success of *Little Women.* Some have seen him as providing a structure and a means of promotion that finally channeled Alcott's energy in productive ways, while others see him as limiting her artistic choices in a negative way by branding her "the children's friend." Although I think it is clear that *Little Women* was not Alcott's first choice of subject matter as an artist, I do not think that it is totally at odds with her other artistic production. Its foregrounding of literary realism as a subject was consonant with many of the ideas in *Moods,* and its setting during the Civil War continued—and indeed culminated—her commitment to working through the violence of that conflict.

At the level of plot, the war drives much of the action of the novel. Specifically, it leads to what Margaret Higonnet calls the "sine qua non of a civil war novel," gender inversions that enable women to experiment with the increased social power occasioned by the departure of male soldiers.[50] In the case of *Little Women*, the March girls and Marmee engage in various work and charity projects because Mr. March is serving as a chaplain in the war. Jo in particular contributes to the war effort by cutting her hair in order to raise twenty-five dollars toward sending her mother to join her sick father in Washington. While the barber cuts, Jo learns that he and his wife have a son in the army. Noting this bond, Jo comments, "How friendly such things make strangers feel, don't they?" Jo is here a stand-in for a male soldier, a link made even more explicit when she reports that having her hair cut felt almost like having "an arm or a leg off."[51]

Such gender inversion continues in the second part of the novel, when Mr. March returns home, weakened by his illness, while the girls continue to participate in charity fairs for the freedmen (319). We also learn that in the three-year gap between the two parts of the novel, Meg's fiancé John Brooke has done "his duty manfully for a year," been "wounded" and "sent home, and not allowed to return" (264). Like Mr. March, John has been weakened by his war experience, allowing Meg to assume more leadership in the household. Yet unlike Mr. March, John suffers no lingering effects from his wound. Instead, he becomes the ideal bourgeois husband: buying a house, fathering twins, bringing work colleagues home for dinner, and being marked by "good sense and sturdy independence" (264). His actions, then, help to restore middle-class gender roles based on the logic of separate spheres. Meg gets angry with him but learns to control her anger by channeling it into more-useful domestic pursuits. In this sense, his position as a veteran highlights the importance of maternal love and discipline to the social order.

By the end of the novel, apart from the sacrificial death of Beth, everyone has joined John in being healed. There have been gendered role reversals, but by the end these have been reversed once more, leading to a restitution of conventional roles. Female self-control and discipline have led to a social stability that has the power to heal wounds and incorporate cultural others. The Bhaers' school serves several disabled students as well as a "merry little quadroon, who could not be taken in elsewhere, but . . . was welcome to the 'Bhaer-garten'" (490). This "garten" is still not perfect—the quadroon is subject to racial stereotypes, especially by those people who "predicted that his admission would ruin the school" (490). Yet any rebellion on the part of individual characters or the nation has effectively been calmed, leading to the kind of universal order that has frequently been cited as a reason for the novel's continuing success. This universal order also distinguishes it from "Pauline's Passion" and *Moods*, both of which give a less utopian vision of civil harmony. "Pauline's Passion" kills off the rebellious slave but shows the lasting effects of slavery and conflict on white womanhood, while *Moods* kills off the Northern man who has (in the 1862 version) been "mastered" by a Southern woman. Neither of these stories imagines the kind of domestic harmony envisioned in the "Bhaer-garten."

Yet all of these works share a commitment to realism as an agent of reconciliation. "Pauline's Passion," while leaving unresolved the lingering effects of civil conflict, nonetheless imagines that writing, and specifically realism, is a crucial means of articulating, and hence understanding, the issues involved. In the case of *Moods*, the move toward reconciliation is primarily generic, showing the connections between Hawthornean romance and the high realism of James. *Little Women* also ends by valorizing a particular kind of realistic writing. Jo, having written sensational tales, ultimately endorses "unromantic facts" and vows to write a "good book" inspired by her "experiences" with her little men (493). In this way the novel practices a kind of realism similar to that we saw represented in Mark's sketches and Adam's and Geoffrey's writing in *Moods*: a realism centered in the everyday lives and values of the middle-class home.

As in *Moods*, however, this domestic realism is ultimately portrayed as inferior to a more fully formed "high realism."[52] In *Moods*, domestic (home-centered) realism is branded as American; recall that Mark wins prizes for a local-color sketch rather than his heroic rendering of Clytemnestra. Although Adam and Geoffrey go to Italy, their travels are less about gaining high culture than about participating in a revolution that takes them away from the problems in their own country. Even when they are in Italy, they are most comforted by maternal miniatures and letters from home, that is, by American culture. As a whole, *Moods* categorizes such domestic art as comforting and meaningful but not great; the greater example consists of intimate, sympathetic engagement with Shakespeare. *Little Women* continues this logic by consistently aligning high class and high art with things European. Laurie, the March family's beloved next-door neighbor, is the son of an Italian woman who has, though she is now dead, presumably invested him with his high culture. Amy travels to Europe in order to study art and becomes engaged to Laurie while there. Jo marries a German professor. Some lower-class European immigrants are problematic; the German Hummels, for example, are the source of the scarlet fever that ultimately kills Beth, and Aunt March's French maid threatens the girls with her Catholicism. However, in general, European culture is portrayed positively: for example, Americans read "rubbish" while Professor Bhaer gives out volumes of Shakespeare,

and Marmee gives copies of Bunyan's *Pilgrim's Progress* to her daughters
as Christmas presents. It is not surprising, given this background, that
Amy—the artist—"in spite of her American birth and breeding," possesses
"that unacknowledged loyalty to the early faith in kings which . . . has
something to do with the love the young country bears the old, —like
that of a big son for an imperious little mother, who held him while she
could, and let him go with a farewell scolding when he rebelled" (316).

This metaphor moves the notion of "rebellion" from either the Confederacy ("rebellious as you are," as Adam says to Ottila) or slavery to the
United States as a whole. In doing so, it also reverts from the Civil War—
the immediate setting of *Little Women*—to the American Revolution.
Moods, as we have seen, evokes the Italian revolution primarily as a way
of making Geoffrey and Adam recognize the value of "home." This metaphor, on the other hand, associates the United States not with "home"
and "mother" (to return to *Typee*'s formulation) but rather with the
"rebellious big son" who has left his maternal home. If the goal of civil
conflict is ultimately to restore domestic harmony, this metaphor reminds
us, the goal of revolution is to create a new order. Such revolution, as
Higonnet puts it, depends on the inequality of the opposing groups and
the fact that "one group is thought to be distinctly inferior in justification
or strength." In this case Alcott represents such inequality by juxtaposing a "big son" against a "little mother." In this respect, it is categorically
distinct from civil conflict in which "the opposed groups are thought
to be moral or military equals." In the realm of sexual politics, as Higonnet points out, such equality does not exist, and civil conflict almost
always becomes revolutionary: an attempt to shift "from subordination
to equality."[53]

Alcott's metaphor of the "big son" and the "little mother," then, supports its larger project of restoring traditional gender roles. Although
Fetterley, Romero, Young, and others have focused on the Civil War setting as an opportunity for Alcott to destabilize gender roles, and hence
effect revolution, the fact remains that *Little Women* is not, in the end, a
revolutionary book in terms of its sexual politics. One could argue that
Alcott's allusion to the "imperious little mother" reveals her critique of
what Mary Ryan would call "the empire of the mother," a phrase that
denotes not only the influence of domestic ideology but also the ways in
which that influence was put into the service of nationalistic ideas about
Manifest Destiny and imperial expansion.[54] Certainly the depictions of
Cuba in both "Pauline's Passion" and *Moods* show the danger of assimilating the colonial other. *Little Women*, however, does not sustain such a
reading. Even if Alcott substitutes a "big man" for the imperial mother,
gender roles are remarkably unchanged by the end of the book. There
is, as I have indicated, some experimentation with gender inversion, but

it is only temporary. By the end, Jo has two sons and a husband and is serving as a teacher, Laurie has married and fathered a (weak) daughter, and so on.

Yet, Amy's—and Alcott's—invocation of the American Revolution remains integral, I would argue, to her understanding of the function of her own writing. If the Civil War has not resulted in a significant change in the sexual or political order, it has resulted in a significant alteration in the history of Alcott's own authorship and in her conception of literary realism. This change, however, is not ancillary to the conflict of the war but rather, in Alcott's words, is conditioned by it. At the level of her career, the war provided access into authorship as she gained fame for *Hospital Sketches*. However, it also provided her with a means to develop her sense of writing's ability to put forward "bitter truths." In some ways her practice of realism paralleled her attitude toward civil conflict, which was to effect reconciliation. She wanted to show that such conflict hurt everyone, not just the "rebels," and that the ideal scenario was to restore order rather than aim for radical change. As demonstrated most clearly in *Moods*, she saw realism as just such a restorative genre, not only because it could portray reconciliation as a theme but also because of its hybridity. Hawthornean romance and European high art can be included in a newly wrought high-art realism that is attentive to social conditions while also encouraging analysis of inner character and moral truth. It is significant, in this respect, that Alcott alludes to the American and Italian revolutions not as models for future radical change but rather as incentives for coming home. Geoffrey and Adam fight in order to be reconciled with their wife and mother, respectively; Amy March goes to England only then to return to the United States and support American art. As Naomi Sofer has pointed out, Amy is particularly eager to support "ambitious girls" and "splendid fellows" who have "genius" (466), thereby providing a model of what Sofer terms "widespread private philanthropy."[55] Revolution, like civil conflict, leads to reconciliation and healing, in this case by bridging the gap between artistic production and the money needed to support it.

As we will see in the next two chapters, other postbellum authors were less sanguine about the ability of conflict to resolve itself so easily. They looked instead to a model of revolution that resulted not in coming home or in generic hybrids but rather in newly formulated theories of authorship and gender relations, including revolutions in publishing practices and in the idea of what Elizabeth Stuart Phelps would term the "coming" (or new) woman. After the Civil War, the notion of parlor literature as an enabling mode of female authorship increasingly gave way to one that insisted on legal and financial rights as well as on authorial responsibility.

Chapter 5

Contractual Authorship
Elizabeth Keckley and Mary Abigail Dodge

In 1870 Mary Abigail Dodge published *A Battle of the Books*, a thinly veiled exposé of a contractual dispute that she had just resolved with her publishers, William Ticknor and James T. Fields. This exposé created a minor sensation, particularly in Boston, where Ticknor and Fields were well known for their successful promotion of Hawthorne, Thoreau, and other important American authors. Both Dodge (whose pen name was Gail Hamilton) and Ticknor and Fields emerged from the scandal relatively unscathed. However, we can associate Dodge's promise to deliver a look "behind the scenes" with another post-Civil War exposé that led to more-disastrous results: Elizabeth Keckley's *Behind the Scenes: Thirty Years a Slave, and Four Years in the White House* (1868).[1] Keckley, a freed slave who was Mary Todd Lincoln's dressmaker and confidante, had ostensibly published her book both as autobiography and as her defense of Mrs. Lincoln's "Old Clothes Scandal," the sale of her wardrobe after her husband's assassination. Having assisted Mrs. Lincoln with many of the details of the auction, Keckley needed to validate her patron's actions and salvage her own career as a dressmaker, which depended a great deal on reputation and word of mouth. For a variety of reasons, as we will see, the book was not received in these terms, instead being seen as a scandalous exposure both of Mrs. Lincoln and of Keckley. Robert Lincoln tried to suppress the book's circulation, but the reputations of both Mrs. Lincoln and Keckley—as well as their friendship—had already been permanently damaged by its publication.

Despite *Behind the Scene*'s limited circulation, its publication was widely noted in national newspapers, and it is certainly possible that Dodge knew about it. Her cousin's husband, James G. Blaine, was a pro-Lincoln Republican who had entered the U.S. Congress in 1863; that connection (she eventually wrote Blaine's biography) would likely have made her attentive to presidential memoirs. Here, however, I am less interested in direct influences between the two works than in their shared authorial concerns. Both women dared to write risky books that they knew might alienate some readers, books that highlighted their authorial failures as much as their successes. In addition, both did so to reveal the corrupt practices of well-known businessmen: Ticknor and Fields, in Dodge's case, and Brady and Keyes, in Keckley's—the latter being the firm that managed Mary Todd Lincoln's clothing sale. The critique of Brady and Keyes, moreover, could also be read as a critique of Keckley's editor James Redpath and his handling of the production of *Behind the Scenes*. Additionally, both women wrote in collaboration with famous widows. Keckley's memoir records her close working relationship with Mary Lincoln and also includes Mrs. Lincoln's voice, in the form of a long appendix of letters to Keckley concerning the clothes sale. Dodge, for her part, wrote *A Battle of the Books* with the support of Nathaniel Hawthorne's widow, Sophia. In 1868, the year that *Behind the Scenes* was published, the two women had a sustained correspondence about their respective treatment by Ticknor and Fields, with Sophia Hawthorne realizing that she too was not receiving the prevailing royalty rate for her husband's books. By the time *A Battle of the Books* appeared, Sophia had moved to Germany, but much of the substance of the book is anticipated in letters that Sophia and Dodge shared in 1868.

These shared concerns reveal the flip side of the authorial optimism that followed Alcott's Civil War writing. The Civil War occasioned Alcott's full entrance into authorship and also motivated her particular construction of realism, which worked to respond to the historical fact of the war by imagining a novelistic form that would effect reconciliation. Her acknowledgment of the need for material support for that writing, marked by her shift from Redpath to Niles as publisher, did not lessen her belief in this reconciling power. There is indeed no easy road to authorship, as she insisted, but the road is still worth taking.

If Alcott by 1868 was beginning to understand the importance of adequate compensation and contracts for authors, Dodge and Keckley—writing at almost exactly the same time—articulated a more explicit argument for that need. Their shared concerns, as outlined above, underscore their specific position as post-Civil War authors. Their decision to reveal corrupt business practices was made more urgent by the precarious economic climate following the war, when rampant inflation was driving up the price of goods and services, including paper for books. Their friendships with two prominent widows—Mary Lincoln and Sophia Hawthorne—point to the shifting social relations that accompanied the war, as women increasingly worked together in the absence and often death of their husbands. To be sure, female authors had worked throughout the antebellum period to negotiate contracts: Stowe, Cummins, and Alcott all signed agreements stipulating a 10 percent royalty on their works. After the war, women began to negotiate contracts more strongly and forthrightly. Elizabeth Stuart Phelps (as I will discuss in the next chapter) flatly refused to publish for editors who would not meet her terms.

In what follows, I will argue that *Behind the Scenes* and *A Battle of the Books* demonstrate a pivotal moment in women's understanding of authorship as a business as well as an aesthetic practice. This understanding, in turn, expands the rubric of authorship. Neither of these women was an author in the same way that Cummins or Alcott was; they wrote nonfiction rather than best-selling novels, and Keckley wrote only one work from which she appears to have made no money. In this respect Keckley might be more properly termed a writer than an author. Yet her concern with issues of professionalization and expertise, as well as with economic rights, links her to authors such as Dodge, who worked to distinguish their labor from amateur writing. Recent critics have discussed Keckley as an "agent" or "producer" of her own valuable labor, locating that agency specifically in her concern with demonstrating the integral relation between black labor and white citizenship.[2] Although this labor is most obvious in her work as a seamstress, I want to apply this concern with labor to her role as author as well, looking at the way in which she demonstrates the competence of her authorial persona in *Behind the Scenes*.

Katherine Adams has read *Behind the Scenes* as a meditation on racialized definitions of freedom in the early Reconstruction era, definitions that ally black freedom with "ownership of labor" and "white freedom with the full exercise of civil and political rights." She locates these definitions specifically in language that President Andrew Johnson used in vetoing the 1866 civil rights bill.[3] This bill was eventually incorporated into the Fourteenth Amendment of the U.S. Constitution, which was ratified in 1868, the same year that *Behind the Scenes* was published and that Dodge and Hawthorne challenged Ticknor and Fields. The Fourteenth Amendment's guarantee of due process and "equal protection of the laws" was also, as Brook Thomas has shown, a "triumph of contract," particularly in its protection of property. Promises that had previously been made on the basis of status or informal relation were now depersonalized and given legal consequences. Yet, as Thomas points out, "the problem was that in the years following the Civil War most freedmen seemed incapable of taking advantage of the moral improvement afforded by newly won economic and political rights."[4] Keckley complicates this formulation. On one hand, she did struggle, as Thomas suggests, to maintain her economic rights; although she ran a small business as a dressmaker, she spent the last years of her life in poverty. On the other hand, as we will see, her printed narrative not only reveals her ability to succeed as a private business owner but also represents such ownership as a constitutional right. Sophia Hawthorne and Mary Abigail Dodge, in contrast, were initially more naive about the process of negotiating their rights, particularly as these related to artistic production.

Their naïveté was, of course, a mark of their racial privilege: as white women who employed household laborers and could, on the whole, avoid doing manual labor, they had a different relation to economic need than did a freedwoman beginning her own business. Dodge, a single professional woman from an upper middle-class family, had cooks and maids around her. Her attitude toward household work and the business end of writing is reflected in her assertion, in *A Battle of the Books*, that "as for business, if I chose to turn my attention to it, I have no doubt I could master all its details, just as I could in cooking. But if you have a cook or a publisher for the express purpose of doing the business for you, what is the use of perplexing yourself about it?" (30).[5] Sophia Hawthorne also took household help for granted; even when she faced financial difficulties after Nathaniel's death, she reported having to fire her maid but still having a "nice laundress, who washes and irons, and one of my old pensioners . . . installed in the kitchen to do small things, for she is feeble and elderly."[6] Keckley, on the other hand, had no resources on which to rely, and did not "know how I was to meet the bills staring me in the face," much less to employ assistants.[7] The writing lives of these women, then, were undertaken from very different class positions that in turn affected their positions on economic rights.

By placing Keckley, Dodge, and Hawthorne in the same historical moment, I mean, first, to emphasize the difference that race makes in conceptions of nineteenth-century female authorship. As Carla Peterson and Frances Smith Foster have shown, African American women struggled as authors not only to receive fair compensation but, even more fundamentally, also to earn the right to get into print and have their voices heard.[8] In this regard, Dodge's and Keckley's respective experiences as authors highlight a structural inequity with regard to contractual freedom. Throughout her disagreement with her publishers, Dodge maintained a belief in the possibility of just, transparent legal contracts. Keckley, on the other hand, ultimately found her only recourse to lie in personal letters, the informal mode of contract that Dodge was advocating moving beyond. At the same time, Keckley's interest in civil and contractual rights suggests the degree to which she was recasting key political debates in her adopted hometown of Washington. If Andrew Johnson was, as Adams suggests, limiting black freedom to the realm of labor, Keckley suggests the ways in which a particular laborer—a seamstress and an author—could use her work to think about civil and political rights as well.

Even as I stress the racial differences that structure these women's authorial experiences, however, I also want to locate these women not only in a shared historical moment but also in a shared conception of authorship. Both articulate the need for a rights-based theory of authorship, a theory firmly rooted in the economics of postbellum publishing. Although there has been increased attention in recent years to the economics of publishing, there is still a tendency to see it, in Mary Ryan's terms, as "only the material scaffolding around which a common culture would be built."[9] The examples of Keckley and Dodge suggest the degree to which that material scaffolding could become the subject as well as the agent of that common culture. The business of publishing, in other words, became a site for articulating authorial rights.

If this articulation helped to provide a common culture for Dodge and Keckley, that culture did not transcend race; as Patricia Williams argues, the "so-called governing narrative, or metalanguage, about the significance of rights is quite different for whites and blacks." This was particularly true after the Civil War, when slaves were "thrust out of the market and into a nowhere land that was not quite the mainstream labor market, and very much outside the marketplace of rights."[10] Grouping Keckley with Dodge runs the risk of subordinating Keckley's authorship, a subordination that is doubly problematic because she presents herself largely in relation to her white patron Mary Lincoln. However, the very fact that it is difficult to examine Keckley in isolation—to separate her from the white culture for which she labored as a slave, seamstress, and author— is finally the defining aspect of her literary production. By juxtaposing the racialized articulation of rights in Keckley's and Dodge's works, I will suggest the ways in which the economics of publishing was central to constructions of authorship in the postbellum period, not only because it sustained authorial careers but also because it defined the rights and responsibilities attendant upon such careers.

Writing and Authorship in *Behind the Scenes*

Behind the Scenes has been utilized most consistently as a presidential memoir and Civil War account, most recently in Jennifer Fleischner's biography of Mary Lincoln and Keckley.[11] As a slave narrative, its fate, as Fleischner puts it, has been "to be overshadowed by Harriet Jacobs's *Incidents in the Life of a Slave Girl*," which is more recognizably a slave narrative.[12] Only about an eighth of *Behind the Scenes* concerns Keckley's life as a slave, and although it is a success story—Keckley becomes Mary Lincoln's personal seamstress and confidante—that success is tempered by the fact that Mrs. Lincoln is a singularly unappealing character. Keckley emerges as an unstable narrator, ranging between candid self-exposure and what Rafia Zafar calls "errors of judgment" about her audience and subject.[13] Some of the most productive readings of the text have placed it in a Gothic tradition by looking at doublings between characters. Keckley and Mary Lincoln, for example, have an inverse relation to each other that makes them foils or even alter egos. Both are mothers whose sons die, although Lincoln is allowed almost excessive amounts of grief while Keckley alludes to her son's death (on a Civil War battlefield) only in passing. Mary Lincoln goes into debt buying clothes, many of which were made by Keckley, while Keckley saves money in order to start her own business. Keckley holds on to her prized possessions as memento mori that should not be sold, while Mary Lincoln sells or discards hers. In addition, Keckley learns the power of fashion to deflect the gaze away from the black female body, while Lincoln goes from being fashionably dressed to being figuratively stripped during the clothing sale.[14]

The generic instability of Keckley's narrative, however, is balanced by a thematic and structural coherence. It is thematically held together by accounts of her sewing, which foreground the material means of its production as well as the metaphor of narrative threads. At a structural level, it is also held together by the letters that Keckley inserts verbatim into the text and attaches in an extensive appendix. These letters range from the highly personal, such as letters from her slave father that were saved by her mother, to the legally binding, such as her emancipation letter. The personal letters gesture toward parts of Keckley's life that she leaves largely untold: watching her parents be separated through slave sales; her four-year relationship with a white man who fathers her child; her marriage to and separation from a dissolute man; the death of her son in the Civil War. At times she encourages reading between the lines of these letters, as when she transcribes the note she wrote to her mother shortly after giving birth to an illegitimate child. "I thought very hard of you for not writing to me," she admits, and she then goes on to describe being an attendant at two weddings—precisely the wedding she, recently with child, did not have (24). As the narrative progresses, she includes fewer intimate letters of this type, turning instead to legal and professional matters.

The need to be fluent with legal language is clear from the beginning of the narrative, when Keckley describes her first master entering her cabin "with a letter in his hand" and the news that her father, George, must return to his master (12). George has no way of challenging the contents of the letter; the letters he writes to his wife after his departure are instead "full of love, and always hoping that the future would bring brighter days" (14). Keckley transcribes one of these love letters, retaining its errors in spelling and grammar in a way that highlights George's challenges—given his legal status—to achieve alphabetical literacy. His writing causes him anxiety: "I have wrote a greate many letter since Ive beene here and almost been reeady to my selfe that its out of the question to write any more at tall: my dear wife I dont feeld no whys like giving out writing to you as yet and I hope when you get this letter that you be Inncougege to write me a letter" (15). He worries that his frequent letters will overwhelm his wife and begs her to reply. It is unclear whether his anxiety stems more from her response or from the dangers that might come from his letters falling into the wrong hands. Either way, he presents letter writing as both a need and a skill.

In contrast to George, Keckley repeatedly establishes herself as a skillful and disciplined letter writer, one who is careful not to reveal too much and is fluent in legal language. Shortly before she purchases her freedom (with the help of loans that she repays from her sewing earnings), she reports that her final master, Mr. Garland, was "so poor that he was unable to pay the dues on a letter advertised as in the post office for him" (27). This moment pits Keckley's business sense against Garland's poverty. Not only can Mr. Garland not write a good letter, but he does not even have the means to receive one. Keckley, in contrast, compiles letters that certify her legal freedom, including Annie Garland's actual letter of emancipation as well as the court documents certifying its validity.

Given Keckley's representation of legal competence in *Behind the Scenes,* it comes as little surprise that her first recorded published writing is a letter printed in the *Chicago Evening Journal* in which she "certifies" that the dress on a wax figure of Jefferson Davis at a Chicago charity ball was in fact a chintz wrapper made by her for Davis's wife. Although she does not include the letter verbatim in her text, she recounts the tale using similarly legalistic language, explaining that her story was not "invalidated" in any way by reports that Jefferson Davis was wearing a cloak instead of a dress when he was captured since "the dress on the wax figure at the fair in Chicago unquestionably was one of the chintz wrappers that I made for Mrs. Davis" (51).[15] By emphasizing the "unquestionable" validity of her claims, she argues for their authority in legal terms.

Later in the narrative, Keckley reprints a copy of her second publication, a letter to the *New York World* explaining Mrs. Lincoln's actions in selling her clothes. By coming into print through writing letters, Keckley gestures toward the trajectory examined earlier, in which privately circulated letters serve as the training ground for entrance into public circulation. As a slave, she had been barred from the coterie circulation that often accompanied such a trajectory. Yet, Keckley's narrative documents this trajectory from manuscript to print not only in her published letter in the *World* but also in her narrative technique, which frequently includes sketches that sound like personal letters. When she describes her trip to Virginia with the Lincolns, for example, she includes dialogue, descriptions of the scenery, and other local-color details (such as the nostalgic playing of "Dixie" on board the Lincolns' boat). She recounts a trip to

St. Louis in similar terms, describing a family reunion with the Garlands, her former owners, that seems to anticipate the regionalist world of Sarah Orne Jewett's Dunnet Landing. It is fitting that her description of this St. Louis trip is framed by letters, having been precipitated by "letters full of tender sympathy and affection" and followed by letters, reprinted in their entirety, from two of the Garland daughters. These letters reveal each daughter's insecurity with the genre of letter writing, with one admitting, "I so seldom indulge in the pleasant task of writing letters that I scarcely know what will interest my correspondent," and the other signing her name "Your child, Mag" (188, 191).

The presence of these letters marks Keckley as a more experienced author, one who is sufficiently adept to incorporate a local-color sketch—complete with amateur letter writers—into a text that is itself packed full of the language of law and business. In this sense Keckley's narrative enacts the moment of transition from a private, domestic model of writing to a model of authorship that understands writing to be both a business and an art. By the time *Behind the Scenes* was published, the business end overcame Keckley's attempts to define herself as an author (as opposed to the less competent writers of the many letters included in her narrative). However, in the narrative, the two concerns go hand in hand.

The preface that introduces the narrative initially portrays Keckley less as an author than as the publisher to Mary Lincoln. "If I have betrayed confidence in anything I have published," she writes, "it is to place Mrs. Lincoln in a better light before the world" (6). Lincoln becomes the author of her own fate ("Mrs. Lincoln, by her own acts, forced herself into notoriety" [5]), while Keckley is the publisher of those actions who will set the record straight. As publisher, she also provides the conceptual frame through which her account should be read. Specifically, she credits the "curse" of slavery not to individual Southerners but rather to "the God of nature and the framers of the Constitution for the United States" (3). This Constitutional reference—printed in the same year as the Fourteenth Amendment—establishes her understanding of the importance of law in framing moral social relations. She describes slavery as a moral wrong that, through a process of legal precedent, has become visible only as a truth: "A solemn truth was thrown to the surface, and what is better still, it was recognized as a *truth* by those who give force to moral laws. An act may be wrong, but unless the ruling power recognizes the wrong, it is useless to hope for a correction of it" (4). In the narrative she repeatedly endorses the efficacy of the law, despite her fundamental belief that the framers of the Constitution had been wrong. In St. Louis, for example, Mr. Garland throws her a quarter and challenges her to run away, but she refuses on legal grounds. "By the laws of the land I am your slave—you are my master, and I will only be free by such means as the laws of the country provide," she replies, and she then proceeds to print the documentation of her legal freedom. Later, when she applies for a pension as the mother of a slain soldier, she quotes a friend as telling her that she "should have [her] rights" since she is "entitled" to the pension (171). She exercises those rights, even receiving help from a Democratic congressman. Legal rights, her story suggests, are not subject to partisan politics.

Keckley finds her most sustained exemplar of the law in the person of Abraham Lincoln. As Priscilla Wald has shown, Lincoln's policies and speeches, while never solving the problem of black citizenship, showed his belief that the Constitution "shapes social identity" and is in this sense prior to subjectivity.[16] Keckley seems to have intuited this view of Constitutional rights, although she presents them through the intersubjective ritual of handshaking. She specifically recalls Lincoln grasping her "outstretched hand warmly" and holding "it while he spoke" on the evening of his second inauguration (117). This event is emblemized in the right-hand glove that he wore that night and that Mrs. Lincoln later gave to Keckley. She also describes other scenes of handshaking, including Frederick Douglass's private audience with the president (119) and Lincoln's exhaustion after greeting Northern troops in Virginia ("I have shaken so many hands today that my arms ache," he complains [127]). On one level, the handshake helps to propel certain democratic ideals across racial lines. As Elizabeth Young points out, for African Americans, it signaled "direct access to the prerogatives, white and male, of citizenship."[17] In another way, the handshake gestures toward the growing legal status of promise. The glove that Keckley inherits links her directly to the president, and it also functions as a kind of contract: the result of a promise made by Mrs. Lincoln to Keckley and an icon of handshaking that promises equal protection under the laws.[18]

However, the handshake as unwritten contract poses particular problems for a black woman. It may point to the efficacy of promise, but as Patricia Williams has forcefully argued, it is an efficacy for whites rather than blacks. Writing 120 years after Keckley, Williams reminds us of the double standard at work in the "trust" behind unwritten contracts. Whereas her male law colleague negotiated a real-estate rental "in cash, with no lease, no exchange of keys and no receipt," she, having grown up in a neighborhood where white landlords refused to sign leases with their black tenants, always insisted on written agreements. A handshake was precisely not enough in a racial relation based on distrust. Although Williams is aware of critical legal studies' analyses of contracts as commodifying personal relations, such commodification becomes empowering, rather than disempowering, for black people who have historically been denied written contracts.[19]

The final chapter and appendix of *Behind the Scenes* provide a case study of exactly the history that Williams describes, as they show how quickly the obligation of a handshake can be undone. In this part of her narrative, Keckley moves from being a publisher controlling the stories of others (especially Mary Lincoln's) to being an author who is not in control of her own story. She loses this control because of two broken promises. The story of the first broken promise, presented explicitly in the text and appendix, concerns Mary Lincoln's and Keckley's experience with Brady and Keyes, the firm that handled the clothing sale. The second story, which is literally behind the scenes of the book, concerns the conditions under which the narrative was published. In this second story, Brady and Keyes are replaced by James Redpath, Keckley's editor, who worked with Keckley as she prepared her book for publication and apparently had complete oversight over the appendix.

In the first story, Keckley reveals Brady and Keyes to be inept businessmen who fail to deliver the promotional circulars they had promised, promiscuously exhibit Mrs. Lincoln's clothes without her permission, and ultimately cost Mrs. Lincoln money rather than generating new funds. Mrs. Lincoln, emphasizing her role as ill-served and destitute widow, did not insist on the terms as clearly as she might have. She employed Brady and Keyes on the basis of a newspaper advertisement rather than client references, and according to Keckley, she traded more on her emotional state than on her rights as the seller. Nevertheless, Brady and Keyes function primarily as con men. At first they want nothing to do with Mrs. Lincoln, who is incognito, but when they discover who she is, they unrealistically promise that they can raise one hundred thousand dollars. Their offices, at 609 Broadway, were close to Mathew Brady's famous daguerreotype studio (359 Broadway) and to P. T. Barnum's American Museum (which had burned in 1865), and their spectacular exhibit of Mrs. Lincoln's clothes was part of the same culture of entertainment that made Barnum's and Brady's spaces into popular destinations.

Given Keckley's emphasis on personal and professional letters, it is not surprising that she is particularly critical of Brady's plan to court buyers through letters specifically fabricated for this purpose. The plan was for Mrs. Lincoln to write letters to Brady that would indicate her financial straits, her pain on having to sell the clothes, and the national obligation to help support her. The superscription would suggest that the letters were written in Chicago, even though they were actually written in New York. Brady would then "show the letters to certain politicians, and ask for money on a threat to publish them if his demands, as Mrs. Lincoln's agent, were not complied with" (214). This political blackmail backfired, however; the letters brought in no money and outraged their recipients, particularly after they were indeed published in a New York newspaper.

Keckley's account of this episode again emphasizes her competence as a letter writer. She stands at Mrs. Lincoln's elbow as she writes, "suggesting that [the letters] be couched in the mildest language possible" (214). Mrs. Lincoln disregards her advice, however, making it clear that Keckley is not to blame. Instead, Keckley ascribes culpability both to Mrs. Lincoln and to Brady. Brady "goaded" Mrs. Lincoln into "desperate measures," while Mrs. Lincoln was willing to do anything that would "raise the wind" (215–16). Keckley, as an expert writer, has more control over the rhetorical situation, understanding the value of the "mild language" that Mrs. Lincoln disdains.

Keckley demonstrates her rhetorical control by extracting an article from the *New York Evening News* that is "based upon the memoranda furnished by me" (221). Here again Keckley models how letters (now in the form of memorandums to an influential editor) can provide an avenue into print. In this case she adopts a measured, factual tone that promises to correct the "many erroneous reports" that were circulated. However, her content amounts to a devastating critique of Mary Lincoln's character and business sense. For one thing, Lincoln is an indiscriminate and hasty letter writer, exactly the opposite of what Keckley wants to be. Lincoln tends to dash off a letter without thinking about its consequences until it is too late, at which point "it is gone, and probably the secrets it contains are not confidentially kept by the party to whom it was addressed, and soon it furnishes inexhaustible material for gossip-loving people" (225). In contrast, Keckley publishes studied letters that correct the errors produced by Lincoln's hastily sent missives.

At the same time, Keckley proves herself to be a conduit of gossip as well, particularly in her report that Mrs. Lincoln justified her behavior by comparing herself to the empress of France, Eugenie, who also "frequently disposes of her cast-off wardrobe, and publicly too, without being subjected to any unkind remarks regarding its propriety" (222). This report only encouraged Mary Lincoln's critics, who saw her as being antinational during a key moment during Reconstruction. Her illusions seem even more poignant when compared to Keckley's earlier account of a recently freed slave who came to Washington and complained that Mrs. Lincoln had not yet given her a shift to wear, as her plantation mistress would have. As Keckley puts it, "she thought the wife of the president of the United States very mean for overlooking this established custom of the plantation" (100). Like the "poor, ignorant woman" in Jacobs's *Incidents in the Life of a Slave Girl* who "thought that America was governed by a Queen, to whom the President was subordinate," the freedwoman in Keckley's narrative is looking for a "Queen Justice" that Mrs. Lincoln is decidedly not. This "Queen Justice" is based on the slave's experience receiving clothing from a supposedly benevolent master—a practice that she has mistakenly converted from a "gift" to a "right."[20]

Keckley's account of the "Old Clothes Scandal" detaches her from the confidence games played by Brady and Keyes and by Mrs. Lincoln, establishing her voice as savvy and truthful as opposed to self-serving and false. She provides an emblem of her technique in her account of one of the trunks that Mrs. Lincoln had brought to New York. "The letters [on the trunk] had been rubbed out, but the faint outlines remained, and these outlines only served to stimulate curiosity" (212). Having come into print through her writing of letters, Keckley retains traces of the form throughout, both indirectly in her technique and explicitly in her printed extracts. She wants her story to excite curiosity but in a properly professional way, revealing only the contents of the trunk that she is prepared for others to see.

Despite this authorial persona, however, Keckley was ultimately not able to retain control over her narrative. This was not because she was afraid of a popular audience; she had already courted that audience in her newspaper contributions and was working in part to ensure a continued audience—or customer base—for her clothes. Instead, she was unable to retain control because of a second broken promise, in this case from James Redpath. Although the publication history of *Behind the Scenes* is still not fully known, scholars have concluded that the appendix was most likely constructed by Redpath, the editor with whom she met daily as she wrote the book.[21] It was not unusual for editors to have such a collaborative relation with their female authors. In 1850, for instance, Susan Warner had completed the proofs for *The Wide, Wide World* while actually living in Henry Putnam's house. Just a few years before Keckley published *Behind the Scenes*, Redpath had worked with Louisa May Alcott on the publication of *Hospital Sketches* (1863). Specifically, Redpath appears to have decided which of Alcott's letters to include; "I enclose some of the letters from which extracts can be made if desirable," Alcott wrote to him. "Will you be kind enough to preserve & return them all when you have made such use of them as you think best as I value some of them very much."[22] As an inexperienced author, Alcott deferred to Redpath's expertise, letting him decide how to use the letters, discussing the payment for the book in what she termed "woman-fashion," and crediting him with helping her find "her style." Keckley, as a former slave, was in an even more vulnerable position as a beginning author. For the decision about which of Mrs. Lincoln's letters to include in the appendix, Keckley—like Alcott—appears to have given him her entire collection. Keckley's preface had promised to exclude "everything of a personal character" from the letters, but when the appendix was actually printed, it apparently included the entire cache of letters that Keckley had given him.

In the appendix Mary Lincoln becomes increasingly shrill in her complaints about the business practices of Brady and Keyes. Her demands for money—and her inability to pay Keckley for her services, essentially treating her as a slave—are interspersed with obtuse insights into her situation. "I begin to think they [Brady and Keyes] are making a political business of *my clothes*, and not for *my* benefit either," Lincoln writes in one representative moment (243). She admits to being suicidal and mentally unstable, and she projects her anxieties onto Keckley, whom she begs to write to her daily. Keckley is her intermediary with Brady and Keyes: she is to prevent some of Lincoln's prized shawls from being "soiled" by the onlookers, and she is to ensure that Brady and Keyes abort their scheme to take their Broadway exhibition on the road. The appendix gives none of Keckley's responses to this, but it is clear that the whole episode hurt her financially more than it did Lincoln. Lincoln received her part of her husband's estate just as *Behind the Scenes* was published, while Keckley had to close her seamstress business while working on Lincoln's behalf in New York. She admits in the final pages of her narrative that "the labor of a lifetime has brought me nothing in a pecuniary way" (235), as she now sits in a garret room sewing by day and writing at night.

The only letter of Keckley's included in the appendix is written to the president of Wilberforce University in Ohio, the alma mater of her son. She writes that she wants to donate "certain valuable relics" to be exhibited as a fund-raiser for the university, which had burned on the day of Lincoln's assassination. Among "many other relics," she wants specifically to donate the cloak and bonnet worn by Mary Lincoln on the night of the assassination, along with the glove that President Lincoln wore at his second Inaugural Ball.[23] This letter clearly presents Keckley as Mary Lincoln's antitype. She wants to donate what Lincoln would try to sell, and she also promises to find a reliable agent, J. P. Ball, to convey the cloak rather than depending on questionable agents such as Brady and Keyes.[24] In addition, she imagines the pieces being shown in a charitable exhibit for the good of educating "the four millions of slaves liberated by our president" (256), instead of in a display meant to fill the leisure time of New York society women and to titillate the men who complained about Mary Lincoln's penchant for low necklines.

This letter so perfectly undermines all of Lincoln's pursuits that it suddenly seems as if Keckley is back in charge of her own narrative, making herself the heroine. She understands the value of relics in a way that Lincoln, Brady, Keyes, and Redpath do not: as something to be honored, preserved, and used for appropriate purposes. Fleischner is surely right in attributing this care for relics to Keckley's displaced mourning; she was never allowed to mourn for all of the losses she endured (her parents, her husband, her child, her president) and so instead displaces that mourning into her account of material relics.[25] However, the letter stands as a kind of authorial relic within the appendix, a reminder of the story that Keckley intended to tell.

Once the book was published, this story was largely lost; instead the book was advertised and reviewed primarily for its revelations about the Lincolns rather than as a narrative of Keckley's life. The *New York Commercial Advertiser* headlined it as "a literary thunderbolt" that would give "startling" information about the White House, while the book's publisher, G.W. Carleton, advertised it as "The Great Sensational Disclosure by Mrs. Keckley." Reviews of the book blamed that spectacle not on Mrs. Lincoln but on Keckley, who was, among other things, a "treacherous creature" given to "back-stairs gossip."[26] Michele Birnbaum has argued that this response stemmed not only from Keckley's clear money-making motives but also from her "breach of the very conditions for women's interracial relations," conditions mandating an "existential absence of the employee."[27] Birnbaum's use of the term "breach" implicitly describes the employer-employee relation in contractual terms, with Keckley's exposure of Lincoln, particularly through the publication of her letters, breaking the terms of yet another unwritten contract. Birnbaum further argues that "whether or not Keckley herself authorized the printing of the letters, whether she was intentionally misled or simply incompetently served by Redpath, seems moot."[28] I would argue that this is not a moot point since it suggests the "breach" of a different kind of contract, that between an author and her editor. *Behind the Scenes* dramatizes Keckley's desire to be able to claim a "moot point"—that is, to have the legal expertise and authority to determine what is and is not a "breach." The fact that she was ultimately unable to gain that right, despite her attempts to gain legal competence, is one of the great tragedies of her experiment with authorship.

A particularly painful and yet illuminating example of the book's reception is a parody entitled *Behind the Seams*, by "Betsey Kickley." This book condenses the action in order to make Keckley illiterate and obtuse even as it also condemns Mrs. Lincoln's behavior. Its conclusion, which merges the story of the "Old Clothes Scandal" and the appendix into one section, does not satirize or mention Keckley's donation to Wilberforce. Instead, it focuses on the social impropriety of Mary Lincoln and Keckley boarding and dining together in New York and ends by reporting that "Mrs. Lincoln has gone to her home and writes to me regularly. I live . . . in a garret-room and I love it." The satirist then seizes on Keckley's dual career and equates writing and sewing: "I write in the night, and sew in the day. Publishers and ladies please take notice. Terms moderate."[29]

This parodic ending crystallizes Keckley's dilemma. She has earned her freedom, established her own business, and become an intimate to the Lincoln White House because of her skills as a seamstress. After the publication of the book, however, she lost the material base for her artistry and became a member of the working poor. The scandal of the book drove away her customers and resulted in no royalties. As the parody suggests, "publishers and ladies" became for her inextricably related; without the support of the ladies, she lost her ability to publish. In this sense, her experience paralleled that of Harriet Wilson, who in the 1850s peddled her narrative *Our Nig* alongside the hats she had learned to make.

Yet, unlike Wilson, Keckley represents herself in *Behind the Scenes* as a professional who has worked throughout her life to claim legal rights to herself and her property, to use letter writing as a training ground for legal competence and for authorship, and to achieve financial independence through her work. Although she recognizes the culpability of the Constitution in perpetuating slavery, she also continues to believe that legal rights are fundamental to individual economic and artistic success. Her narrative posits those rights in contractual terms as she negotiates her freedom, her pension, her business, and Lincoln's settlement with Brady and Keyes. Given her endorsement of contractual thinking, it is ironic that in the end she was unable to negotiate payment from either Mary Lincoln (for her services in the clothing sale) or her publisher. The reception of her writing was instead ultimately controlled by Redpath's indiscretion, Robert Lincoln's anger, Democratic newspaper editors' bias against the Lincoln presidency, and Mary Lincoln's demands.

The end of this story may be ironic, but it is not particularly surprising. Throughout *Behind the Scenes*, Keckley replaces the heartfelt and ungrammatical writing represented by her father with her own polished, quasi-legal language. In this way, her book advocates the particular importance for a black woman of written contracts—precisely the contracts that she failed to receive from Mary Lincoln or Brady and Keyes. The importance of written contracts that she implicitly endorses is constantly undercut by unwritten contracts carrying no legal authority. Although from a white point of view unwritten contracts might be celebrated as occasions for increased interpersonal relations in which persons are not equated with property (a handshake rather than a piece of paper), African Americans such as Keckley presented such "progressive" contracts as denials of civil rights.

Patricia Williams argues that the ongoing task for contract theory is "to expand private property rights into a conception of civil rights, into the right to expect civility from others."[30] Elizabeth Keckley, I believe, understood this connection quite well, even though she was not able to achieve it. Mary Abigail Dodge and Sophia Hawthorne also experienced problems with unwritten contracts, as I will argue in the rest of this chapter. Their stance complicates an easy equation between race and legal issues of trust since as white women they also rejected the promise of unwritten contracts. However, it also highlights the class privilege and race privilege that were necessary to advocate successfully for economic rights. Both Dodge and Hawthorne were able to employ servants who not only carried out domestic tasks but also made it possible for them to have the time to write. This is a far cry from "Bitsey Kickley's" writing during the night and sewing during the day. The profession of authorship depended on an underclass of workers, many of them women, who provided everything from household help to the labor to manufacture paper and books.[31] Dodge and Hawthorne did not engage this class issue, but they did begin the long process of exposing what lies behind (and beneath) the scenes of authorship—in their case focusing especially on economic arrangements between authors and publishers.

Reserved Rights in *A Battle of the Books*

A Battle of the Books, like *Behind the Scenes,* created a scandal when it was published in 1870. Its author, Mary Abigail Dodge, deflected some of this scandal by writing under the pseudonym Gail Hamilton. Although her real identity was, like Maria Cummins's, an open secret in her local community (Hamilton was the name of her home town), she adopted a pen name in order to signal the difference between her authorial rights and her private rights. As she put it in a letter to Fanny Fern (another pen name): "I consider no crime more radically heinous than the violation of privacy. You must have suffered from it too severely yourself to be surprised at any abhorrence of it on my part. . . . Of course, if you judge from my writings that I am a woman, you can say what you please about that woman, that writer, and I have neither the wish nor the right to say you nay. So much of the woman as appears in an author's writings is public property by her own free will. All the rest belongs to her reserved rights."[32] This letter, published in 1869, is saturated with the language of the Fourteenth Amendment, balancing privacy ("reserved rights") and personal liberty ("free will") against the legal right to speak and to create "public property" through published writing. Her private and public names correspond to this division. Yet, Dodge recognized that such a division could not always hold, as when property rights lead to an infringement of privacy. For that reason, she was willing to air her grievances. The revelation is in the service of a public good, although Dodge also realized that "there is nothing the public so dearly loves . . . as private affairs" (10).

In making this statement, Dodge could have been describing her own reaction when, in 1867, she read an article in the *Congregationalist and*

Boston Recorder on "The Pay of Authors." This article made an open secret of pay practices by reporting that the "ordinary remuneration" paid by publishers to authors was 10 percent of the retail price of the book.[33] Dodge realized that she was being paid only fifteen cents a copy, or 6.6 to 7.5 percent, on her books. Having corroborated this percentage with other authors, she requested that Ticknor and Fields pay her the market rate, first through letters to Fields and eventually through an arbitration panel. She received $1,250 from the publishers in back pay, along with an agreement to be paid a 10 percent royalty on all future sales of her Ticknor and Fields books. She had learned to "deal with publishers, not like women and idiots, but as business men with business men" (*Battle*, 285).

This lesson did not come naturally to her; prior to 1867 she had tended to ignore business matters. Commenting on the history of her authorship in "My Book" (1866), she summarized the publishing process this way: "I threw out a bottle of papers, less out of regard to friends than to myself. They floated into a printing-press, and came forth a book."[34] Immersed in this seemingly effortless writing, she claimed not to have time for the everyday details even of housekeeping and bill paying, preferring to delegate those to servants and family members with whom she lived, such as her sister Augusta and her cousin Harriet Blaine. On a typical day, she reported, she would get up at dawn, "write or work till eight, then breakfast, P.O. letters, papers, etc., out-doors, walking, rambling, etc., as long as I like, then come in and do what I like till dinner at five—then do what I like again till nine, when I go to bed. It's a charming life to me."[35]

Her trips to the post office seem to have been especially important. Like Keckley, she recognized the value of letters, which she described as "the cream of social intercourse."[36] As with cream, there is also something decadent about their richness, and Dodge occasionally describes them with the air of a guilty addict. "I believe it is a weakness," she wrote, "but still I like to write letters and especially I like to write where there is a little unexplored ground."[37] Her weakness in this regard links her to Mary Lincoln's profligate letter-writing habits, although Dodge tended to use her letters as occasions to explore philosophical and religious topics rather than to wage complaints. She prized intimate correspondence in which her "very own self" could speak "without embarrassment or distraction," as she wrote to Henry James, Sr.[38] But like Keckley, she also recognized that a certain amount of correspondence was incumbent upon her as a professional woman. This was particularly true during her time coediting magazines, including *Our Young Folks* (1865–67) and *Wood's Household Magazine* (1870). She maintained editorial correspondence and also had to reply to philanthropic requests, such as writing letters to be sold at a fair sponsored by the American Sunday School Union in Boston.

One of the booths at the fair was to be a post office at which patrons could buy letters from various celebrities. If Dodge were to write some, the organizers explained, they "could charge an extra price for them" as there are "any number of young men and young ladies, unmarried, who would pay well for letters."[39] Letters here are less the "cream of social intercourse" than objects in an economic exchange that will bring profit to the larger community.

Having learned the business of letter writing while an editor, however, Dodge ultimately focused less on this philanthropic model than on a contractual model that would guarantee a certain compensation for her work. She did so in part through a sustained correspondence with Sophia Hawthorne that began as social discourse but gradually transitioned to legal matters, as both women realized that they had been similarly mistreated by Ticknor and Fields. It was as a reader of Hawthorne's situation that Dodge gained the confidence to take legal action against Ticknor and Fields. She converted letters from the "cream of social intercourse" into experiments in legal discourse that in turn helped her define her rights as an author.

Fields had introduced Dodge to the Hawthornes in 1863. They warmed to each other immediately; Nathaniel wrote to Fields that "she is just as healthy-minded as if she had never touched a pen," and Sophia called her a "blessing to our literature, of which literature I am sometimes woefully weary."[40] Since both Nathaniel Hawthorne and Dodge published with Fields, their writings sometimes appeared together in the same issue of his house magazines. For example, they each had a piece in the August 1863 issue of the *Atlantic Monthly*—Hawthorne's on "Civic Banquets" in England and Dodge's on Harvard University's senior class day.[41] Both articles give satirical looks at venerable institutions, the lord mayor's dinner and Harvard, respectively, and both put the authors in the position of the outsider who neither can nor really wishes to join the institution.

Given these connections, it is not surprising that much of Dodge's initial correspondence with Sophia centered on Nathaniel. Dodge begins by portraying him as the incarnation of the romantic genius, with a little teasing about what such a position entails. "I think it is very demoralising for a man of genius to be so happily situated as he is," she wrote in 1863. "A little irritation is necessary to promote healthy circulation." She goes on to describe a photograph of Hawthorne in which he "sits like a great dream in the doorway of darkness glowing out, phosphorescent. . . . What a remarkable derangement of things there is in this world! I would give the whole of it for the sake of looking romantic and Mr. Hawthorne agonises to bring himself down to commonplace—and I look as romantic as a healthy pumpkin and he cannot open his eyes without seeming the very Spirit of Imagination."[42] As a "healthy pumpkin," she can offer this

imaginative genius real-world sense, and her comments combine amusement and admiration. Immediately after Hawthorne's death, his wife and
Dodge continued their admiration for his majestic artistic powers. "We
have often wished you would come," Sophia wrote to her friend. "But I
have feared you would hardly like to be here now that my King has . . .
passed beyond the Golden Gates up into his Palace."[43]

Dodge did come to visit, however, and on one of those visits—in the
summer of 1868—they began their critique of Ticknor and Fields. Susan
Coultrap-McQuin has described Dodge's conflict with Fields as a "battle
over the philosophy of author-publisher relations under the reign of
Gentleman Publishers."[44] Fields, especially, had cultivated a familiar relation with his authors that made them hesitant to bring up their business
concerns. A few months before Sophia and Dodge began their critique,
Rebecca Harding Davis—who also felt betrayed by Fields—admitted that
she had remained loyal to the *Atlantic* "even at a pecuniary loss because
it was my oldest friend." She complained about Fields's decision to drop
her without warning from his list of contributors (a move prompted in
part by her decision to publish in other magazines) as being neither
"business-like" nor "friendly."[45] Her terminology suggests the extent to
which, for her, business was connected with more intimate feelings of
friendship. Sophia Hawthorne and Dodge too had made this connection.
As they came to question it, however, they associated it with Fields's practices in general rather than just with his relation to his female contributors. In their view, Hawthorne had become a feminized and infantilized
victim of publishers, someone who was duped by confidence men (his
publishers) and relied on oral promises rather than written contracts.
"The great romancer is so nervous that he wants as much kindness of
management, as much mental nursing as a sick child," *A Battle of the
Books* reports (278).[46] His childlike lack of business skills, Dodge learned
from Sophia, made him overly passive in his relations with his publishers. "Mr. Hawthorne never had a single paper given him or signed by
[Ticknor and Fields] from first to last," Sophia complained to Dodge.
"Ah—they took advantage of his delicacy and confidence. They knew he
would continue to trust and to be silent."[47]

Critical assessments of Sophia's relation to her husband have often
centered on her conventional domestic role and the threat she would
pose were she to become an author. Julie Hall, for example, suggests that
Nathaniel felt that a "publishing wife" would be "an emasculating threat,"
a suggestion that she draws from a quite startling letter from him to
Francis Bennoch in which he admits not knowing "whether I can tolerate
a literary rival at bed and board; there would probably be a new chapter in the 'Quarrels of Authors.'"[48] Yet, Sophia's assessment of her husband's treatment by Fields locates such "emasculation" not in her own

literary practices but rather in the practices of the publishers who controlled many aspects of their literary promotion and distribution.

Even as Hawthorne and Dodge represent authors as feminized by their publishers, they also show that the "gentlemanly" publishing practices of Ticknor and Fields are themselves feminized. "What they adduce as evidence—elegant extracts from Mr. Hawthorne's letters—are utterly worthless," Dodge writes. "They might just as well bring forward extracts from my letters to show that they have done right by me. . . . Their assertion that they are quite content with these friendly and familiar assurances of Mr. Hawthorne's as evidences that he had nothing to complain of is quite feminine in its simplicity." In this way, Dodge uses her letters to Sophia as a platform from which to spell out the reasons why letters are not valid legal documents. Personal letters and oral agreements—Hawthorne's mode of business—are "the friendly and familiar style of doing business," but she vows to exchange such a style for "a little hostile and formal accuracy."[49]

This last phrase anticipates Patricia Williams's insistence on a "detailed, lengthily negotiated, finely printed lease firmly establishing me as the ideal arm's length transactor" as opposed to her white male colleague's informal cash arrangement.[50] Dodge understands that what might seem to be a position of trust and respect—Fields's "gentlemanly" agreement with Hawthorne—is in fact a way of disempowering him, a fact that becomes all the more harmful when it comes time for his widow to negotiate her rights. At the same time, Dodge's insistence on "formal accuracy" suggests a concern not only with lawfulness—as in a formal contract—but also with the structure through which she will achieve that lawfulness.

A Battle of the Books is explicitly presented as an allegory, with Dodge placing the events a century before they actually happened and giving all of the major players in the saga fictional names. Ticknor and Fields, for example, become Brummell and Hunt. Yet, the book highlights its factual accuracy. It incorporates many of the letters that Dodge wrote to her publishers and to others as she went through her legal arbitration, changing the names but not the facts. It also equates accuracy with business savvy. "A man innocent of business capacity, is far more innocent than any woman can be," Dodge writes. "A woman may be never so silly, but there is generally a substratum of hard sense somewhere. A man may be never so wise, and yet completely destitute of this practical ability" (253). Women here become the sensible sex. They are not the sentimental romantics or hysterical neurotics but rather the purveyors of "hard sense." In this way Dodge also understands realism in gendered terms. Publishers and hopelessly romantic male writers live in an idealized world that nonetheless has very real consequences for those women who are dispossessed by it.

In *A Battle of the Books,* Brummell and Hunt try to detach the market from Dodge's legal concerns, challenging her to test their practices by taking her work to other publishers. "I hope that after you have put other publishers to the *real test*," Brummell writes, "you will find as complete satisfaction from the general average of your next *five or six* years, as I am inclined to think you might derive from a consideration of a similar period just ending" (57–58). The "real" market will prove that Dodge was not being discriminated against in her pay. Dodge counters such logic by detailing the publishers' fuzzy math as well as the advantages that the publishers have already had by gaining an unfair share of the profits. She also insists that the market does not determine legal rights but rather that legal rights stabilize market fluctuations. She repeats throughout *A Battle of the Books* that Brummell and Hunt justified their change in pay rates (from a percentage to a fixed sum per copy) by appealing "to fluctuation of prices and general uncertainties," or what she elsewhere terms "fluctuations of the market" in which higher prices decrease sales (25). Dodge argues for legal rights that are prior to the vagaries of the market, that are, in her words, "back of the contract" (15). She finds no grounds on which she is not worth as much as (or more than) other writers, and to correct this wrong she thinks "that the law is the shortest cut in the known world" (263). She mourns the writing time she loses while pursuing justice, but she retains her belief in the efficacy of the law. "The rules which obtain in courts of justice and which seem to the unprofessional mind a mere medley of arbitrary vexations and restrictions, are the result of the experience of the ages; and with all their short-comings and their long-comings do probably present the most expeditious and unerring mode of reaching truth which human wit and wisdom have yet devised" (263).

Critics dismissed Dodge's legal positions and "hard sense," judging the book to be overly harsh on the publishers. Although Dodge later said that she wrote the book to reform certain "sinners" and help their "sufferers," reviewers of the book depicted Dodge as the sinner and the publishers as the sufferers. Just as reviewers of Keckley were harsher on her than on Mary Lincoln, so too the reviewers of Dodge were harsher on her than on Ticknor and Fields. The *Overland Monthly* noted that literary women tend to invest author-publisher relations with "a certain confidential mystery" that forces the publishers "into somewhat of the attitude of trifling with female trust and confidence."[51] The reviewer picks up on the gender constructions that Dodge presents but misses her main point: that all authors, not just "literary women," are feminized when they mystify contracts; and that the "confidential mystery" is the creation of the publishers, not the authors. *Harper's* similarly defended publishers, saying that their editors' experiences with publishers were "very different from the very unbusiness-like business relations in which she became involved with the house which has hitherto published her works."[52] Although both journals faulted Dodge for airing her private grievances, their own domestic metaphors collapse the public into the private. *Harper's* emphasizes the "personal experience of some years" that its editors have enjoyed with their publishers, and their substitution of "house" for "publisher" reminds us that publishing was allied with "unbusiness-like" domestic relations rather than with the business relations that Dodge supports. Another review, in *Lippincott's*, shares this domestic metaphor, comparing Ticknor and Fields (which it calls "the house in question") to "the man who was asked why he allowed his wife to beat him. 'It pleases her,' was the reply, 'and it don't hurt me in the least.'"[53] The husband-publisher and the author-wife are here in a hierarchical power relation in which the author's rights, even if violent, have no effect on the publisher. In fact, the whole business dispute is one that readers should care about "no more" than they do "Gail Hamilton's washing bill," as the *Galaxy* put it.[54]

Sophia and Dodge tried to put the experience behind them. Sophia traveled to Germany after successfully getting Ticknor and Fields to agree to give her a fixed percentage of the retail price on all of her husband's books as well as on her own *Passages from the American Note-Books of Nathaniel Hawthorne* (1868). In Germany she did not dwell on the experience, although she did write to her sister Elizabeth Peabody—perhaps rather wistfully—that she had heard that the firm of Ticknor and Fields was "dissolved."[55] (In fact, Fields was simply retiring from the firm, which continued under the name of Fields, Osgood and Company.) It is significant that while in Dresden, she revised her letters and journals into *Notes in England and Italy* (1869), her only single-authored book. Julie Hall and Annamaria Formichella Elsden have recently argued that the move to Europe freed her, finally, to become the author she had long wanted to be.[56] However, I would argue that her collaborative effort with Dodge to claim contractual rights—an effort that Hall does not mention—is an even more significant factor in her turn to authorship.

Dodge, for her part, continued to write for other publishers, being forthright in her correspondence about what the payments would be. She lost $750 of her own money in publishing *A Battle of the Books* but subsequently was satisfied with her income. One of the editors she worked with most was James Redpath, who had moved to editing the *North American Review*. He and Dodge maintained cordial professional relations. In 1886, for instance, when she returned the proofs for "An American Queen" to the *Review,* she praised his abilities to withstand "the numberless vexations of editorism" and to remain "still humane." After its publication, she joked that he must treat her "civilly" because she had received many compliments on the article and felt "rather lofty."[57] This refers in part to the article, in which Dodge refers to Zilpah P. Grant, founding president of the first American women's college, Adams Female Academy, as an "American Queen." It also becomes an ironic follow-up to Sophia's earlier comments about Hawthorne as "King," as well as to Keckley's association of Mary Lincoln with the "Queen of Justice." Dodge feels "lofty" not because she is an isolated romantic genius or imperial ruler but rather because she has found the right combination of wit, subject matter, and market. She has won "the right to expect civility from others," in Williams's words, precisely through her successful legal confrontation with Ticknor and Fields.

"An American Queen" ends with details about how Grant—now married to a Massachusetts senator—lost her retirement income after being swindled out of stocks by a "business agent" who "betrayed his trust," "using her stocks without her knowledge to aid a member of his own family, who naturally became bankrupt."[58] As in *A Battle of the Books*, Dodge makes her case by inserting as proof the actual letter that Grant (now Mrs. Banister) had written to this "wicked servant." She writes, "I want to know what is knowable about my funds," and "I believe you will state to me the facts." Once again Dodge shows how hard the facts are to come by for those who are mistreated by evil editors or business agents. Dodge praises Grant for not complaining about her loss, but she appoints herself as the champion of business sense. She requests from Redpath some offprints for "private circulation" by a former pupil of Mrs. Banister's who "would like to send around to her comrades the wide world over, copies of this article."[59] This article, which quotes a letter, will now be privately circulated as a letter by one of Mrs. Banister's devoted followers. Dodge, still writing under her public name of Gail Hamilton, thus moves toward understanding correspondence and its private circulation as being in tandem with and supported by the market, not prior to it. Having once insisted that feminized authors relate to their publishers as "business men with business men," she ultimately identifies a middle ground that sees business and femininity as allies rather than as dichotomies. It is not the market that is the problem for authors; it is their unwillingness to confront its vagaries and demand written contracts. Letters, while not substituting for contracts, provide some evidentiary authority that in turn allows authors such as Mary Abigail Dodge and Sophia Hawthorne to negotiate the market on their own terms.

Elizabeth Keckley, as we have seen, also imagined letters as a gateway to legal rights. As a slave, she witnessed the ability of a letter to break up her family, and she learned to write letters that borrowed the language of the law. Yet, her inclusion in her book of nonlegal letters—particularly those by Mary Lincoln—ultimately led to hostile reception for the work

and its removal from the literary market. As an author, she was ultimately no more in control of her rights than she was as a slave girl, and
yet *Behind the Scenes* stands as a testimony to the importance of those
rights. For Keckley, the expectation that Redpath (and Mary Lincoln and
Brady and Keyes) would treat her "civilly" is secondary to the fact that
they would grant her civil and legal rights at all.

Mary Abigail Dodge, in contrast, reversed Keckley's experience. Dodge
first distinguished letters from contracts, focusing in particular on the
failure of letters to uphold authors' rights with their publishers. She recognized this failure, however, by writing letters to Sophia Hawthorne
and other writers and by reprinting much of her correspondence with
Ticknor and Fields in *A Battle of the Books*. In this way, she was able to show
the ability of letters to support her authorial rights, even as Keckley's
use of letters ultimately undermined hers.

It would be tempting to understand Keckley's and Dodge's endorsement of letters as a distinctive feature of their status as female authors: a
trace of the "parlor literature" that marked their entrance into authorship (and, in Keckley's case, an exit from it as well). However, Dodge
challenges such an interpretation at the end of *A Battle of the Books* when
she endorses a book trade that transcends gender. "[I]n literature as in
the gospel," she writes, "there is neither male nor female" since "trade
laws know no more of gallantry than trade winds"; indeed, they know
"no sex, no chivalry, no deference, no mercy. There is nothing but supply
and demand; nothing but buy and sell" (287–88). Personal correspondence assumes a relation between authors that is based on status ("sex"
or "chivalry," in Dodge's terms) as well as on mutual obligation, and it
is therefore an insufficient model for the kind of legal competence that
Dodge is advocating. In this sense, Dodge differs from the many postbellum novelists, according to Brook Thomas, who worked to stabilize
trade laws and their concomitant trade anxieties by reinserting interpersonal relations between characters.[60] Those interpersonal relations are
for Dodge an insufficient mode of achieving justice, even if they are important—as in the case of her correspondence with Sophia Hawthorne—
in the decision to pursue it.

Those who understand basic laws of supply and demand can, Dodge
argues, use them as "a chariot of state" that leads to "fame and fortune,"
while those who do not will find the laws "a car of Juggernaut" that will
crush the ignorant "beneath its wheels, without passion, but without pity"
(288). It is not the market per se that is the problem, in Dodge's view,
but rather the lack of authorial-contractual justice. *A Battle of the Books*
represents Dodge's attempt to define what such justice would look like,
and she does so on behalf of all authors—men and women—who have
followed the "Juggernaut" instead of the "chariot of state."

Dodge's chariot metaphor reminds us that legal rights are the purview of the state, and as Keckley's history reminds us, that state can use those rights for oppressive as well as liberating purposes. "In the law," Patricia Williams writes, "rights are islands of empowerment. To be unrighted is to be disempowered, and the line between rights and no-rights is most often the line between dominators and oppressors. Rights contain images of power, and manipulating those images, either visually or linguistically, is central in the making and maintenance of rights."[61] Keckley and Dodge attempt to manipulate those images through their use of letters, legal language, and contractual relations. Although Keckley is on the losing end of the laws of supply and demand that Dodge endorses, both women show their full engagement with the promise of rights to be "islands of empowerment." They understand that the history of oppression is intimately connected to the history of individual rights, but they also understand that to reject the promise of rights because of that oppressive history would be only to replicate it. Instead, they offer a model of authorship that merges legal competence with character formation and never loses sight of writing's material foundations.

Their models of authorship, however, have not played as well in our own time as one might expect. Dodge calls for authors to write as "business men to business men," and yet the business underlying book production remains a challenge to our literary aesthetic practices. Current critical practices are more conducive to reading *Incidents in the Life of a Slave Girl*, which leaves untold the story of Jacobs's postslavery experiences, including the publication of her book, than to reading Keckley's account of her work as a seamstress and of Mary Todd Lincoln's dress sale. Michael Berthold exemplifies this challenge when he writes that Keckley's "mastery of an economic discourse [dress-making] in fact makes possible the autobiographical occasion; having obtained some economical freedom for herself, Keckley has the luxury to consider, through her text, subjectivity's slipperiness and perils."[62] Such a statement creates a hierarchical progression from economic discourse to the "luxury" of subjectivity. Yet, Keckley's narrative arguably reverses this hierarchy. Her greatest perils as a subject come when she is a slave trying to earn her legal and economic rights, and once she "masters" those rights, she makes them central to her story. Dodge found one of her greatest "luxuries" to be the writing of *A Battle of the Books*. She, like Keckley, incurred debt while writing it, but she balanced that debt against the "luxury" of thinking about her reserved rights. Like James G. Blaine, whom she described as having "scrupulous regard to the rights and interests of the individual," she believed in a "principle of protection" that was "sinuous and flexible" enough "to be complemented by [a] principle of reciprocity" with other individuals.[63] In articulating this belief, she, like Keckley, in turn encourages us to articulate models of authorship that do not subordinate the extratextual (economic, material, and/or legal) to the textual but rather attend to their reciprocal relations.

At the same time, the connections among Keckley, Dodge, and Hawthorne urge us to think about racial difference even as we think about how reading across that difference might lead us to new insights. Here I am sympathetic to the historian Sylvia Hoffert's recent claim "that however privileged one group of women has been over another, however much race, class, ethnicity, or sexual preference may appear to have separated them, their consciousness of those differences and the way they exploit that consciousness to serve their own ends testifies [*sic*] to the degree to which their lives were connected. In terms of understanding those lives, appreciating what they shared may be as important as acknowledging how they differed."[64] Hoffert's particular example of such shared concerns also pairs Keckley with a white woman: the abolitionist journalist Jane Grey Swisshelm, who was at one time thought to be Keckley's ghostwriter. Swisshelm, Hoffert argues, was able to articulate grounds for a divorce by borrowing the language of emancipation, and Keckley achieved "success" by acknowledging white perceptions and desires. Her point is not to elide difference but to ask what each woman did with the fact of that difference.

In the cases drawn here, such an understanding illuminates the logic of rights-based theory in the late 1860s and beyond. They suggest the complex ways in which the presence of unwritten contracts motivated women to agitate for transparency and "formal accuracy" even as it virtually guaranteed that those agitations would not be successful. The challenge for current literary history is to avoid replicating this process by focusing on these women's claims as authors rather than on their failure to succeed in meeting those claims. Failure, in this case, can be seen not only as a problem of audience but also as an important moment in the shift in female literary production from informal to formal contractual relations. The American literary canon as it developed over the twentieth century is full of famous examples of authors who failed to reach an audience: Melville with his post–*Moby-Dick* writing; Hawthorne with his Civil War writing and unfinished romances; Dickinson with her poetry. Such authors have conventionally been seen, in William Charvat's classic phrase, as understanding "reader resistance . . . as a challenge to their ability as craftsmen" and as being "at their best when they accepted the challenge."[65] Keckley and Dodge, for different reasons, also had a conflicted relation to their audience—a conflict greatly increased, in both cases, by cultural prescriptions about what it was proper for them to put into print. If the goal for Cummins and Alcott was to maintain their authorial rights in the wake of the massive popularity of their works, the goal for Dodge and Keckley was to claim those rights even in scandalous writing that was almost guaranteed to hurt their reputations. Their willingness to do so offers strong testimony to their desire to claim authorship.

Chapter 6

Elizabeth Stuart Phelps's Ethical Authorship

In 1893 Elizabeth Stuart Phelps published a story in *Harper's New Monthly Magazine* entitled "The Rejected Manuscript."[1] Written near the end of her career, the story is a meditation on the difficulties of being a "one-book author" in postbellum America. The author in the story, Mary Hathorne, is depicted as having just moved to a small New England town. She is desperate to get another book into print because her husband has failed as a school principal and is struggling to keep the few students remaining under his care from defecting to a Harvard tutor. Although Hathorne had initially "stumbled upon what is called literary success," she has now developed the practiced eye of an author; her "occupation had accustomed her to take running notes of the most unpromising situations" (286, 284). Her latest manuscript, "Love's Daily Bread," is repeatedly rejected until she finally takes it to the "prince" of Boston publishers, who eventually accepts it with a thousand-dollar advance and a contract giving her 10 percent royalties. This happy circumstance not only helps the Hathornes out of their financial straits (even the grocer suddenly starts being nice to them) but also heals the strained marriage between Mary and her husband.

This story is quite extraordinary not only as a commentary on Phelps's own experiences as an author but also for its insights into authorship in general. Its autobiographical parallels are unmistakable. First, Mary was Phelps's birth name; when her mother died, Mary assumed the name Elizabeth Stuart, calling it a "name I am proud to wear."[2] Second, Phelps and Hathorne are both frequently mistaken for other authors. In Phelps's case, it is her mother; in Hathorne's, it is "another woman of the same name" who wrote *The Innocent Sin* (283). Third, Phelps's first book, *The Gates Ajar* (1869), was her most popular, as is the case with Mary Hathorne's first book, *A Platonic Friendship. The Gates Ajar* spawned not only large sales but also a host of related items, including specially packaged cigars and hats. Yet, this success also created another kind of conflict for Phelps and for Hathorne: that between writing sequels to the first book or writing in other kinds of modes and on other kinds of subjects. Fourth, this conflict was particularly stressful because Phelps, like Hathorne, assumed most of the financial responsibility for her family. Phelps married Herbert Ward in 1888 when she was forty-four. Ward, seventeen years younger, was the son of the editor of the *New York Independent* and an aspiring writer who preferred yachting over working: just the kind of ineffectual dreamer that Demosthenes Hathorne is purported to be. Hathorne's last name links him, of course, with Nathaniel Hawthorne, who as a young man had added the "w" to his name. By 1893, thirty years after Hawthorne's death (and thirty years after Phelps's first publication), this association is important but also dated. Demosthenes is labeled an "anachronism," and Mary too is working to resuscitate her authorial image.

For Phelps, as for Hathorne, being married to a dreamer meant being aggressive in selling her writing. For the most part, Phelps was successful in insisting on fair contracts. For example, she received five thousand dollars for serialization and book rights to *A Singular Life*, her major novel of the 1890s, making Hathorne's thousand dollars pale in comparison.[3] But like Hathorne, she also faced stiff competition from other best-sellers. She sold fifty-four thousand copies of *A Singular Life* in four years, while Lew Wallace's *Ben Hur* sold that many in a year.[4] Although she acknowledged the presence of such competition, Phelps was vexed when some editors began to reject her work or insist that she submit a completed manuscript before receiving a contract. She was particularly irritated when her own father-in-law, who was also one of her editors, requested that she reduce her fee. "I cannot remember that a *reduction* of my price has even been offered me," she wrote him. "I cannot, of course, afford to write for your columns upon the terms proposed."[5]

This comment, written eight months after the publication of "The Rejected Manuscript," glosses the tension between corporate and gentlemanly publishing evoked by the story. The Hathornes are living in a highly industrialized economy in which writing is paid per column and corporate earnings affect workers' salaries. The story begins with an allusion to the importance of the punctuality of the P and Q Railroad, which the "corporation looks upon . . . as a duty to this fattening suburb" and its citizens regard as a "sacred privilege" (282). When Demosthenes fails to attract students, he accepts a position working for the H. T. Wire company, where he hopes to serve "the science of electricity . . . with the honor and the intelligence of an educated gentleman" (291). His desire to bring his genteel background to a new science tempers the impersonality of this corporate world (his employer is also his neighbor), just as the gentleman publisher who finally publishes his wife's manuscript takes concern for her health and welfare as well as for her literary productions.

Prior to calling on this publisher, Hathorne has received rejection letters that focus more on sales than on literary merit. The firm "Bind and

Blow," for example, reports that the manuscript "does not present itself to the judgment of the house as possessing the popular qualities of your former book; and we fear that its publication would disappoint both yourself and us" (288). Her gentleman publisher, on the other hand, regards it as "a story of a high order, and a great advance upon your first" (292). This publisher—who is surely based on James T. Fields, the publisher of Phelps, Hawthorne, and Dodge—also has a family history with Mary. He has known her late father, who was himself an editor; the professional networks established between publishing houses lead to a gift economy that exists alongside the corporate one. At the same time, Phelps underscores the relative fragility of this gift economy in times of corporate loss. Her father has left only a small inheritance at his death: "There had been one of those large salaries which stop when the managing editor does, and which are responsible for the habits of ease that have no backers in accumulation or inheritance" (285).

At the end of the story, Hathorne receives a thousand-dollar advance for *Love's Daily Bread* and, later, a letter from her publisher noting that "orders are coming in by telegraph" and that the book will be the "novel of the year" (292). This move again collapses the distinction between corporate and gentlemanly publishing: the same publisher who is "tender" with Mary is also adept at manipulating new technologies, compiling orders by a telegraph that runs just as efficiently as does the P and Q Railroad. It is not clear whether Mary's literary success will mean that her husband can give up his job at the electric company. However, it is clear that Phelps wants to claim that sympathy and benevolence—exemplified in Mary's relation to the "prince of American publishers" and to her own husband—can go hand in hand with technological progress and business savvy.

Even as "The Rejected Manuscript" can be read as an autobiographical account of Phelps's relation to her publishers in the 1890s, however, it also highlights another significant aspect of her authorship: her rejection of what she takes to be false binaries. One of these is the distinction between corporate and gift economies. Another is between productivity and leisure. The story includes an illustration (see Figure 16) that depicts Hathorne at the moment of receiving the thousand-dollar check, or what her daughter terms a "good luck letter"—a formulation that itself points to the merging of social writing and economic currency. This illustration echoes Pre-Raphaelite portraits of prostrate women—John Everett Millais's painting of Ophelia, for example—and converts Hathorne the author into a work of art.

Yet, the story complicates this aestheticization. As long as Hathorne's manuscript is being rejected, she is a woman in constant motion, multitasking so much that she takes "running notes" for her writing even as she is arriving into town (284). However, as the story nears acceptance, she becomes increasingly immobilized: first assuming a veil to go speak to its eventual publisher; then suffering a severe illness and stillbirth of a baby; and finally waiting for news while sitting "idly on the lounge" (291). When we realize that the paper she idly holds in the illustration is a thousand-dollar check, however, we begin to see that idleness not only as a precursor of death but also as an image of success.[6] Once a manuscript is accepted, leisure becomes a positive virtue rather than a sign of dejection, not least because it turns Mary Hathorne the producer of fiction into Mary Hathorne the reader. Phelps anticipates this earlier in the story when she shows Mary twice in the "show window" of the post office (which had previously been a shoe store) reading her rejection letters. While on display in the post office window, she reads the rejection letters in between running errands and caring for her children. Lying on her lounge, however, she is able to read "the letter leisurely" (292). In this way, the illustration serves as an apt emblem of the way in which the idea of leisurely reading could be represented as an image of middle-class success.

"'MUMMER,' SAID POPSY, SEVERELY, 'YOU'VE DROPPED A GOOD-LUCK LETTER.'"

Figure 16. Illustration from Elizabeth Stuart Phelps Ward's "The Rejected Manuscript," *Harper's New Monthly Magazine* (1893). Courtesy The Ohio State University Cartoon Research Library.

This leisurely image of authorship would seem to be in utter conflict with the orderly image of Phelps in her study (Chapter 2, Figure 12), and yet what is ultimately most striking about these opposing tableaux is how they deconstruct their own logic. The reclining Mary Hathorne is in fact holding a check in her hand, showing that even the most romantic notion of the enervated author (or neurasthenic woman) could incorporate a materialist vision of authorship. Similarly, the image of Phelps in her study combines the amenities of the parlor with the seriousness of an office. Portraits and photographs, a dog, a work basket beside a comfortable chair—all suggest that this is a domestic space in which can intrude only small triangles of light from the three windows. At the same time, the solidity of the desk and the thoughtful profile of Phelps suggest a woman hard at work, too busy to look directly at the portrait painter or even at the domestic comforts surrounding her. There is a hammock on which she might rest, but it is hard to imagine it in use. Professionalism dominates a domestic image here, just as a professional "good luck" payment becomes the focal point of the otherwise domestic scene in the *Harper's* illustration.

Twentieth-century scholars studying Phelps's authorship tend to describe her as a demanding author with whom, like Mary Abigail Dodge, publishers often found it hard to work.[7] Her occasional antagonism toward her publishers is, in this view, a sign of authorial weakness rather than a problem with audience. She does not fit easily into the romantic rejection model associated with Melville, Hawthorne or Dickinson, all of whom in various ways defined their creative success by how much they could antagonize all but their most ideal readers and develop an ironic relation to the literary market. Phelps, in contrast, was quite up-front about her dependence on that market. She would never have become an author, she confesses in her memoirs, *Chapters from a Life* (1896), if her first story had not been accepted and her early writings well compensated by *Harper's*. Amateur parlor writing was for her never an option. "It may be a humiliating fact," she wrote, "but it is the truth, that had my first story been refused, or even the second or the third, I should have written no more. For the opinion of important editors, and for the sacredness of market value in literary wares . . . I had a kind of respect at which I sometimes wonder; for I do not recall that it was ever distinctly taught me" (76). Her conversion of literary commodities into "sacred" values suggests the convergence in her mind of high art and an appreciative— and paying—readership. Throughout her career she was consistent about demanding adequate compensation for her literary labor, even though those demands earned her a reputation as a difficult complainer. The market that brought increasingly large numbers of readers also made it possible to have a relatively comfortable life as an author. Phelps did not see this fact as compromising her position as a Christian woman and did not shy away from the privilege that it brought her.

Even as Phelps questioned the distinction between corporate and genteel values, and between productivity and leisure, she also explored and ultimately rejected other existing models of authorship: a Calvinist belief in labor, including writing, as valuable only as a form of God's glory; private manuscript writing as the obligatory starting mode for the woman writer; the Civil War as a metaphor for conflicting artistic demands; and a romantic notion of genius that links artistic production with isolation and its consummation with death. In place of these models, she adopted a form of ethical realism that rejected the more dominant "scientific" realism of the time. This realism, she believed, would allow her to find professional acclaim while also maintaining certain literary standards. Like Mary Hathorne, who combines "genius enough to possess fine instincts" with a knowledge of the importance of being paid for her work, Phelps found a mode of authorship that allowed her to combine aesthetic, experiential, and financial success. When asked in 1890 to explain her literary methods as part of a book entitled *The Art of Authorship*, she attributed her style to "downright hard work . . . and the experience of life."[8] Disciplined work and real-life experience, in turn, become the cornerstones of her ethical realism.

In the rest of this chapter, I will examine Phelps's construction of this ethical realism by looking at works written at three key points in her career: her early Civil War texts, including three stories published in *Harper's*; *The Story of Avis* (1877), which was in many ways a memorial to her mother; and *A Singular Life* (1894), her late temperance novel. In *Chapters from a Life*, she identified these works as pivotal, with the Civil War stories marking the beginning of her career (74), *Avis* producing her "favorite heroine" (157), and *A Singular Life* being the book that she most hoped to find "friends for" and not "to have seriously misunderstood" (74, 157, 272). In all of these works we can see Phelps rejecting alternate authorial positions in order to move toward a productive ethical realism.

Civil War Writing in the 1860s

Mary Hathorne stumbles onto her career with almost no effort, but Phelps traced her decision to write as a response to a series of traumatic events: the death of her mother in 1852, the outbreak of the Civil War in 1861, and the death during the war of Lt. S. H. Thompson, her first love.[9] Her autobiography describes her mother, whose "last book and . . . last baby came together, and killed her," as having "one of those rich and piteous lives such as only gifted women know; torn by the civil war of the dual nature which can be given to women only" (12). Her mother's internal conflict, in Phelps's analysis, led directly to her death. During the war Phelps remembered watching the professors at Andover Academy, where her father taught, cry as they read reports of the dead at Bull Run. However, she worried most about the effects of the war on women: "the helpless, outnumbering, unconsulted women; they whom war trampled down, without a choice or protest" (98). The national devastation of the war was linked for her to the perpetual conflict that women experienced because of their gender, a conflict that she had begun to understand as an eight-year-old grieving for her mother. Since the trauma of her mother's death and that of the Civil War were for her inextricably connected, it is not surprising that she began her career by writing war stories that were published under her mother's name. It is also not surprising that the work for which she was best known in her lifetime—*The Gates Ajar*—records the experiences of a grieving sister coming to terms with the death of her brother during the war.

Phelps considered her war writing a form of benevolence akin to other Andover women's sewing for soldiers or missionary appeals. It was also, as she said in *The Art of Authorship*, a form of "downright hard work." When *Harper's* paid her twenty-five dollars for her first story, she saw it as a means of financial independence. "It occurred to me, with a throb of pleasure . . . , that I could take care of myself, and from that day to this I have done so" (*Chapters from a Life*, 79). By supporting herself through her work, Phelps implicitly rejected the model of authorship practiced by her mother. The elder Phelps had, like Maria Cummins, first written stories meant to be read aloud, in her case to her children, and then moved on to ever increasing circulations. Indeed, according to Austin Phelps, the elder Phelps's best-selling *The Sunny Side; or The Minister's Wife* was "originally written with no distinct intention to publish it, but simply to portray for the gratification of the author, the character of a deceased friend."[10] Having witnessed this model, however, Phelps rejected the localized practice of parlor literature (she confessed to hating to read her works aloud) in order to take up what she considered a particular kind of realistic writing. This writing, in turn, was largely a response to the trauma of the Civil War—the same war that enabled her and many other women to broaden their social roles and become wage earners for the first time (recall Jo March's excitement in being able to sell her hair). Phelps presents the war as a crisis of representation as well as of the nation, linking that crisis to the maternal loss that was so intrinsic to her authorship. In the course of writing these works, Phelps also rejected the work ethic of her father's strict Calvinism.

Phelps's first published stories appeared in *Harper's* in 1864.[11] The first, "A Sacrifice Consumed," appeared immediately following a chapter from the serialized version of Trollope's fifth Barsetshire chronicle,

The Small House at Allington. Like Trollope's novel, Phelps's story depicts a virtuous heroine, Ruth, who remains single when she cannot have the man she loves. However, Ruth is separated from her beloved, John Rogers, because he is killed at Antietam, not, as in Lily Dale's case, because a man jilts her. As such, Phelps puts what Trollope calls a story of "ordinary life" into the service of the national crisis, lifting the stakes of martyrdom in the process.

Phelps's narrator emphasizes the realism of the story throughout. "I am giving you no sickly sentimentalism when I let you into the secret of her moment of pain," she says of Ruth as she waits to hear from John (236). Later, after John and Ruth have become engaged but before he has enlisted in the Union army, we are told that "in a truthful story of such a life as hers you must not expect excitement or change of scene" (238). Although such avowals of truth telling were somewhat formulaic in 1864 (Stowe, Fern, Alcott, and Jacobs all made similar proclamations), they have a particular significance for Phelps. In her mother's case, the connection between sickness and sentiment was quite literal: Phelps believed, as did her father, that her mother had died as a result of the strain of writing a successful sentimental work, *The Sunnyside*, while also being a wife and mother.

Given the resonance of the phrase "sickly sentimentalism" for Phelps's mother, it is striking that maternal power has an important role in the plot of "A Sacrifice Consumed." John proposes to Ruth by giving her his mother's wedding ring (engraved with an image of an anchor), and once she is engaged, she lets her memories return her to her happy childhood with her mother. She "slips back through . . . the wretched, toiling years" and remembers "playing among the butter-cups and daisies at her mother's door" (237). The soldier who informs Ruth of John's death has himself come home to be nursed by his mother. "I've just come home on furlough to git my arm cured up," he says; "thought mother could do it better than those doctors" (239). Ruth does not have the opportunity to become a mother, but she ends the story vowing to continue her work as a seamstress and also to be faithful in her suffering. Like mothers who have lost their sons in battle, she "lived very patiently at the foot of the altar where the ashes of her sacrifice lay, and knew that God had accepted it for the blessing of her country, herself, and John" (240).

Even as Ruth sacrifices her chance to be a mother, that sacrifice converts her into a writer. Specifically, she writes letters to John while he is at the front, joining what Mary Abigail Dodge called "the great army of letters that marches Southward with every morning sun," a "powerful engine of war" that is full of "details of the little interests of home."[12] She becomes, in other words, the kind of local realist endorsed by a parlor culture but now extending to the battlefield. As is appropriate for someone enlisting in an army, Ruth is such a diligent letter writer that she stays up late at night and "cramp[s] her already tired fingers" in order to maintain their correspondence. She kisses John's name when she writes it, and he understands the sentimental importance of the letters; his dying words are a request that his fellow soldier return all of Ruth's letters to her. These letters become a metonymic embodiment of John: "she took up her letters and kissed them hotly—they were the last thing John had held—staggered to the bed, and buried her face in the pillows" (239).

Phelps's title has echoes to the Old Testament and the Hebraic belief that God would reveal himself by sending fire that would consume offerings or sacrifices. The story of Elijah the prophet, for example, includes a moment when "the fire of the Lord fell, and consumed the burnt sacrifice, and the wood, and the stones, and the dust, and licked up the water that was in the trench."[13] More immediately, Phelps may have derived the title from Jeremiah Taylor's *The Sacrifice Consumed: Life of Edward Hamilton Brewer, Lately a Soldier in the Army of the Potomac* (1863). This book, written by a Connecticut minister, was published by the Boston religious publisher Henry Hoyt, a publisher whom Austin Phelps, a theology professor in nearby Andover, would likely have patronized. Taylor portrays the death of a young Union soldier as a sacrifice "in the cause of right." Taylor also devotes a long chapter to the sacrifice of Brewer's mother and others like her, who reveal "the truly heroic" to be "the amount of sacrifice which love is ready to make in accomplishing the end proposed." The "sphere" of such women is "preeminently one of endurance," and as in Phelps's story, Taylor demonstrates this endurance in part through reprinting excerpts from the letters that Brewer wrote home to his mother.[14] Phelps builds on Taylor's views by writing a story focusing wholly on women's "sphere of endurance" and the strength and patriotism emanating from that sphere. That endurance comes largely through the writing and reading of letters that in turn become synonymous with John. Ruth sacrifices her writing after John's death, moving not into print but rather into her isolated "sphere of endurance."[15]

Phelps's next *Harper's* story continues her concern with maternal sacrifice and writing. In "The Bend," a young Tennessee girl named Hetty falls in love with a "Yankee abolitionist," Richard Deane, who is boarding in her town. The town seems to be removed from the immediate conflict of the war; there are "battles and sojers tearin' through the country," as one native puts it, but they are "shet up here atween the mountains" (323). Eventually the soldiers descend from the mountains, and Hetty becomes a nurse in a hospital serving both Confederate soldiers and Union prisoners. In the meantime, Richard Deane has left town, aided by Hetty, who has already saved him from being murdered by a group of townsmen. He eventually returns to Tennessee to propose to Hetty, leading to a union of a Southern girl and a Northern man that could become a model for national healing.

Like "A Sacrifice Consumed," "The Bend" is also heavily influenced by the absent presence of a mother. Hetty is orphaned and does not know her mother, but she resolves to be courageous in order to honor her memory, and she has a moment of Christian revelation when she calls out to her dead mother. The maternal is there but only as a ghost; Hetty's role is to move beyond it. "The Bend" also foregrounds the central importance of letters. Here, however, the letters do not reach their intended audience. Rather than become a physical surrogate for the beloved other, the letters are intercepted by Richard Deane's romantic rival. This makes her reunion with Deane all the more surprising and satisfying, but it also represents the fragility of epistolary relations. Letters here do not go to a dead-letter office, but they do become associated with a paradoxically productive rejection: Hetty does not receive her love letters but still ends up with her lover. In this way, too, Phelps forecloses the notion that letters can lead to print, instead highlighting her authorial prerogative to create a surprise ending that is based on failed communication.

Phelps's third *Harper's* story, "My Refugees," is also set in Tennessee. It features a first-person narrator who shares certain characteristics with Alcott's Tribulation Periwinkle: she is an independent, opinionated nurse who has what she terms a "natural perversity," at one point even admitting to wanting to tie a sheet over a particularly recalcitrant patient (754). The refugees she encounters, however, have a story more tragic than those of the soldiers that Tribulation recounts. They have lost four children trying to escape from the South and are in danger of losing their only surviving child, an infant. The narrator lets the refugee woman tell the story in her own voice. In the end there is again reconciliation; Stephen, her husband, recovers from his critical condition, willed back to life by a young drummer boy who dies in his place.

The narrator of "My Refugees" comments on the letters she needs to write on behalf of the soldiers, but letters function less here as a plot device than as a narrative one. The narrator, speaking in the first person of "my refugees," assumes an epistolary intimacy with her readers, as does the refugee Mary in narrating her own tale. The narrator admits that she had imagined that Mary would tell a more romantic story: "In fact, I may as well acknowledge that I am naturally of a romantic turn of mind, and had anticipated the recital of her adventures in various forms; as, for example, whether she might be a spy, or a Southern aristocrat in disguise; and I believe I even speculated upon the possibility of a chalked negro" (756). The irony of these speculations, of course, is that they have more basis "in fact" than in "a romantic turn of mind" since the war did in fact produce disguises of exactly the type she mentions. But the story aims to capture a human dimension of the war that goes beyond these more spectacular disguises. The tragedy of these refugees' story is that they are not at all disguised but in fact have watched four of their children die, often without even a shelter to deflect the tragic ugliness of death.

When the narrator says that she is "naturally" of a romantic turn of mind, she presents the story as an experience with effects that were profound enough to change her natural inclinations. Her experience, in other words, has turned her from a "romantic turn of mind" to a realistic one. Phelps's first two stories, while foregrounding their own truthfulness, appeal to this "romantic turn of mind" as they turn the pain of death on a battlefield into an example of heroic Christian suffering on the part of the beloved left at home or give occasion for a classic love triangle to be resolved in a happy ending. "My Refugees" signals the beginning of her emphasis on the facticity of her narrative.

If telling the facts of the story converts the narrator from her "romantic turn of mind," so too the experience of loss converts the refugee mother, Mary, from a sentimental true woman into a more autonomous, hardened figure. In Mary, the narrator tells us, "what we mean by the innate religion of a woman was with her dimmed or missing" (760). Her husband, in contrast, maintains his Christian faith throughout, buoyed by the even more ardent prayers of a dying drummer boy. In this way the story reenacts the "natural perversity" that the narrator sees in herself. This fact emphasizes, on one hand, the fact that the story is shaped by her telling of it. On the other hand, it shows that the destabilizations of war are working to effect not only gender inversions—what Margaret Higonnet calls the "sine qua non" of the Civil War novel—but also racial ones.[16] The narrator thinks not only about the passing of the "chalked negro" but also about how the white and mulatto children playing together outside the hospital are "hardly indistinguishable" (761). She also watches Mary Rand kiss a baby who is representative of "Young Africa," a scene that recapitulates Alcott's depiction of Tribulation Periwinkle holding "Baby Africa" in *Hospital Sketches*.[17]

Such scenes highlight the shift that "My Refugees" makes from an emphasis on the power of private correspondence—whether received or not—to one on the importance of oral performance and storytelling. The most painful scenes in the story are out in the open, for the narrator and for the readers, including watching the death of two of the children and hearing the story that Mary, the refugee mother, needs to tell. Ruth, in "A Sacrifice Consumed," reads, writes, and sews in a "room which served her as parlor, kitchen, and work-room," but she gestures toward the middle-class ideals of parlor culture (237). Mary has no such privilege, signaling Phelps's continuing rejection of the model presented by her own mother.

After the war Phelps wrote her most famous Civil War work, *The Gates Ajar*. The most immediately noticeable fact about this work is that is does not engage in civil conflict: between the North and South, between generations of women, or within the soul. Instead, it depicts heaven as a kind of conflict-free zone in which earthly dreams are fulfilled and families are reunited. In the book, the bereaved sister, Mary, comes to terms with her brother's death through extended conversations with her Aunt Winifred, who believes in the materiality, and domesticity, of heaven—so much so that when she dies of breast cancer at the end of the book, it seems a happy ending. The spiritualist and sentimental work of this novel have been well documented and discussed, particularly the way Phelps deploys the rhetoric of domesticity to create a consolatory vision of heaven.[18] This deployment, in turn, signals a break with the strict Calvinism advocated by her theologian father, who would have depicted heaven in much darker terms. If Phelps had begun breaking away from her maternal model of authorship even as she assumed her mother's name, so too she broke away from her father's theology by writing a spiritualist novel. (He had published his own best-selling tract, "The Still Hour," in 1858.)

What has been less noted is Phelps's novelistic form. Mary narrates it by writing in a private journal, the same one in which she had recorded the weather and her lovers as a schoolgirl. She takes it up in lieu of the packet of her brother's letters, which she deliberately does not read: "the packages in the yellow envelopes I have not been quite brave enough to open yet" (3). On the day she receives a telegraph announcing his death, she had been overjoyed by a letter from her brother, "bright and full of mischief" and announcing a furlough in a few months. But after his death, Mary rejects not only letters but reading in general, only rarely glancing at the "Telegraphic Summary" newspaper. "You used to be fond enough of books," her neighbor Mrs. Bland says, a "regular blue-stocking, Mr. Bland called you (no personal objection to you, of course, my dear, but he *doesn't* like literary women, which is a great comfort to me). Why don't you read and divert yourself now?" (21). Instead of reading, Mary writes in her journal. By turning to a less public display of her literary propensities, she is able both to assimilate Winifred's lessons and to gather a reputation as an appropriate guardian for Winifred's daughter Faith. In other words, Mary uses writing not as an entrance into authorship but rather as an escape from it. That Phelps did the opposite ironizes her popularity: the book succeeds in the voice of a woman who will no longer be a "literary woman."

During the course of the 1860s, then, Phelps succeeded in writing well-compensated texts that thematize the problems with conventional women's writing. Letter writing is presented as problematic, either because the letters are too personal and emotional, fail to reach their intended recipient, or are not as conducive to truth telling as oral conversation or private journal writing is. In this respect, Phelps echoes Lamb's *Elia* essays (the only book that Mary Cabot can force herself to read), in which he complains about the inherent belatedness of letters. "This kind of dish, above all, requires to be served up hot," he says, thinking in particular about the expression of sentiment.[19] Literary women are marked as having too much time on their hands; Phelps suggests in their place the images of working women (seamstresses, guardians, refugee mothers, women working for magazines) who, although not maternal in the traditional sense, are nonetheless working toward a social good.

Phelps emphasized this again in her most overtly realist text of the 1860s, the "Tenth of January," published in the *Atlantic Monthly* in 1868. It focuses on the January 10, 1860, collapse and fire in the Pemberton cotton mills in Lawrence, Massachusetts, three and a half miles from Phelps's home in Andover, in which 750 workers were buried and 88 died. Phelps reports doing meticulous research in order to write the story, including spending a month visiting the rebuilt mill and interviewing workers, engineers, and officials. She also read newspaper accounts of the disaster and incorporated portions of actual names into her story.[20] Phelps's labor was repaid after its publication when she received letters of encouragement from two male mentors, Thomas Wentworth Higginson and John Greenleaf Whittier. Writing a memorial of Whittier in 1893, Phelps reported that this unsought letter she received from him about the *Atlantic* story "was the beginning of an inspiration covering a space of almost thirty years."[21] The presence of these mentors, in turn, signaled another important step in her separation from her father. She continued to live with and support him, but she discussed her literary concerns with others. In *Chapters from a Life*, she indicates that this separation also enabled her to think about realism as a literary mode. Prior to the Pemberton fire, she "did not talk about realism" and "had heard nothing . . . about 'material,' and conscience in the use of it, and little enough about art. . . . Of critical phraseology I knew nothing; and of critical standards only what I had observed by reading the best fiction. Poor novels and stories I did not read" (91). Phelps's use of "poor" here denotes her subject as well as her form: she had not read of "poor" or working people in the "poor," or less privileged, mode of realism. The fact that she decided to take on such a subject and form, then, presents a turn away from her parents (her father had rendered "poor" reading "absent from [her] convenience" [92]) and toward the support of mentors such as Whittier and Higginson.

By the end of the 1860s, then, Phelps had begun the process of detaching herself from the literary legacy of her parents ("You come of a family of large circulations," the publisher James T. Fields told her) and also of redefining the work of the "literary woman" (*Chapters from a Life*, 10).

This woman would be neither a letter writer nor a sentimental romanticist. Instead, she would work hard to produce her work, and to gain adequate compensation for it, while also moving toward an increasingly realist aesthetic. This aesthetic, in turn, would lead her to reject two other received models of authorship: that of an author ravaged by civil conflict and that of the solitary genius. These rejections would be the particular subjects of her greatest work of the 1870s, *The Story of Avis*.

Revolution in *The Story of Avis*

Phelps published *The Story of Avis* in 1877, but it is set during the Civil War; Avis Dobell decides to marry Philip Ostrander only after he has been wounded at Bull Run.[22] Granted, Philip is probably the most unheroic soldier in all of American literature. He enlists to escape personal difficulties; he is harmed not because of a gunshot but because a horse falls on top of him; he comes close to being seduced by his nurse, Barbara Allen; and he ultimately dies when he falls off a horse while on a rest cure in Florida. However, his status as a soldier remains central to the plot, particularly since, as Naomi Sofer points out, Avis sees her marriage to him as "her contribution to the war effort," sacrificing her art as a form of penance.[23] Phelps makes this connection explicit when Avis responds to his proposal as itself a "civil war" since she has "two natures" (later defined as "art and love") "warring against each other" (107, 122). In the end, however, Phelps uses such competition to reject civil strife as her primary metaphor for artistic production, turning instead to a metaphor of social and personal revolution. At the same time, she builds on her previous work by continuing to reject her father's Calvinism as well as her mother's form of "local" writing.

Avis's father, like Phelps's own, is a professor (in Hegel's case of ethics and intellectual philosophy) who tends to remove himself from concern with everyday realities. Hegel Dobell reads about the war rather than participating in it directly, spending most of his time sitting at a desk in front of a portrait of the philosopher William Hamilton (see Figure 17) and writing brochures with titles such as "Was Fichte a Mystic?" and "Identity of Identity and Non-Identity" (20). Hamilton (1788–56), whom Hegel physically resembles, was a member of the common-sense school of Scottish philosophy whose main theological belief was "the law of the conditioned." This law concluded that God was unknowable through reason since "the Conditioned or the thinkable lies between two extremes or poles," while the "Unconditioned"—such as God—is inconceivable by reason.[24] This law was consonant with Calvinistic concepts of justification by faith, and to that extent Hegel Dobell and Hamilton are both allied with Austin Phelps.

Figure 17. Portrait of Sir William Hamilton, by John Ballantyne. Courtesy The National Gallery of Scotland.

Yet, one of the stories of Avis concerns her ability to domesticate her father's Calvinism. When we first meet him, he is an intimidating presence, a widower who shows no warmth toward his daughter. As a child, she announces to him that she wants to be an artist, which he immediately dismisses as "womanish apings of a man's affairs, like a monkey playing tunes on a hand-organ" (33). Thinking about her mother, however, who had wanted to be an actress, he decides that Avis can go study art in Europe, particularly since she has impressed him with her own copy of the portrait of Sir William. Once she returns, however, she ministers to him, reminding him of her mother (115). She also teaches him the importance of sympathy as well as of intellect. Having returned from Florida after Philip's death, Avis presents to him a "frosted future" that "chilled him like some novel defect in the laws of nature; as if the sun should elect upon whose roof it would shine, or the rain pass him by to visit his neighbor's field" (244). This chill signals his sympathy with her tragedy, but the metaphor of the sun and "election" signals a subtle shift in his own Calvinist thinking. Predestination, a central tenet of Calvinism, includes the belief that divine election is an inescapable fact. However, here election is shown to be an unnatural defect, an inconsistency that can lead to a "frosted future." His last words to Avis are "Your little daughter speaks" (244). The philosopher has ceded his authority to that of a small child with the Puritan name of Waitstill. Named after her paternal grandmother but emblematic of what Phelps calls "the coming woman," Wait signals a shift in the Dobells' Calvinism, one that puts authority in the domestic world of childhood as well as in theological tracts.

This shift is also seen in the other minister in the novel, John Rose. The husband of Avis's best friend, Coy, John moves beyond doctrine to enact a more hands-on ministry, one that includes holding regular "office hours" as a "soul doctor" for those in need as well as visiting the tenements of Harmouth. Avis accompanies him on one such visit and discovers the limitations of her previous practice of being "a little colorblind to misery for beauty's sake" (159). Her art has been false insofar as it has not included "the moan of human famine" (160). As such, John's modified Calvinism—one interested in the immortality of all souls rather than merely those of the elect—in turn signals a shift in Avis's aesthetic vision from the heroic or mythic to a realistic concern with the pain of the lower classes. Austin Phelps had preached that it "will be a happy day for the church when questions of social reform . . . shall no more embarrass the distinctive enterprises of Christian benevolence," but Avis—the daughter of an ethics professor—increasingly sees social reform as integral to her calling.[25]

Avis's aesthetic shift signals Phelps's gradual move toward what she would eventually term an "ethical realism": an effort both "to tell the

truth about the world [she] live[d] in" and to "write with an ethical purpose" (*Chapters from a Life*, 259, 257). Her ethical realism constituted a
break with the Calvinist attitude toward social reform endorsed by her
father as well as a further rejection of the parlor literature that her mother
had practiced. The novel literally begins in the parlor, with a meeting of
the Poetry Club at Chatty Hogarth's house. Chatty is the hostess because
she is an invalid who cannot move beyond her home, further reiterat-
ing the confines of this domestic space. It is, like Stowe's Semi-Colon
Club, a coed group; we hear John Rose reading Spenser and Philip
Ostrander reading a paper on Spenserian meter. Yet, the "high literary
virtue" practiced by the club does not necessarily produce its intended
results; it becomes more an occasion for courtship and flirtation than
for scholarly exchange, with the result being that at least one of its members—Coy Bishop—can never remember whether a particular quotation
came from Galileo, Socrates, Newton, or her beloved John Rose. "What
was the use of reading-clubs, and suffering such anxiety about the coffee,
when one took one's turn," she wonders, "if one could not tell whether
one owed an idea to an old Greek, or to an evening caller?" (4). By the
end of the novel, Coy and Avis no longer attend the club, though they
do gossip about its most recent incarnation in the "Odyssey Club" (247).
The parlor culture associated with female art and literacy has proven to
be irrelevant to Avis's story.

If Phelps uses *Avis* to reject this culture, however, she is no less optimistic about a romantic model of artistry. Avis enters the novel having
just returned from studying art in Europe, ready to commit herself to a
career that has already received positive notice in the newspapers. However, the novel works as a whole to demonstrate the limitations of such
a career. For one thing, it requires a problematic solitude, as Coy notes
when she reproves Avis "for staying so much by herself since she had
come home" (5). For another thing, as we have already seen, it fosters
a certain "color-blindness" that renders artistic revelations "false." Phelps's
primary emblem of this blindness is the character of Susan Wanamaker
Jessup, a former lover of Philip's whose life is a kind of undertow to Avis's.
Whereas Avis is a producer of art, Susan labors selling it by working as a
traveling book agent. The difficulty of this labor is underscored by the
fact that her last name is Wanamaker, linking her with John Wanamaker,
who had opened his famous department store in 1876, the year before
Avis was published. Given the increasing incorporation of America, agents
such as Susan Wanamaker seem doomed to failure. Like Avis, Susan then
enters an unhappy marriage, following her husband to the South (the
Jessups go to Texas rather than to Florida). Unlike Avis, however, Susan
has a husband who is physically abusive rather than just a bad match.
Susan eventually returns to Harmouth to work as housekeeper to the

affluent Stratford Allen, who has, among other things, bought Avis's most prized painting: an allegorical work about the Egyptian Sphinx. Susan's story, then, demonstrates the human cost of artistic isolation, not only in terms of unspoken subjects but also in terms of the work—the book peddling and house cleaning—that must support it. If parlor literature is an empty model, the romantic artist is even more problematic insofar as it naturalizes social privilege, erasing the presence of the workers who must support it.

Phelps repeats this pattern of deconstructing the romantic ideal of art throughout *The Story of Avis*. Avis paints portraits, including one of Philip, but finds that the process leads to "self-distrust" (57), with the "nervousness" that accompanies a portrait's completion being the equivalent of "the ending of a life" (62). This reverses the romantic trope equating perfect art with the death of the subject, as in Poe's "Oval Portrait," Hawthorne's "The Prophetic Portrait," or Harriet Prescott Spofford's "The Amber Gods," each of which imagines a portrait supplanting the real person it depicts. The metaphorical death of the artist is no better; it is little wonder that Avis stops painting portraits and turns to more allegorical subjects. Allegory too proves problematic. The only way to earn money through her allegorical painting is to sell photographic copies of it, a form of reproduction that Avis admits is "not best for the picture" but is "best for us all now" (215). Avis's decision to photograph her painting is particularly painful given that it follows on the heels of her son Van's death. Van is now memorialized only in a tintype, the least-expensive form of reproductive portraiture. "I've kept the tintype you sent—see—in my wallet," Philip tells her when he returns from Europe, not yet knowing about Van's death. "I've carried it all about. I was sorry you couldn't afford a photograph" (211). In order to afford high-quality photographs of her children, Avis needs to compromise the originality of her painting by issuing photographic copies.

Given these various artistic impasses, it is perhaps inevitable that Avis ends up renouncing art altogether, deciding to teach at the art school rather than produce the paintings that might be studied there. We might read this as a bitter commentary on the difficulties of being a female artist, of claiming originality in a world that assumes, in Hegel Dobell's words, that such claims are nothing more than "womanish apings of men's affairs." After all, Avis's primary artistic lesson comes from her marriage to Philip, whom she ultimately realizes is not a "divine ideal" but an "unheroic human reality" whose "worst is the real of him" (178, 230). The text, however, discourages this reading, focusing instead on the way in which this rejection of art can paradoxically lead to a rejection of civil strife as the primary analogy for women's experience.

Hegel Dobell again provides a key point in this shift away from civil conflict. When Avis announces to him that she has resolved her own "civil war" (106)—the debate about whether or not to marry—by deciding to accept Philip's proposal, Hegel's thoughts immediately return to his philosophical hero, William Hamilton. "'The conceivable,'" he murmured, "'lies always between two inconceivable extremes. Such we find in the law of the conditioned'" (115). This line, taken from Hamilton, underscores the idea that human experience, including thought, cannot hold together two extremes simultaneously. Since Avis, and her world, cannot imagine her being a wife and an artist simultaneously, the "law of the conditioned" stipulates that she will gravitate toward one in order to move forward with her life. Although Hamilton insisted that one extreme must always be true, since they are mutually contradictory, Phelps's use of him suggests that her own vision was somewhere in the middle, with the "conditioned" existing as the antithesis of civil conflict. In this way her use of Hamilton echoes her later invocation of Aristotelian ethics, when she reminds us—following Philip's feeble attempts to confide in Avis about Susan Wanamaker—that "Aristotle ranks confidence as one of the passions" (167). The *Nicomachean Ethics* stipulates that moral virtue will always lie between the extremes of passion and the faculties by which we process them. Confidence, as an excess of self-assurance, is a passion whose opposite faculty is fear, with courage being the virtue in the middle. Courage, for Phelps, seems to occupy something like the "law of the conditioned" since its virtue arises from its ability to exist between extremes.

In *The Story of Avis,* Phelps replaces civil conflict—both national and gendered—with a revolutionary courage that allows Avis to move forward. In one of the final scenes of the book, Phelps depicts the need to move beyond conflict in a conversation between Coy and Avis. On one level, this conversation seems to reinvoke Phelps's critique of parlor culture: the women sit in the parsonage parlor, with Coy sewing baby clothes, engaging in random gossip. Little seems to have changed since the opening scene in Chatty Hogarth's parlor, but there are small signs of change. Avis's daughter plays with a screwdriver—hardly normal parlor furnishing (248). The women have decided not to attend the weekly Poetry Club meeting. In addition, their conversation goes beyond local details to talk "of matters of which they did not often speak" (247). Conversational intimacy replaces scripted poetry lessons. Coy, the perfectly contented wife, even admits to disliking asking her husband for money, a small sign that she is even more coy than we thought (248). Avis looks at her "as the country, wasted by civil war, pauses to look off upon the little neutral state" (249). Avis here becomes a stand-in for the country in need of healing after the war, and Coy—the devoted mother and minister's wife—becomes the "neutral" state that will aid that healing.

Civil conflict is ultimately not endlessly sustainable, leading to waste above all else.

At the same time, Phelps suggests the revolutionary move that will follow the neutral state. Avis's daughter Wait—named after her Puritan grandmother—will become the New Woman whom Avis cannot, with "intellectual command" as well as physical strength and health (246). Such a woman engages in "sweet warfare" at the end of which she ultimately "vanquishes" her man through "generosity" (247). Waitstill Ostrander (Philip's mother), Susan Wanamaker, Coy Bishop, and Avis Dobell all combine in this coming woman to define femininity not as civil conflict but as a revolutionary hybrid of individualism and benevolence, strength and generosity.[26] Civil wars, as Higonnet reminds us, usually assume that the opposed groups are "moral or military equals," while in revolutions "one group is thought to be distinctly inferior in justification of strength," with "the stress on reversal of a political order."[27] According to this logic, which Phelps seems to share, civil conflict will never lead to true social change since it does not acknowledge difference. Phelps's investment in this difference did not make her a modern feminist since she continued to believe, as Nina Baym puts it, that although not "all women like to do housework[,] . . . they are most fulfilled when they occupy a protected home space."[28] Coy and Avis, sitting in such a space, nonetheless enact an important critique of civil conflict, thinking about how women, rather than monkey grinders, can engage in "sweet warfare."

Phelps imagined *The Story of Avis* as a whole as doing revolutionary work. Writing to George Eliot about their mutual interest in depicting strong "coming women," she noted that a "woman's personal identity is a vast undiscovered country with which society has yet to acquaint itself, and by which it is yet to be revolutionized."[29] Unlike Alcott, who imagines revolution only through memories of an "imperious little mother" scolding a "big son," Phelps imagines a future revolution. Her British "little mother" takes the specific form of George Eliot, who inspired her to write *The Story of Avis.* "If I overstep my rights [in writing to you]," she wrote Eliot, "you will remember that I am an American and that it is the birthright of Americans to be 'agitators,' and so, pardon me I am one!"[30] In this comment Phelps again frames her future work by appealing to the revolutionary energies of the American War for Independence. During the Civil War, writers had frequently turned to the Revolution for images of heroism. In *The Sacrifice Consumed,* for example, Taylor compares Union mothers to "the American women in the period of the Revolution, . . . the women of the times of Washington and Bunker's Hill," specifically invoking Abigail Adams's resolve to sacrifice "selfish passions to the general good."[31] Longfellow wrote "Paul Revere's Ride" in 1860; Hawthorne spent the early 1860s planning a series of romances based around a Revolutionary soldier, Septimus Felton; Lincoln famously invoked the Revolution at the beginning of the Gettysburg Address. Lyde Cullen Sizer has claimed that women writers did not "generally invoke the legacy of the Revolution, as men North and South did."[32] Yet in *Avis*, at least, Phelps rejected the revolutionary logic of the Civil War and replaced it with a vision of a unified nation of agitators: the "vast undiscovered country" of women that will not remain a neutral state but will "yet" revolutionize society. In doing so, she also defined novel writing as a revolutionary act. In this respect *Avis* anticipates the turn-of-the-century commentator Annie Nathan Meyer's assessment of the novel as a literary form: "it has developed into a vast mirror that reflects not only the gay, tripping, bepowdered figures of the past, but the whole trend of Life to-day; —not figures only, but thoughts, aspirations, revolutions."[33]

A *Singular Life* and the Legacy of Ethical Realism

In the final decades of her career, Phelps channeled these revolutionary propensities in quite specific directions, working on behalf of dress reform, antivivisection laws, and temperance. Like Mary Hathorne, the reborn author of "The Rejected Manuscript," she reinvented herself through her reform writing, which she allied with a particular form of ethical realism. This reinvention gave her great personal satisfaction, particularly with the writing of *A Singular Life* (1894), her most sustained temperance novel. She registered this satisfaction, for instance, in her comments about the novel in a letter to the publisher Henry Oscar Houghton. "The book is twice as long as any I have written, and my soul is in it," she wrote.[34] *A Singular Life* tells the story of Emanuel Bayard, a minister murdered while doing missionary work in Angel Alley, the bowery district of a New England fishing town called Windover. His church, Christlove, takes away business from the taverns, and Bayard is killed by the son of the local liquor dealer. Bayard's story in many ways culminates the trajectory of rejection that we have been tracing. It is, as a nineteenth-century commentator put it, "the story of a cumulative agonism."[35] It also constitutes a significant shift in Phelps's conception of that rejection. Instead of seeing it in oppositional terms, as a reaction against something else, she sees it as socially productive. If Avis gives up her art in order to make way for the coming generations, Bayard represents something like that future ideal. The law of the conditioned moves, in this case, to a bridging of oppositions. Instead of imagining that only one extreme can be known at a time, Phelps projects onto Bayard a more Aristotelian vision of a heroic mean.

Avis ends, we recall, with Phelps's admonition that it will take three generations to make the coming woman. *A Singular Life* begins with a group of seminary students noting that it takes "three generations to make a gentleman" (3). The students, eating at a club dinner, essentially restage the Poetry Club meeting that begins *Avis*. As this is an all-male group, it is significant that they are still engaged in a kind of neoparlor culture, a semipublic sphere that understands conversation to be a key to intellectual and moral growth. The fact that the generational discussion has shifted from Coy and Avis to a group of seminary students signals the beginning of Phelps's conciliatory vision in this work. Men and women may have different gifts, but they also share a fundamental progressive urge. One might argue that it is a sign of the failure of the coming woman to have a man appropriate her role. However, the logic of Phelps's novel, and career, suggests that she is less interested in showing female oppression than in establishing a common ground or mean between the sexes, albeit one that retains the idea of sexual difference.

Having begun *A Singular Life* by making this key connection to *Avis*, Phelps then continues to break down the oppositions she had earlier established. If John Rose is a kind of antitype to Austin Phelps, Emanuel Bayard merges the two types. Like Austin, he is never happier than when he is studying or writing, and he marries the daughter of a theology professor who is much like Austin. However, like John, he realizes the limits of theological education, noting that "no curriculum recognizes Job Slip," the alcoholic whom Bayard succeeds in reforming (153), and that "it is not so hard to endure suffering as to resist ease" (213). Bayard's merging of these two types may have been particularly important to Phelps in the wake of the highly publicized "Andover Controversy" in the late 1880s and the death of her father in 1890. Although her father had left Andover in 1879 after serving as its president for ten years, he still spoke out on the conservative side of the controversy. During the controversy Andover's board of visitors put some professors on trial for heresy to determine whether they had broken their contracts by breaking the Andover Creed. The particular issue at stake was the question of future probation, or whether one could come to know Christ after death even if not hearing the gospel during life and hence be saved from a life in hell. Austin Phelps believed that the founding creed was more important than any revisionist revelations about it. The controversy pitted old orthodoxy—those believing in a Calvinist creed that discounted works—against a new orthodoxy that endorsed a concern with social reform and science as well as future probation. Although Austin sided with the old, his daughter was interested in the new, particularly since it was fighting for a vision of heaven that more nearly aligned with the one she had depicted in *The Gates Ajar*.[36]

Bayard also helps his father-in-law, the stuffy Professor Carruth, move toward the new orthodoxy. When Christlove church is rededicated after an arson fire, Carruth abandons a prepared doctrinal sermon in order to give an extemporaneous one that is widely seen as his best ever. He who "had been so occupied with the misery of the next world that he had never investigated the hell of this one" finally understands the importance of social action (385). After this rededication, the services at Christlove increasingly attract not only the lower classes but also the upper classes from the nearby First Church (which had originally refused to hire Bayard). They also attract members of what the townsfolk call the "summer people": the wealthy New Englanders who come to the seaside not to make a living but for an extended summer vacation. In the final scene of the book, as Bayard lies in state at the church, one of these summer residents talks to an Italian immigrant, a clear rewriting of the first scene in Angel Alley, in which a fisherman fights with an Italian laborer (57). All is not healed—Bayard has been murdered, after all, by a representative of the group that resents the business he has taken away—but the clear suggestion is that even a Calvinist minister such as Bayard can move beyond doctrinal abstractions to promote social reconciliation. Bayard shows, we are told, the "power of an elect personality" (264). However, his singular election does not remove him from a concern with the people.

Another sign of Bayard's election is his ability to move beyond the social restrictions imposed by his background. Although he is the son of a socially mixed couple—a carpenter and a Boston Brahmin's daughter— he is raised in the Back Bay by his decidedly upper-crust uncle. (Both of his parents, predictably named Mary and Joseph, die when he is a toddler.) This background also eventually merges with Christlove; although his uncle first disinherits him, a visit to Windover changes his mind, and he leaves his nephew the Back Bay house, the sale of which helps fund the rebuilding of the church. It is only at this point that Bayard marries the professor's daughter, whom he teaches to move beyond the ivory tower of her father's seminary. When he first meets Helen at a seminary tea, she immediately shows him her photograph book—exactly the kind of book that Avis Dobell, who can afford only tintypes, does not have. *A Singular Life* sympathizes with Helen despite her class status.

By current literary standards, *A Singular Life* pales in comparison to *Avis*; its plot is more formulaic and the interior of its central character less fully drawn. However, it is crucial, I believe, to understanding the shape of Phelps's career. As is the case with many characters in her books, Bayard is a creative double who clearly mirrors some of her concerns as an artist, particularly balancing his love of solitude with his dedication to social service. (He longs to be "curled into the shell of his solitude contentedly," echoing Phelps's comment to Whittier that she was "made to live curled up in a shell somewhere (an oyster shell perhaps!) on the seashore" [10].[37]) He is also concerned with the finances of his ministry.

Although he is ultimately saved by his uncle's bequest, along with some stock he inherits from his mother, he worries about how he can support his social work. At one point we are told that the "subscription list for his quarter's salary lay across the manuscript notes" for his sermon; as is the case with Phelps's works, his writing would be to no avail if no one subscribed to it (175). Also like Phelps, he believes that his writing serves an important social and moral function.

This function is ultimately related, to Phelps, to her particular practice of realism. Realism was for her a matter of heart and soul as much as of mimetic accuracy, and she worried about the overly clinical approach she saw in the prevailing objective mode of high realism. In this respect she saw herself following the English school of realism as practiced by George Eliot rather than the French school that valued scientific intellectualism. She would again have agreed with Annie Nathan Meyer, who wrote in 1896 that "the novel is not psychology, it is applied psychology; it is not social economics, it is applied social economics."[38] Her views were also similar to those of William Roscoe Thayer, who believed that fiction should "discover the secret of the heart of man, who is spiritual," rather than be, in Thomas Sergeant Perry's words, a "fellow-worker" of "the scientific spirit."[39]

In *Chapters from a Life,* Phelps hints at her divergence from this scientific approach when she emphasizes the importance of writing "with an ethical purpose" (257). Truth-telling, for her, necessarily includes an attention to the moral struggles of life. In her view—following the law of the conditioned—there is ultimately little difference among the "contending schools" of "the realist," "the romanticist," and "the idealist." If there is any distinction, it is "not so much one of artistic theory as of the personal equation," the artist's "personal impression as to what life is" (259–60).[40] Reviews of *A Singular Life* praised her attention to such impressions, pointing to the fact that Bayard was a "man" with "anguish and suffering" rather than a "psalm-singing hero" full of "ardor" but "no pietistic gush."[41] They also found it more "worthy" and "forceful" than work appearing at the same time by authors we now associate more clearly with realism.[42] One reviewer praised the "symmetrical form" of Phelps's writing, for example, right after dismissing Stephen Crane's *The Red Badge of Courage* as an "unconvincing . . . account, in roughshod descriptive style, of the thoughts and feelings of a young soldier."[43] Another critiqued the "prosy realism and vague, find-it-if-you-can meaning of Mr. [Henry] James' style" while praising "the many exquisite little touches of character, dialogue, and incident in a style peculiarly Miss Phelps' own."[44]

In a work written a hundred years later, Brook Thomas labels Phelps's work "nonrealist" because it presents "a world in which social relations are regulated by a transcendental principle" as opposed to laissez-faire market relations.[45] Yet, Phelps, like many of her reviewers, did not find that such a principle barred her from being called a realist. Her personal regret at the increasingly distant relations between authors and publishers could, in fact, be seen as proof of her belief in what Thomas calls the "promise of contract" and its optimism about professional relations creating equitable treatment between persons. Indeed, her belief was so strong that she was even willing to pitch her brand of realism against that practiced by William Dean Howells, whom she called the "chief exponent" of realism in America. In *Chapters from a Life*, she explicitly challenges a passage in *Literary Friends and Acquaintance* in which Howells claims that the work of Hawthorne, Emerson, and many celebrated New England authors was "marred by" an "intense ethicism. . . . They still helplessly pointed the moral in all they did. . . . New England yet lacks her novelist, because it was her instinct and her conscience to be true to an ideal of life rather than to life itself" (260–61). Phelps disagrees, arguing that "moral character is to human life what air is to the natural world;—it is elemental" (261). Since moral character is part of "the truth," there is no conflict between being a realistic "truth-teller" and having moral influence.

Even as Phelps was willing to challenge Howells's definition of realism, she also realized that his comment in *Literary Friends and Acquaintance* was only one of "the latest phrases of the school of art" associated with realism (260). For this reason, it would be misleading to take this comment as the definitive word on Howells's critical stance. What interests me is the fact that Phelps chose to read Howells in this way, setting her own emphasis on writing with an ethical purpose against his criticism of an "intense ethicism." She distinguished herself from Howells not in order to denigrate her own art but rather to make a claim for its importance within theories of realism. In this respect her position complicates Michael Davitt Bell's assumption that women writers at the turn of the century failed as realists because they "were more concerned with achieving distinction as 'serious' artists than with securing wide moral influence."[46] Serious art and moral influence were not antithetical concepts in Phelps's view, and she was willing to take on Howells precisely because he seemed to suggest that they were.

Phelps's disagreements with Howells are also revealed in their correspondence during the ten years that he was editor of the *Atlantic*. In 1874, for example, she sent him some poems that were, as she told him, "in punishment for the bad opinion you expressed of some verses" she had sent earlier. "If you do not like these," she continued, "I shall write you an epic, and so on till you treat me better."[47] She was even more annoyed with him in 1881 when he asked her to cut her serialized novel *Friends: A Duet* in order to make room for a piece by Henry James. "The very fact that there is so much of Mr. James makes it more important to me that my story should have its fair artistic effect. You will know, from your own experience, how vital these matters are to the author."[48] That same year Howells published *Dr. Breen's Practice*, an account of a woman doctor who ends up forgoing her career in order to get married. When this novel appeared, Phelps already had in press *Doctor Zay*, an alternate account of a woman doctor who manages to combine marriage and career. Acknowledging the similarity of the books, Phelps wrote to Howells with her blunt assessment of Dr. Breen. "I don't feel that Dr. Breen is a fair example of professional women," she wrote; "indeed I know she is not for I know the class thoroughly from long personal observation under unusual opportunities." Yet, Phelps felt that this was "all the better for *my* doctor, who will contrast as gloriously in that respect, as Alas! She will suffer in comparison with your work in others."[49] Phelps neither trashes Howells's novel nor assumes a false modesty; she is a peer who, in this case, has a certain narrative authority based on "personal observation." Phelps's complaint with Howells here is not so much about ethics as it is about the powers of observation—precisely the powers that, as we saw in Chapter 1, had led to a critical commonplace equating women with "natural" propensities toward realism. ("Mrs. [Phelps] Ward has always been a keen observer," notes a reviewer of *Chapters from a Life*.[50]) Phelps ends her letter by quoting Herbert Spencer's praise for novels that "diverge from those 'plots' which rarely occur in actual life." In this case Phelps claims to know more about such actuality than Howells does.

Although many of Phelps's disagreements with Howells sprang from substantive differences of opinion about the nature of her art, they were also motivated by her loyalty to other authors whom she saw as writing with an ethical purpose. The list of authors whom Howells identified as marred by "the New England mind" included not only Phelps but also some of her friends, including Harriet Beecher Stowe, Oliver Wendell Holmes, and John Greenleaf Whittier, and Phelps was eager to defend these allies. She was especially adamant in her defense of Stowe, whom she called "the foremost woman of America" (*Chapters from a Life*, 138). Phelps saw herself as continuing Stowe's tradition of social writing, wanting in particular to "do for these poor slaves [to drink] what Harriet Stowe did for the black [slaves]." As one reviewer put it, *A Singular Life* "may be related to the moral welfare of to-day as Uncle Tom's Cabin was to the slave issue."[51]

Rethinking Phelps in relation to authors such as Howells and Stowe leads us to ask fundamental questions about literary history and the classifications that we employ to structure that history. Given that Phelps was one in a circle of authors that included Stowe and Howells, why did she lose the battle for literary recognition? Her decision to retreat to her study, rather than to work as an editor (like Howells) or a lecturer (like Stowe), may have weakened her ability to make her ideas have critical currency. Nineteenth-century critics wished that she had continued to write in the vein of *The Gates Ajar* and complained about her negative depiction of marriage in *The Story of Avis*.[52] Yet, her religious writing then made it difficult to place Phelps in the realist canon as it came to be formed in the early twentieth century. She is neither a "pure" sentimentalist nor a "pure" realist. Even critics and publishers who respected her moral purpose did so on the grounds that it remained understated. In 1905, for instance, the editor of *Harper's* admitted to her that in general he was against "any moral preachment as a main *motif*, in fiction," but that he would continue to accept her work as long as she continued to write "a sympathetic human story of such spiritual value that the reader forgot the moral, it was so beautifully veiled."[53]

After Phelps's death, such moralism—veiled or otherwise—became increasingly distasteful to modernist critics. By 1930 Vernon Parrington could identify her as one of New England's first industrial novelists while also condemning her as "an emotional woman who lived in a world of sentiment rather than reality."[54] By the end of the twentieth century, of course, sentiment had again become a privileged term within gender studies. Ironically, at that point Phelps became too clinically realist; her characters do not have the kind of strong, sympathetic attachments that are central to most sentimental texts, and Phelps herself seems too remote and class-conscious. In the first three conferences of what is now the Society for the Study of American Writers, there was only one panel devoted to Phelps, and it focused on her relation to other women, working to make her authorship less anomalous within literary history by categorizing her with other authors.[55] It is of historic interest to me that *The Story of Avis* was reissued by Rutgers University Press in 1985 but was not included in its American Women Writers Series; although Nina Baym reported in a 1985 *Legacy* article that the work would inaugurate the series, it has a different cover and size than the rest and is not included in lists or advertisements of the series.[56] This graphically illustrates the difficulty of making Phelps fit into the current canon of American women's writing.

Yet, I would suggest that her authorship—complete with its dynamics of rejection, both by herself and others—is crucial in challenging us to expand the usual categories through which we organize postbellum American literature and women's literature in particular, categories that classify authorship, for example, as low or high, popular or elite (and antimarket), sentimental or detachedly realistic. Phelps is difficult to classify within these familiar rubrics. Her work encompasses spiritual novels as well as "problem novels" focused on marriage; she thought of herself as an artist but also courted an audience and was willing to do "hack work"; she wrote best-sellers and experimental works. As one of her colleagues summarized her contradictions, she was "solitary of soul, yet going out to others in fullness of sympathy, profoundly spiritual, yet rebellious toward creeds of man's device, hating wrong and espousing the cause of the weak and oppressed, coloring all things with her own thoughts, and writing pages in her heart's blood."[57] However, she did not have such trouble placing herself, understanding her work of ethical realism as occupying a middle ground or "law of the conditioned" between extremes. These extremes, theorized in the periodical press but also practiced by other authors, put solitary private (and romantic) writing and Calvinist dogma on one side and audience-driven mass production and social reform on the other. By finding a middle ground between these extremes but still always defining herself as an author, Phelps shows the importance of understanding the practice of nineteenth-century female authorship as constantly negotiating and traversing its own organizing paradigms.

Chapter 7
Epilogue
Amateurs and Professionals in Woolson and James

In an 1885 letter to the author and diplomat John Hay, Constance Fenimore Woolson describes "stand[ing] before her . . . a three-divisioned
velvet frame" in which she has placed Hay's photograph beside those of
William Dean Howells and Henry James. "I have tried the three pictures
in every sort of combination. But do what you will, you all stand with your
backs to each other; or at least cold-shoulders," she writes.[1] These men
are not giving Woolson but rather each other the cold shoulder. This
wonderful anecdote goes far in reminding us that Woolson, like Phelps,
saw herself as a peer of Howells and James, one who worried as much
about their relation to each other as she did about their relation to her.
In a letter to Howells, James points to this interconnection when he
claims that Howells and Woolson are the only two novelists in English
that he reads, and that he values in particular her intelligence and her
ability to "understand[] when she is spoken to."[2] Like Phelps, Woolson
sometimes felt envious when such "understanding" meant that these
men's works displaced hers in a given magazine. In 1876, for instance,
she complained to a friend that "Howells has 'favorites' [at the *Atlantic
Monthly*]. Chief among them at present, Henry James, Jr."[3] However, the
fact that she kept their photographs on her writing desk goes far to underscore the importance of understanding the reciprocal relations between
male and female authors.

In the case of Woolson, it is virtually impossible not to study this relation
since much scholarly interest in her has revolved around the question
of her particular friendship with Henry James. The two met in Florence
in 1880 and became close friends who visited Italian landmarks together,
shared a common social circle and an extensive personal correspondence, and for a time rented neighboring apartments in Florence.[4] The
fact that James burned most of his correspondence with Woolson immediately after her death, by suicide, in 1894, led a generation of James
scholars to portray Woolson as James's protégée and unrequited lover
who always wanted more attention than she received. A more recent
generation of feminist critics has shifted the conversation from whether

Woolson and James were romantically attached to how they influenced each other's work. Cheryl Torsney and Anne Boyd, in particular, have gone far to challenge what Torsney calls "the legend of the lonely spinster who carries a torch for the icy James all over Europe," focusing instead on their literary companionship. In the process of doing so, this group of critics has tended to portray this literary companionship in oppositional terms, with Woolson attempting to subvert James's "bias toward 'authoresses,'" as Boyd puts it.[5]

One of the primary sites for locating Woolson's critique has been her story "Miss Grief." First published in *Lippincott's* in 1880, this story has been frequently anthologized in recent years.[6] In the story Woolson, a grand-niece of James Fenimore Cooper, depicts a woman, Aaronna Moncrief, who tries to find an audience for her literary manuscripts by appealing to a successful male writer. The story's conclusion, in which the woman dies with her work unpublished and the writer lives to tell (and publish) her tale, seems to support reading the story as a meditation on the inequities of a gendered construction of authorship in the final decades of the nineteenth century. In the past fifteen years, such readings have tended to locate their critique of this gendered construction in a hostile, patriarchal marketplace. Cheryl Torsney, for example, has argued that Woolson's disagreements with two of her publishers, the Osgoods and D. Appleton, provide a context for seeing "Miss Grief" as a story implying that "many powerful works by women were, in effect, suppressed by those male readers, editors, and publishers in positions of power."[7] Joan Myers Weimer makes a similar statement when she concludes that "Woolson believed in women's genius, but saw it as so compromised by the patriarchy of her time that it could appear only in distorted forms, and could bring only grief to its possessors."[8]

If "Miss Grief" articulates a gendered construction of authorship, however, it does so in a way that complicates an easy analogy between female constraint or oppression and male power and success. For one thing, as I will show, the story portrays the male author-narrator primarily in feminine terms, as a kind of woman writer: a latter-day example of the *cacoëthes scribendi* examined in the first chapter. At the same time, Moncrief shares many qualities that had come to be associated with authors, as opposed to writers; she also is repeatedly described in masculine terms. Such gender crossing does not, of course, necessarily militate against an antipatriarchal reading of the story; the fact that Moncrief has to assume certain masculine traits in order to attain high literary seriousness is a sign of the increasingly clear alliance in the late nineteenth century between male privilege and structures of literary taste and production.

For my purposes, however, I am most interested in what this gender inversion signifies for the history of authorship that I have been tracing.

This significance becomes particularly clear when we read "Miss Grief" alongside James's "The Real Thing" (1892). As I have already indicated, it is a familiar move to place Woolson and James together. Critics have read Woolson's story "Rodman the Keeper" (1880) as an inspiration for James's "The Altar of the Dead" (1895), for example; Woolson is also commonly cited as a source for the character May Bartram in "The Beast in the Jungle" (1903). James's influence on Woolson too has been well documented, particularly in "A Florentine Experiment" (1880), which fictionalizes many of Woolson's experiences with James as she recorded them in her notebooks.[9] "Miss Grief" was written before Woolson had met James, but she may have had his work on her mind since she had recently reviewed *The Europeans* for the *Atlantic Monthly*. The fact that "Miss Grief" first appeared in the May 1880 issue of *Lippincott's Magazine*, a few weeks after James and Woolson had met in Florence, also links it with James, although it is clear that she had finished the story before their actual meeting.[10] "The Real Thing," written twelve years later, is not commonly associated with Woolson, although its subject—a painter struggling to tell the story of some visitors to his studio—has clear analogies to "Miss Grief." By bringing the stories together in this final chapter, my purpose is less to revisit the relation between Woolson and James than to think about what these stories suggest about the history of authorship in the nineteenth century.

The most striking aspect of the James-Woolson relation, in my view, is the similarity with which they described each other's work, a similarity that ascribes to each of them a keen eye for detail. In a review of his works in the *Atlantic Monthly*, for example, Woolson identified James's "talent" as being "that of keen observation and fine discrimination of character, which he portrays with a subtle and delicate touch." He is not a great storyteller; indeed, Woolson finds (as have many subsequent generations of James's readers) that "Mr. James, as far as possible, has *his* people do nothing at all." Instead, the interest of his stories lies in the "minute details" he gives about his characters.[11] A decade later, when James published an essay on Woolson in *Harper's Weekly*, he praised her in almost identical terms. In particular, he commented on the "minuteness of observation and tenderness of feeling" that characterize her regionalist fiction about the American South. Although her "delicate manipulation of the real is mingled with an occasionally frank appeal to the romantic muse," James admires Woolson for giving sympathetic expression to a region that has remained largely "voiceless" during Reconstruction.[12]

James was not alone in praising Woolson's powers of observation; indeed, this was a nineteenth-century tag line for her work. An 1886 advertisement for her work in *Harper's*, for instance, featured extracts from reviews praising the "author's acuteness of perception" and the way in which she "adds to her observation of scenes and localities an unusual insight into the human heart," an insight that the reviewer compares to that of George Eliot.[13] Nor are these terms unique to Woolson; as we have seen, such terms were routinely employed to justify and define female authorship. James had provided such a justification in the 1860s when he predicted in the *Nation* that women's ability to draw would make them prominent practitioners of realism.[14]

The fact that Woolson endorses James in nearly identical terms could be read as a sign that components of women's fiction had been naturalized into theories of realism by the 1880s. This naturalization led to ever-finer discriminations of exactly what constituted "the real" and a resulting division between high realism—meant to inoculate the masses against the sentimentalism that James notes in Woolson—and a domestic realism that privileged observation over inner character.[15] This distinction, in turn, complicated theories of female authorship that gave women a privileged role as observers and producers of detail. The last two decades of the nineteenth century, as we have seen, saw the consolidation of female authorship as a critical category. Such consolidation, however, increasingly blurred gender distinctions: recall Annie Nathan Meyer's assertion that "the very subjects upon which one would naturally expect women to throw a new light have really inspired the masterpieces of men."[16] Such gender crossings are also evident in Elizabeth Stuart Phelps's contextualization of her vision of realism with that of Howells, and in Woolson's photographs of Howells and James on her desk.

As we saw in the first chapter, this blurring was greeted by some women as a positive development, with Rebecca Harding Davis in particular being quite optimistic about the "quickening movement" that was opening writing up to an increasingly diverse group. However, for Woolson, as for Phelps, the erosion of the idea of women's authorship as exceptional was experienced as a loss. One manifestation of this loss, for Woolson, was the fact that her portrait image was widely circulated as part of what she termed, in a letter to John Hay, "a fancy at present for bringing out 'series' of 'authors' likenesses.'" As we saw in Chapter 2, for much of the nineteenth century, portraits of women authors—if circulated at all—presented women as models of sincerity and domesticity rather than as distinct personalities. For Woolson, though, the "fancy" for portraits now means that "a photograph of some sort is sure to be obtained of everybody, somewhere; & the thing done whether the victim likes it or not." For her, "it is a pang to every nerve in my body, to be produced in public in that way"; or, as she wrote to James, just "because a woman happens to write a little" should not mean that she necessarily "becomes the property of the public." If she was to be photographed, she preferred a profile shot that would hide some of her facial features.[17] This preference suggests that she has some nostalgia for an earlier form of authorship that maintained the privacy of the author, the form that allowed Maria Cummins, for example, to become a best-selling author while still publishing anonymously. At the same time, her insistence on the "property" of the writer—and what can justifiably be claimed by the public—shows that Woolson has benefited from the increasing concern with authorial rights in the postbellum years, a concern that we see manifested, for example, in the careers of Dodge, Sophia Hawthorne, and Phelps.

Woolson's response to authorial publicity, then, registers the success of female authorship over the course of the nineteenth century, on the one hand, and nostalgia for an earlier model of female production, on the other. This nostalgia was also apparent in Woolson's fantasies about returning to an amateur status. Writing to Hay in 1890 (two years before her death), she responds to his comment that "it is amateurish to have one's books printed according to one's own taste, and for one's family and friends" by praising such amateurism: "If Fate would only turn *me* into an Amateur! I am afraid I shall be dead before, in the natural course of trade, I can get poor Rodman the Keeper revised. By misunderstanding, the new edition (Harper's) was brought out just as it stood when recovered finally from the piratical Appletons. No one minds it but the author. But oh! how she squirms!"[18] Woolson, as "the author," has nostalgia for amateurism because she is frustrated with her publishers: Harper's has reissued a book, *Rodman the Keeper*, without letting her make any changes to it. Even worse, the previous publisher, D. Appleton and Company, has not paid her for its two editions of *Rodman*; in an earlier letter to Hay, she notes that Appleton has not provided her with "the usual ten per cent" because they have not yet recovered their own expenses.[19] Dodge had to submit Ticknor and Fields to arbitration in order to get this "usual" 10 percent, and the fact that Woolson recognizes it as "usual" testifies to the importance and success of such struggles. Woolson's experience, however, also shows that a contractual promise of 10 percent is useless if it is given only out of publishers' profits, particularly when those publishers are not required to document those profits.

Woolson's frustration, then, is one of an "author" who has signed contractual agreements with publishers and wishes to maintain some editorial control even within "the natural course of trade." Her acknowledgment that it does not ultimately make much difference to anyone else, however, suggests that she knows the limits of her authorial powers: few readers would notice or care about any changes. This is not a complaint about readers as much as an acknowledgment of the realities of actual reading practices, but Woolson's solution—to become an "Amateur"—points to her nostalgia for the kind of parlor literature that had originally enabled much of nineteenth-century women's authorship. When she imagines printing a book "for one's family and friends," she recalls the rhetorical occasion that was said to have inspired *The Lamplighter*, or that gave Sophia Hawthorne early experience with writing (as her Cuban journals were privately bound and circulated in Boston), or that occasioned Alcott's first published book (culled from letters written home from a Civil War hospital). As a solution to a dispute with a publisher, the idea of "going amateur" is impractical. However, as a solution to the problem of maintaining authorial control, it provides an enabling fantasy.

As I will argue in the next section, "Miss Grief" represents both the allure and the dangers of this fantasy, as it traces the "fate" of an "amateur" who goes to a published writer in order to try to get her work into print. If this story is an exploration of male (and specifically Jamesean) bias toward "authoresses," as Boyd puts it, it is also a nuanced exploration by one such "authoress" of what that category entails. Seen this way, the story is not so much about an opposition between masculine and feminine modes of production as it is about the perceived opposition between amateur and professional writing, an opposition that the story ultimately works to destabilize.

Woolson's key means of achieving this destabilization is through her questioning of the limits of print. The story concludes that there is a certain reality beyond print that can never be fully represented in it. In this way, the story also articulates—and perhaps grieves—the loss of a "finely perceived" observation and detail that can be represented in print. It is in this respect that I think it most clearly anticipates the concerns of "The Real Thing." James too focuses on amateurs' attempts to represent "the real thing," although in this case the amateurs—Major and Mrs. Churm—desire to pose as models for a successful male artist. While Woolson focuses on the production of art, that is to say, James focuses on its appropriate subjects and the extent to which it must have a direct relation to the "real thing." Both stories, however, serve as meditations on the successes of female authorship, meditations that also serve as an elegy for a domestic amateur production now thoroughly mediated by the world of print.

Reading "Miss Grief"

One of the most striking aspects about "Miss Grief" is how little we know about its title character. She appears unbidden to Woolson's unnamed male narrator, a Jamesean figure living in Rome who is happy to live up to his reputation as a reader of Balzac and "that quiet young fellow who writes those delightful little studies of society."[20] Like many female novelists, this "young fellow" specializes in sketches of "real life," but he does so without much real passion. He writes his sketches with a professional detachment, looking for personal stimulation instead in the company he keeps and the women he hopes to court. Eventually he becomes interested in the tragic figure of "Miss Grief," but only after first turning her away from his house seven times.

When the narrator finally meets this woman, he constantly misreads her and her situation. This misreading is most obvious in his insistence on allegorizing her as "Miss Grief," even after she tells him that her surname is "Crief." (Only later, after she has died, does he realize that neither name is correct: it is actually Moncrief.) For him, she is a type more than she is a person, a walking embodiment of a certain kind of sorrow. He also misreads her social situation, imagining that the woman who accompanies her to his home is her maid, named "Serena," when in fact she is later revealed to be her Aunt Martha.

Kristin Comment has suggested that the narrator's confusion about the identity of this companion stems from the fact that Moncrief may have ended a lesbian relationship with "Serena" a few weeks before the story opens.[21] This reading suggests a plausible motivation for the narrator's confusion; Comment argues that he may have been particularly threatened by Moncrief's allusion to "smoking" with Serena since this could be a code for sexual activity. Comment also sees Moncrief's masculine character traits as part of this lesbian subtheme, noting that the narrator's beloved—Ethelind Abercrombie—presents a strong contrasting femininity and that Moncrief's first name, Aaronna, results from the fact, as she reports, that her father "was much disappointed that [she] was not a boy, and gave [her] as nearly as possible the name he had prepared—Aaron" (310).

If Moncrief crosses lines of gender and sexuality, it is important to ask what this crossing signals in terms of the story's representation of authorship. An initial answer to this question lies in the relation of these terms to representations of amateurism and professionalism in the story. In many ways Moncrief is the masculine professional and the narrator is the feminine amateur—though these terms, in this case, are related to a prophetical model of authorship rather than a market-driven one. Aaron, Moncrief's namesake, is identified in the Old Testament as the first high priest and brother and spokesman of Moses. In this sense, Moncrief is allied not only with masculinity but also specifically with biblical prophecy.[22] In the nineteenth century a freshly articulated sense of what Richard Brodhead terms "prophetical authorship" had led Melville, Hawthorne, and Thoreau, among others, to create a "prophetic self" in which a "driven or compelled speaker, wildly unpopular in his conceptions," writes in order to "deliver knowledge of [an] alienated reality back to the world that would forget it."[23] Moncrief, through her name and her actions, seems to embody this ideal of prophetic authorship. Her

artistic power lies in her originality and her willingness to create an "alienated reality." The narrator compares her creations to jewels that are not
quite wearable: "each ring unfinished, each bracelet too large or too
small for its purpose, each breast-pin without its fastening, each neck-
lace purposely broken" (311). She takes objects known in the real world
and uses them to a less practical, more prophetic end. Rather than spe-
cializing in "delightful little studies of society," as the narrator does, and
using the keen powers of observation frequently ascribed to female
authors, Moncrief explores the limits of realism by making jewelry that
is "purposely broken."

As this image suggests, such art does not court readers who are used to
wearing ready-made jewels. Yet, Moncrief, the prophetic author, initially
attracts the narrator's attention by modeling for him an ideal audience,
positioning herself as the narrator's spokeswoman. She recites all of his
works by memory, improving on his words by virtue of her reading. (In
this respect, Moncrief echoes Woolson, who describes in a letter to James
her admiration for his essay on Venice, "whose every word I know, almost
by heart."[24]) As the narrator listens to these words, his vanity leads him to
believe that Moncrief "understood me almost better than I had understood myself" (305). Like Hilda in Hawthorne's *The Marble Faun*, who
improves on artworks as she copies them, Moncrief improves on her reading as she recites it.[25] Yet, her skills go beyond merely reading his works
better than he could himself. Moncrief also intuitively identifies or proph-
esies what the narrator secretly thinks is his best work. Most of his writings are, as she points out, "interiors—exquisitely painted and delicately
finished, but of small scope." They are, in other words, "feminized" pieces.
Rather than admiring these qualities, however, as a good woman reader
and writer might, Moncrief seizes on a bit of the narrator's writing that is
more "masculine," work that she identifies as "a sketch in a few bold, masterly lines" and that he considers a "little shaft" with a "higher purpose"
aimed "toward the distant stars" (305). As his interpreter, she constructs
aesthetic criteria that celebrate masculine purpose and height rather than
mere observation. The feminine reader here works to heighten the "masterly" accomplishments of the feminized male narrator.

Moncrief's reading, then, enacts a strategic gender inversion in which
she uses her masculine powers (and name) to support "bold, masterly
lines" that "reach to the stars." She offers this support, moreover, when
she appears unbidden from the streets of Rome to the narrator's "bachelor's parlor" (307). The parlor is again presented as an originary site of
literary production, but here it is associated with masculine rather than
feminine literary production. Moncrief's performative reading puts her
in the position of a professional expert mentoring the narrator. He eventually comes to admire her so much, and to defer to her age (she is

forty-three, while he is just over thirty, although he thinks of her as much older [310]), that he feels "as if [he] ought to go down on [his] knees before her and entreat her to take her proper place of supremacy at once" (308). This does not entirely balance the power relations between them—in fact the narrator never does kneel before her—but it does strengthen the gender inversions occurring between them.

These inversions continue even after Moncrief has finally convinced the narrator to read her literary manuscripts. She brings them to him protected in a box, and the narrator first imagines that this box will contain a collectible antique, such as old lace. Again the narrator is making Moncrief into a type rather than an individual; it does not occur to him that she would be a writer. Even more significant, however, is the fact that his misreading allies him with an old-fashioned domestic sphere; he is hoping for antique lace. When the narrator actually reads Moncrief's manuscript, a dramatic tragedy entitled "Armor," he reads it because he "could not be in a worse mood" (307). This "moodiness" also emphasizes his feminine qualities, as he uses reading in a stereotypically feminine fashion to compensate for emotional instability and emptiness.[26] In this capacity the tragedy succeeds brilliantly; the narrator is so impressed by its "earnestness, passion and power" that he sits up half the night reading it (307). He then communicates his approval by writing a letter, participating in the tradition of fan mail to authors discussed in Chapter 2. His letter proposes that he come visit her, but she replies that she would "prefer to come to [him]" in his parlor (310). This insistence again emphasizes his domesticity; she is mobile while he is not.

The narrator's domesticity is also nurturing; at his home Moncrief begins to eat after a long period of fasting. "It was good and rich food. It was so long since I had had food like that!" she later remembers (315). Although Moncrief enters wearing "an old-fashioned lace veil with a heavy border shad[ing] her face" (304), she is not a dematerialized, veiled female body but rather someone whose physical presence is increased through the aid of a domesticated man. Even when she is dying—now in her "bare chamber"—she undergoes a "sudden animation" (had Woolson been reading Poe?) in which the soul returns to the body, and she asks for food for the first time "in weeks." The narrator terms this "animation" "the most wonderful thing I ever saw" (314).

The narrator's domestic nurture is ultimately insufficient, however, and Moncrief dies in spite of her efforts to gain physical strength. When she dies, she asks that her manuscripts be buried with her. Ultimately the narrator finds an audience for her through his own story, but he does not attempt to publish her works after her death. Instead, he keeps the manuscript of "Armor" in a "locked case," deciding not to publish it because of its slight faults (315). Not surprisingly, given the gender inversion I

have been tracing, the narrator's representation of these faults marks
Moncrief as contributing to a masculine aesthetic of originality and mastery rather than a feminine one of quotidian observation. The narrator
comments on the tragedy's "originality" and "force," and he privately
admits to himself that in her case he thinks less about formal execution
than overall force (308–9). Even as he appreciates these qualities, however, he supposes that the reading public will not. He can "forget the
dark spots," the "glaring impossibilities of plot," but he knows that the
public will not. Moncrief has lived up to her association with Aaron: she
is telling a truth that the public does not want to hear.

Yet, just as she has been an ideal reader for the narrator, so too he
provides a model of ideal reception for her art. As he reads her collected
works, including poetry and a prose sketch, he thinks of her repeatedly
as a genius, and he is aware of the irony that "she, with the greater
power, failed" whereas he, "with the less, succeeded" (315). Her poetry
is "like the work of dreams; they were *Kubla Khan*, only more so" (311).[27]
The narrator finds Moncrief's prose sketch powerful but more flawed
than her poetry, with an implausible character in a doctor who "practised
murder as a fine art, and was regarded (by the author) as a second Mes-
siah" (311). Yet, when the narrator tries to rework this sketch to omit
the doctor, he realizes that he cannot. Her works form a coherent, brilliant whole. Even unrealistic characters such as the murderous doctor are
"so clearly interwoven with every part of the tale that to take [them] out
was like taking out one especial figure in the carpet" (313). The narrator's phrase here anticipates, of course, James's short story "The Figure
in the Carpet" (1896). This "fable for the critics," as F. O. Matthiessen and
Kenneth Murdock have described it, was written in part to critique the
growing popularity of mass-produced fiction and to close "the widening
gap between the slick popular magazine and the serious reader."[28] This
gap also characterizes the disjunction between Moncrief's prophecy and
the narrator's "delightful little studies of society." In Woolson's story, the
author with the "secret" to the figure in the carpet is a woman.

On her deathbed Moncrief listens to the narrator tell her a "romance
invented for the occasion." Ironically, this oral romance is much better
than his actual published work. "None of [his] published sketches could
compare with it" (314). Just as Moncrief has earlier encouraged him
to "reach for the stars" rather than settle for publishing second-rate
work, so too she now inspires him to do that best work through his oral
"romance." As Paul Crumbley points out, this moment of inspiration
gratifies Moncrief because it signals the narrator's participation in a "gift-
based distribution" of stories that is "an alternative to consumer-based
print publication."[29] This passing of inspiration, however, also marks the
end of the gender inversion in the story as Moncrief is redomesticated

as a woman writer. As the narrator pleases her with his oral romance, he also falsely tells her that he has found a publisher for her work. This lie underscores not only his power over her but also the fact that she will never move into print publication. Instead, she insists that her manuscripts not be removed from her and beseeches the narrator not to "look at them—my poor dead children!" (314). In a familiar trope of female artistic production, she has dedicated her maternal instincts to her art, but her children have been stillborn.[30]

Her solicitousness for her children marks her as a domestic woman, as does her final wish that the narrator help her aunt return to America. The aunt, aptly named Martha (one thinks not only of the Martha who tended Jesus at the cross but also of Martha Washington), has been outspoken in expressing contempt for the "literary men" who have "racked and stabbed" her niece (313). However, Moncrief feels guilty for ever having asked her to leave the United States; it is important that she return to her homeland. Moncrief is buried abroad, but her actions on behalf of her "children"—her manuscripts—and her aunt identify her as a good domestic woman, in terms of both home and nation. In this sense, the ending anticipates the homesickness that Woolson expressed in a letter to Henry James two years later. Having been in bed feeling ill, she had almost decided "that I must go home; go home, get my precious books, and little household gods together, a dog or two, and never stir again."[31]

In the last lines of the story, the narrator reveals that he has abandoned his bachelor ways and married Ethelind. He refuses to show Moncrief's manuscript to his wife, but his whole experience has helped him to reestablish his expected role as husband. Formerly a bachelor who dreams of old lace and writes social sketches, he is now a doting husband who is charged not only with doing his own writing but also with keeping Moncrief's legacy alive, ensuring that no one "should cast so much as a thought of scorn upon the memory of the writer, upon [his] poor dead, 'unavailable,' unaccepted 'Miss Grief'" (315). As the narrator specifically categorizes her as a writer, he emphasizes his own position as a published author. He polices her one remaining manuscript, "Armor," by keeping it in a locked box, signaling the ways in which the male literary establishment controls female production.

How do we balance this ending against the beginning image in which Woolson "encases" Howells, James, and Hay in a frame in her own writing desk? Is it merely an inversion of authorial control? Is it the dark underside of the professional camaraderie that she imagines with her male colleagues? How does Moncrief's status as a writer at the end of the story play into Woolson's fantasies—however fleeting—of returning to amateur status? One approach to answering these questions is to read "Miss Grief" as working to destabilize the categorical distinctions between male and female, professional and amateur, and author and writer that were become increasingly rigid by the end of the nineteenth century. Just as Woolson could simultaneously complain about her royalties and wish to be an amateur, so too "Miss Grief" shows how an author can simultaneously lament her lack of audience through print and define a prophetic model of authorship that values a more informal gift exchange between author and reader. It is for this reason that the story asks us to grieve Moncrief's lack of access to a network of publishers and also to respect her declaration, in her final meeting with the narrator, that she now knows what it is "to be fully happy" (314).

James's posthumous essay on Woolson begins by proposing that "the work of Miss Constance Fenimore Woolson is an excellent example of the way the door stands open between the personal life of American women and the immeasurable world of print."[32] She is an excellent example, in other words, of the trajectory from the private world of parlor literature to print that was so often ascribed to nineteenth-century female authors. Yet, like Phelps, Woolson ultimately debunks this trajectory, using "Miss Grief" to close the door between the personal and the world of print. Moncrief remains throughout an enigmatic figure about whom we know certain details (that she was forty-three years, two months, and eight days old when she died) but not others (for example, her entire history before meeting the narrator and her rationale for coming to the narrator). In this sense she resists circulating her private life in print. She writes, but she does not have the *cacoëthes scribendi* that imagines her experiences, and her words, as being immediately worthy of print. Instead, her acts of oral memorization and recitation move her reading away from the disembodied world of print into her own body and voice.

It is not surprising, given this transition, that the narrator eventually becomes more impressed with "the woman . . . than the writer—the fragile, nerve-less body more than the inspired mind" (307). Far from entering the anonymous world of print, Moncrief stands as a kind of prophetic singer, one whose bodily presence, marked by her fragility and even her small hands, demands as much attention as does her work. She does not alienate her body from her labors but incorporates it into them. Even her manuscripts, although "written in pencil upon a piece of coarse printing-paper," have the appearance of something finer: "the handwriting was as clear and delicate as that of the manuscript in ink" (307). The physical labor of her *hand*writing transforms cheap printing paper—the stuff through which mass-produced writing is disseminated—into a more valuable manuscript. Not only does Moncrief, like Melville's Bartleby, "prefer not to" enter the immeasurable world of print, then, but she also transforms that world into something more contained and measurable, into "children" that she can bury or lock in a box.

The logic of such a move—that the most "original" writing is that which is not mediated by the world of print—is part of the grief that is expressed in Woolson's story since it means that the best writing is also necessarily the most unread, the least available to an audience. At the same time, however, the story testifies to the importance of the "immeasurable world of print." If the narrator had not been willing to enter that world, Moncrief's entire production as an author would remain unknown. If Woolson asks us to be aware of the limitations of print—and of the publishing companies that support it—she also warns against a too-easy valorization of the pleasures of amateur writing. If her own publishing struggles occasionally make her wish to be an amateur, she also realizes that she can make such a wish only within the context of her own position as a published author. In "Miss Grief" she offers one way of contextualizing this position even further as the narrator's "memory of a writer" presents a model of prophetic authorship that is codified neither by gender nor by particular professional affiliation.

Exploring "The Real Thing"

The artist narrator of "The Real Thing," like that of "Miss Grief," focuses on memory: in the last sentence of the story he admits that he is "content to have paid the price [of his experience]—for the memory."[33] In addition, the story, according to James's notebooks, was based on his memory of an anecdote that George du Maurier had told him about a well-born but "ruined" English couple who came to him for a modeling job.[34] Within the context of James's career, the story is typically read as a parable about psychological realism. My interest, however, lies less in James's overall aesthetic theories than with the ways in which this story revises some of Woolson's claims about authorship and the mediation of print.

The two stories share some obvious similarities. Both feature unnamed first-person narrators who are artists (literary and visual, respectively), bachelors, Europeans (living in Rome and in London), and successes in the marketplace. Both are also ambivalent about that success. Woolson's narrator recognizes that his best work—the passage that Moncrief first recites and the romance that he invents and recites to her—is either unrecognized by his reading public or unpublished. James's artist, similarly, makes a living providing black-and-white illustrations for magazines, storybooks, and "sketches of contemporary life" but admits that he considers these his "potboilers," in the meantime dreaming of being known by connoisseurs as a "great painter of portraits" (a questionable goal, given that portraiture was often regarded as a lesser art) (235). In addition, both narrators are highly affected by their encounters with protégés who arrive uninvited at their homes and then continue to appear for an extended period of time. In "The Real Thing" these supplicants are Major and Mrs. Monarch, who come hoping to make money by working as models for the artist's illustrations. Eventually the artist dismisses them because they prove to be singularly bad models.

In a notebook entry about the story, James insisted that "The Real Thing" is a "picture" that "must illustrate something" rather than a "story" in the vulgar sense of the word; he wants to ensure that the tale is in the service of a higher point.[35] The Monarchs' problem is their inflexibility as models; they are always the same, no matter how the artist clothes them or poses them. Yet, their effect is to create images that are patently unrealistic and inappropriate for the "edition de luxe" of "the rarest of the novelists" that the narrator has been employed to illustrate (239). In the illustrations Mrs. Monarch always appears to be "too tall," putting the artist in the dilemma of "having represented a fascinating woman as seven feet high" (244). Similarly, the Major's trousers and fingers turn out to look "colossal" (245, 249). The disproportionate excess of these figures anticipates the emphasis on the grotesque that would become a feature of modernism, and they stand in stark opposition to the "small scope" of the "little studies" that Woolson's narrator publishes.[36] They are more like the "jewelry" that Moncrief creates, which looks beautiful but is entirely nonfunctional. Just as Moncrief's handwritten manuscripts and oral performances are not easily assimilated into the "immeasurable world of print," so too the Monarchs' monstrous bodies are not easily assimilated into black-and-white drawings.

If the Monarchs' physical monstrosity renders them unfit for that world, so too do their reading habits. They dutifully pick up *Rutland Ramsay*, but to no avail; "they had dipped into the most brilliant of our novelists without deciphering many passages" (251). Their resistance to the world of print is also reflected in their previous experience in the world of photography. "We've been photographed, *immensely*," Mrs. Monarch reports (237). Presumably the very qualities that make the Monarchs poor subjects for black-and-white illustration also make them good subjects for photography, which tends to want "the real thing" rather than an idealized type. Yet, in the same conversation in which Mrs. Monarch makes this admission, we also learn that at the time of her marriage she was known as "the Beautiful Statue" (237). Statues, as three-dimensional, and often colossal, works of art, are not easily captured by the flattened photographic image. The experiences of seeing a photograph of a statue and of walking around the statue in person are very different.

We learn from the Monarchs that although they have been photographed innumerable times, they have few photographs of themselves left because they have "given quantities away" with their "autographs and that sort of thing" (238). At one time these photographs, at least of Mrs. Monarch, were available in shops, but "not now," as Mrs. Monarch reports "with her eyes on the floor" (238). To the extent that one is known through one's "real" body, age becomes a liability, and Mrs. Monarch's shame seems to stem from the fact that she has deteriorated physically and the fact that she and her husband have fallen on difficult economic times. Although the Monarchs are clearly not royalty, despite their name, they do appear to have been social butterflies (a different kind of "monarch") at one time. Their current economic status, however, means that they are no longer celebrities sold in a shop; they can only give their pictures away. Unlike Woolson, who disliked having her likeness circulated as part of a series of authors' likenesses, Mrs. Monarch mourns the fact that no one now wants to purchase her image.

Within the history of authorship that I have been tracing, what is most striking about the Monarchs' "fall" is that it signals a move from a consumer-driven print publication to the exchange gift economy that was shared by Moncrief and her mentor and by Woolson in her fantasy about retreating to amateur status. Not only do they give their pictures away, but they also autograph them. These autographs personalize the images and give them status as manuscripts as well as mass-produced photographs. Antebellum female authors often complained about what Lydia Sigourney described as "album persecution"; the incessant requests for autographs were part of a nascent celebrity culture that these women often viewed as compromising feminine propriety. As Caroline Kirkland put it, the mania for autographs was proof "that our instinctive modesty has suffered some abrasion from contact with the public."[37] By the 1890s, however, the Monarchs' autographs are less about publicity than a return to an earlier form of parlor culture.

Indeed, by the end of "The Real Thing," the Monarchs, having given up on being models, literally produce that culture: they serve tea to the narrator and his new models, the Cockney maid Miss Churm and the Italian peasant Oronte. The narrator's friend Jack Hawley compares the Monarchs to a "pair of feather beds" (251). This metaphor, with its association of softness and old-fashioned values, intensifies their domesticity even further: their impulse, in any space in which they find themselves, is to cover and comfort others with a misplaced nurturing spirit.

Katherine Grier has argued that the parlor died out as a central space in Victorian culture because of the advent of the automobile. The middle- and upper-class consumers who had previously made their parlors into social theaters now turned their attention (and their money) to buying the nicest automobiles they could afford—automobiles that carried them away from the home, and the parlor, and that changed the nature of social interaction.[38] Miss Churm and Oronte prefigure this shift. They are always moving—on an omnibus, with an ice cart—and are marked more by their itinerant habits than by a sense of place. They can pose as domestic figures but do not live as ones. Oronte, indeed, barely knows how to serve tea, thinking it a "queer process" (247).

The Monarchs, then, baffle the narrator in several ways. First, they challenge his expectations about social class. When they first arrive, he expects that they are coming to commission a portrait and is disappointed to learn that they want to be hired as models. As sitters, they appeal to the artist's higher image of himself as a portraitist, but as models, they remind him that he is only a "mere" illustrator. Second, even as models, they embody a monstrous physicality that makes it impossible for them to "disappear" into a black-and-white illustration. Third, they conserve an ideal of domesticity that is about to be as anachronistic as featherbeds: a middle-class view of domesticity that by the 1890s was being superseded by the ideals of cosmopolitanism and mobility.

The intractability of these features is signaled in the last paragraphs of the story, when the Monarchs make one final appearance at the artist's studio. Rather than disappearing into the streets of London, they reassert their presence by coming in and quietly taking charge. Mrs. Monarch rearranges Miss Churm's curls in order to make her "twice as charming" (253). Rather than doing her "harm," as the narrator has feared, Mrs. Monarch has doubled her charm. She does so by "quieting" the narrator with a "glance [he] shall never forget" and that he confesses he "should like to have been able to paint" (253).[39]

In characteristic fashion, James here points to the limits of representation, offering us a moment of catachresis in which he suggests what cannot be painted, which is the reality that lingers just beyond the page. In doing so, he recalls Woolson's narrator: just as the artist can remember but not paint the "glance" that Mrs. Monarch gives him, so too Woolson's narrator can remember but not fully describe the "memory" of "Miss Grief."[40] In this sense, both of these stories dwell on the limits of representation, on the physicality and memories of women that are not easily assimilated into the world of black-and-white print. In doing so, they also both suggest a nostalgia for modes of artistic production that are not directly tied to print production. In a culture where sketches of everyday life vie with "de-luxe editions" of acclaimed novelists for the attention of the book-buying public, Woolson and James understand the attractions of alternate models of authorship: the prophetic mode of Moncrief; the oral romance mode of Woolson's narrator; the antiquarian mode of gift exchange endorsed by the Monarchs; the high aesthetic mode aspired to by James's narrator. At the same time, they understand that all of these various modes are, as with their own authorship, supported by the culture of print—the same culture that had, over the course of the second half of the nineteenth century, naturalized female author-ship as a category of literary production.

Conclusion: Beyond Grief

In 1882, two years after publishing "Miss Grief," Woolson wrote to James about her experience reading his recently published novel, *The Portrait of a Lady*. The letter is very much one of solidarity and sympathy, not only about his specific achievement in *Portrait* but also about the difficulties of being appreciated by a "careless public" and by "jealous" critics.[41] The problems of authorship here begin to be less about gender than about the increasing divide between a "careless" popular public and a more "caring" or elite one. The implications of such a shift—that male and female "high-art" authors increasingly shared common concerns by the end of the century—are twofold: first, that women had succeeded so well in becoming "authors" that it was no longer as necessary to talk about "female authors" specifically; and second, that gender had been replaced as a key term in discussing authorship by hierarchies of taste and artis-tic production. These hierarchies of taste, in turn, came from continu-ing efforts to define the proper subject of art, including its complex relation to the category of "the real."

In "Miss Grief" and "The Real Thing," as we have seen, Woolson and James make such definitions in part by imagining a gift economy in which manuscripts and autographs circulate apart from commodity print cul-ture. With the origins of—and justification for—female authorship fully decoupled from amateur writing, such a gift economy becomes a newly attractive—if necessarily limited—alternative. At the same time, these stories take pains not to glorify this alternative. The narrators of these two stories, who have been fully successful in a commodity print culture, are more conventional than Moncrief or the Monarchs, and yet it is be-cause of this convention that they are able to tell their stories at all, to be the conservers of a particular memory even as they go about making their "slight" sketches. Indeed, it is the writing of the story for print that unleashes their memories. As such, they support Lawrence Buell's call to question "the usual assumption that [commodification] must entail some sort of aesthetic debasement" by looking at the way that writing for a particular niche audience can "unleash creative energies."[42] This idea is supported, in turn, by other authors whom we have seen: *Little Women,* for example, represented just such an "unleashing" for Alcott.

Yet, "Miss Grief" and "The Real Thing" also exemplify the complica-tions of viewing market status as the key component of authorship since both stories ultimately imagine amateurs to be the "real thing" that in turn cannot be fully represented by professionally successful artists. Moncrief, who finds happiness in her writing, has more talent than the narrator whom she looks to for publishing advice, and in turn he is able to tell her story only obliquely. The Monarchs, who are amateur sitters, are more interesting (and colossal) than the professional models (Oronte and Churm) whom James's artist hires, and that artist too is only able to capture that interest indirectly, focusing primarily on their effect on his "memory." The fact that Oronte, Churm, and Woolson's narrator can all "succeed" is a sign of increasing access to literary culture: Oronte and Churm, although not of a high social class, can nonetheless "pass" in deluxe editions; and Woolson's narrator, although not of the highest talent, has a satisfying and profitable career.

Throughout this book I have similarly tried to separate authorship from the literary market, while also recognizing it as a material component. As we have seen, female authorship in the second half of the nineteenth century was about self-naming and identification; about social structures that facilitate authorship and writing more generally; about specific political events—in this instance most significantly the Civil War—that help shape professional careers and opportunities; about legal and civil rights; and about the ethics of writing and of realism in particular. This is only a partial list, and yet it shows how authorship as a professional category assumed a wide variety of meanings for the women who aimed to fall within it.

In examining these various meanings, I have tried to highlight the success of individual women in fulfilling their own authorial practices. The reception of Maria Cummins's work was shaped by the publicity practices of Jewett and other publishers, but *The Lamplighter* was also in many ways successful on its own textual terms, as a book that moved beyond parlor literature to invite multiple levels of engagement. Similarly, Louisa May Alcott's experiences with Redpath, Niles, and other publishers shaped her career and encouraged her to write to a wide spectrum of literary niches. This spectrum does not have to be a sign only of conflict or internal division; it can also be a sign of an opportunity to experiment with her particular type of domestic realism in a wide variety of venues. Elizabeth Keckley's racial difference is crucial to understanding her particular construction of authorial rights, but her articulation of those rights gives a way to think about *Behind the Scenes* as something other than a failed narrative of a slave's success. Mary Abigail Dodge and Sophia Hawthorne struggled for more specific contractual rights, but this struggle can be read as an important chapter in the history of authorship as well as a transparent attempt to represent the "business of writing." Elizabeth Stuart Phelps's anomalies as an author can be read not only as anachronistic demands but also as a successful engagement with—if also a rejection of—cultural conversations about authorship that had been on-going even during her mother's career.

The preceding summary leaves out one figure whose work I have touched on in this book: Sophia Hawthorne. Her case too demonstrates the limitations of reading authorship primarily in terms of social or economic difference as well as the possibility of other models of success, some of which I have traced in this book. Sophia Hawthorne was a particularly polarizing figure in twentieth-century American literary study. Several generations have castigated her for her editorial practices, particularly in relation to the editing of her husband's notebooks, and a more recent one has castigated that generation—as well as nineteenth-century culture—for making it a "transgression" for her to be an author in her own right.[43] Yet, this debate obscures elements of Hawthorne's career that make her fascinating as an author. She came into authorship by writing voluminous letters and diaries, challenging distinctions between private and published writing. Her most energetic writing occurred when she was out of the country, in Cuba as a young girl, in England and Italy with her husband, and in Germany as a widow. This fact is important not only for the history of travel writing but also because of what it contributes to current theories of transnationalism. Although she was able to travel because of her particular national status (especially in her position as a diplomatic wife), it is important to think about the relation of this status to her "freeing" as an author—particularly in colonial Cuba. She also provides a collaborative model of authorship, both in her Cuban journals (read aloud by her sister Elizabeth Peabody) and in her editorial work with her husband. In addition, she exemplifies the relation between literary production and the material support necessary for that production in her attempts to move beyond informal and oral agreements to contractual rights.

Of these various alternative ways of thinking about authorship, transnationalism perhaps has the most promise in contributing to "the ultimate project of defining new kinds of social organization that will dispense with the hierarchies, exclusions, and fears of the past," as John Carlos Rowe recently concluded in a *PMLA* article on the subject.[44] Here the study of women authors may be in the vanguard rather than struggling to catch up. Although theories of domesticity and women's work were intricately tied to theories of nineteenth-century nationalism, they did avoid the particular confluence of self-reliance and nationalism that has been a long-standing legacy of nineteenth-century American men's writing. Woolson, like Phelps, was as apt to look at George Eliot as a point of reference as she was to look at Henry James as such, and to some extent gender concerns were inherently transnationalist. A quick glance through the authors studied here suggests the manifold ways in which a transnationalist lens might produce fresh readings. What does it really mean that we know that *The Lamplighter* was read in Norway or that it became part of an Irish author's novel? How might we read Alcott's treatment of Cuba and the Italian revolution as something other than displacements of American nationalist concerns? Who made the cloth that was imported for Keckley's use as a seamstress? To what extent does Avis Dobell's European education (and use of an Egyptian figure) point to a transnational aesthetic? What is the significance of the Italian setting of "Miss Grief"?

That is, of course, the subject for another book. I point to it here as an extension of my own call for a nonoppositional theory of female authorship. Nineteenth-century women themselves sometimes established certain oppositions, working at points to distance authors from writers; to anatomize the ways in which women were sometimes subordinated to men, in both editorial and economic decisions; and to justify their own art by constructing it in contrast to other forms (the romance, portraiture, realism, and so on). But through their various claims as authors, they were also able to show a variety of ways in which authorship could be personally and professionally sustaining and rewarding. By putting the literary women studied here in conversation with each other, I hope to have begun to show how an attention to these authorial claims can help us move beyond grieving the limitations placed on women writers, even as we continue to respect the terms of that grief.

Notes

Preface

1. Judith Fetterley and Marjorie Pryse, *Writing out of Place: Regionalism, Women, and American Literary Culture* (Urbana: University of Illinois Press, 2003), 13.

2. Michel Foucault, "What Is an Author?," in Foucault, *Language, Counter-Memory, Practice*, ed. Donald F. Bouchard (Ithaca, N.Y.: Cornell University Press, 1977), 123.

3. Anne E. Boyd, *Writing for Immortality: Women and the Emergence of High Literary Culture in America* (Baltimore: Johns Hopkins University Press, 2004), 249, 9.

4. Naomi Sofer, *Making the "America of Art": Cultural Nationalism and Nineteenth-Century Women Writers* (Columbus: Ohio State University Press, 2005), 11.

5. Catherine Gallagher, *Nobody's Story: The Vanishing Acts of Women Writers in the Marketplace, 1670–1820* (Berkeley: University of California Press, 1994), xv.

6. Pierre Bourdieu, *The Field of Cultural Production*, ed. Randal Johnson (New York: Columbia University Press, 1993), 40, 42.

7. Elizabeth Ammons, *Conflicting Stories: American Women Writers at the Turn into the Twentieth Century* (New York: Oxford University Press, 1991); Richard Brodhead, *Cultures of Letters: Scenes of Reading and Writing in Nineteenth-Century America* (Chicago: University of Chicago Press, 1993).

8. Bourdieu, 30, 42.

9. Sean McCann emphasizes this point in his review of *The Field of Cultural Production* in "Reintroduction of the Specialists," *American Quarterly* 49 (March 1997): 185–86.

10. As early as 1825 a contributor to the *United States Literary Gazette* had outlined these functions in an article entitled "Authors and Writers." Authors are original "producers" of "higher and brighter thoughts," while writers combine "suggestions" and "matters of mere observation." "Prophetic authors," in particular, "live in the future of their own minds" and "go habitually before time" ("Authors and Writers," *United States Literary Gazette* 1 [March 1, 1825]: 346–47).

11. Jennifer Cognard-Black, *Narrative in the Professional Age: Transatlantic Readings of Harriet Beecher Stowe, George Eliot, and Elizabeth Stuart Phelps* (New York: Routledge, 2004), 10.

12. Judith Fetterley, "Plenary Remarks," *Legacy* 19 (March 2002): 6.

13. For a description of this style, see Jeffrey D. Groves, "Judging Literary Books by Their Covers: House Styles, Ticknor and Fields, and Literary Promotion," in *Reading Books: Essays on the Material Text and Literature in America*, ed. Michele

Moylan and Lane Stiles (Amherst: University of Massachusetts Press, 1996), 84–92. Ticknor and Fields editions measured 3 ¾ by 5 ¾ inches; each book in the Schomburg series measures 6.84 by 5.06 inches.

14. Nina Baym defended this approach in the inaugural volume of *Legacy*: "The author-by-author approach of *LEGACY* seems not only useful and necessary, but corrective to the tendency to absorb women authors into one or another idea of the 'female'" ("Rewriting the Scribbling Women," *Legacy* 2 [1985]: 10).

15. The programs for the 2001 and 2003 SSAWW conferences are archived at http://www.unl.edu/legacy/SSAWW_conf.html. The program for the 1996 Hartford conference is reprinted in *Legacy* 15 (1998): 10–14.

16. Nathaniel Hawthorne to William D. Ticknor, January 19, 1855, in Hawthorne, *The Letters, 1853–1856*, vol. 17 of *The Centenary Edition of the Works of Nathaniel Hawthorne*, ed. Thomas Woodson et al. (Columbus: Ohio State University Press, 1987), 304. The hesitation in using "author" as a "master term" is implicit in Cognard-Black's note that she chooses "artist" rather than "author" because "the position of author is a highly invested cultural site—a nexus of power dynamics that maintain a notion of authorship that is, of course, as privileged as any God might be" (155).

17. An article in an early issue of *Legacy*, for example, acknowledges that "there are good arguments for refusing to canonize certain nineteenth-century writers at the expense of others, even if we could agree on the criteria," but then goes on to say that it may be time "to risk putting some judgments . . . into print" (Barbara A. White, "Notes toward a Bibliography: Some Sources for the Study of Women's Fiction, 1790–1865," *Legacy* 2 [spring 1985]: 7).

18. This panel, moderated by Frances Smith Foster and including Lois Brown, Jennifer Fleischner, Xiomara Santamarina, and Sarah Robbins, took place at the Society for the Study of American Women Writers Conference, Fort Worth, Texas, September 26, 2003.

19. Robert Darnton, "What Is the History of Books?," in *The Book History Reader*, ed. David Finkelstein and Alistair McCleery (London: Routledge, 2002), 18.

20. Roland Barthes, "The Death of the Author," in *The Book History Reader*, ed. Finkelstein and McCleery, 224; Susan T. West, "From Owning to Owning Up: Authorial Rights and Rhetorical Responsibilities" (Ph.D. diss., Ohio State University, 1997), 27.

21. Christine Battersby, *Gender and Genius: Towards a Feminist Aesthetics* (Bloomington: Indiana University Press, 1989), 146. See also Cheryl Walker, "Feminist Literary Criticism and the Author," *Critical Inquiry* 16 (spring 1990): 551–71.

22. Foucault, 120.

23. Ibid., 115.

24. William L. Gibson, "Writers behind Barbed Wire," *New York Review of Books* 10 (March 14, 1968): 35. The Center for Edition of American Authors (CEAA) was established by the MLA in 1963; it was succeeded by the Committee on Scholarly Editions in 1976—precisely the time when the recovery of women authors was in full swing. See John Unsworth, "Reconsidering and Revising the MLA Committee on Scholarly Editions' Guidelines for Scholarly Editions," http://www.iath.virginia.edu/~jmu2m/sts2001.html, accessed January 30, 2004.

25. It is heartening, in this respect, to note that some scholars who have published multiauthor studies of women are now turning to book-length studies of individual authors: Melissa Homestead, for example, has started one of Catharine Sedgwick.

26. Mrs. A. J. Graves, *Women in America: Being an Examination into the Moral and*

Intellectual Condition of American Female Society (New York: Harper and Brothers, 1847), 190–93.

27. Foucault, 124.

28. Nina Baym, "Melodramas of Beset Manhood: How Theories of American Fiction Exclude Women Authors," *American Quarterly* 33 (1981): 123–39.

29. Examples of the former include Linda Grasso, *The Artistry of Anger: Black and White Women's Literature in America, 1820–1860* (Chapel Hill: University of North Carolina Press, 2002); and Nancy Walker, *The Disobedient Writer: Women and Narrative Tradition* (Austin: University of Texas Press, 1995). Examples of the latter include Brodhead, *Cultures of Letters*; Michael T. Gilmore, *American Romanticism and the Marketplace* (Chicago: University of Chicago Press, 1985); and Michael Newbury, *Figuring Authorship in Antebellum America* (Stanford, Calif.: Stanford University Press, 1997).

30. Michael Davitt Bell, *Culture, Genre, and Literary Vocation: Selected Essays on American Literature* (Chicago: University of Chicago Press, 2001), 184.

31. "Female Authors," *North American Review* 72 (January 1851): 162.

32. "National Literature, and the International Copy-Right Treaty," *United States Review* 2 (August 1853): 99. This gendered rhetoric is, as the title suggests, in the service of advocating an international copyright, a reaction that, as Meredith McGill points out, is in reaction to the success of Stowe's *Uncle Tom's Cabin* abroad and fears of an alliance between British aristocrats and effeminate American abolitionists (*American Literature and the Culture of Reprinting, 1834–1853* [Philadelphia: University of Pennsylvania Press, 2003], 275).

Chapter 1

1. Fanny Fern, *Ruth Hall*, ed. Susan Belasco Smith (New York: Penguin, 1997), 225.

2. Augusta J. Evans, *St. Elmo* (New York: Grosset and Dunlap, n.d.), 489.

3. Mrs. M. L. Rayne, *What Can a Woman Do; or, Her Position in the Business and Literary World* (Detroit: F. B. Dickerson, 1883), 30.

4. Carol Shields, *Unless* (London: Fourth Estate/HarperCollins, 2002), 1, 5.

5. Louisa May Alcott to Abigail May Alcott, December 25, 1864, in Alcott, *The Selected Letters of Louisa May Alcott*, ed. Joel Myerson and Daniel Shealy (Boston: Little, Brown, 1987), 106.

6. Sarah Orne Jewett to Sarah K. Bolton, n.d., Bolton-Stanwood Family Papers, vol. 27, p. 93, American Antiquarian Society, Worcester, Mass.; Rebecca Harding Davis, "Women in Literature," *Independent* (May 7, 1891): 2; R.W. B. Lewis, *Edith Wharton: A Biography* (New York: Harper and Row, 1975), 297.

7. Gail Hamilton, *A Battle of the Books* (Cambridge: Hurd and Houghton, 1870), 266.

8. Bell, *Culture, Genre, and Literary Vocation*, 184.

9. See, for example, Brodhead, *Cultures of Letters*; and Nancy Glazener, *Reading for Realism: The History of a U.S. Literary Institution* (Durham, N.C.: Duke University Press, 1997).

10. Susan Coultrap-McQuin, *Doing Literary Business: American Women Writers in the Nineteenth Century* (Chapel Hill: University of North Carolina Press, 1990), 6. Coultrap-McQuin in turn cites J. C. Derby's *Fifty Years among Authors* (New York: Carleton, 1884), 283–85, which unfortunately does not say which "western paper" this "bagatelle" is taken from.

11. Grasso, *Artistry of Anger.*

12. Thrace Talmon, "The Latest Crusade: Lady Authors and Their Critics," *National Era* 11 (June 5, 1857): 101. A few weeks later the *Era* reprinted part of the *Observer*'s reply, which noted that it had "not sought to deter women from the use of the pen, to promote the good and the true and the beautiful" ("Female Authorship," *National Era* 11 [August 6, 1857]: 126).

13. [Hannah Farnham Sawyer Lee], "Female Authorship," *Monthly Miscellany of Religion and Letters* 2 (May 1840): 249; "Literary Success of Female Writers," *Harvard Register* 2 (April 1827): 55, 58. Lee's later article on "Female Authorship" in the *Monthly Miscellany of Religion and Letters* uses the term "author" exclusively (3 [September 1840]: 151–54).

14. "Cacoethes Scribendi," *Boston Medical Intelligencer* 2 (August 3, 1824): 50.

15. "The Victim of a Proof-Reader," *Atkinson's Casket* 9 (September 1835): 486–88; "Cacoethes Scribendi," *Harvardiana* 2 (September 1, 1835): 21–26; "True Republicanism," *Current Literature* 37 (November 1904): 470.

16. Ronald J. Zboray and Mary Saracino Zboray, *Literary Dollars and Social Sense: A People's History of the Mass Market Book* (New York: Routledge, 2005), xiii.

17. Charlotte Forten, *The Journals of Charlotte Forten Grimké,* ed. Brenda Stevenson (New York: Oxford University Press, 1988), 156, 236; Zboray and Zboray, 44. On Forten, see also Carla L. Peterson, *"Doers of the Word": African-American Women Speakers and Writers in the North (1830–1880)* (New York: Oxford University Press, 1995), 176–95.

18. Xiomara Santamarina, "Black Hairdresser and Social Critic: Eliza Potter and the Labors of Femininity," *American Literature* 77 (March 2005): 151–77.

19. Lulie, "Persevere: Or, Life with an Aim," *Godey's Lady's Book* 68 (March 1864): 254–58; Fannie Aymar Mathews, "When I Was a Man: A True Story," *New Peterson Magazine* 2 (October 1893): 1033.

20. Catharine Sedgwick, "Cacoethes Scribendi," in *Provisions: A Reader from 19th-Century American Women,* ed. Judith Fetterley (Bloomington: Indiana University Press, 1985), 53.

21. P. Thorne, "Cacoethes Scribendi; and What Came of It," *Lippincott's Magazine of Literature, Science and Education* 6 (December 1870): 645.

22. Ella Rodman, "A Fragment of Autobiography," *Graham's American Monthly Magazine of Literature, Art, and Fashion* 45 (November 1854): 451.

23. "Female Authorship," *Littell's Living Age* 9 (May 23, 1846): 345.

24. Alice Neal, "American Female Authorship," *Godey's Magazine and Lady's Book* 44 (February 1852): 146.

25. *Daily Alta California,* October 22, 1854, in Elizabeth Stoddard, *The Morgesons and Other Writings, Published and Unpublished,* ed. Lawrence Buell and Sandra A. Zagarell (Philadelphia: University of Pennsylvania Press, 1984), 314. See also Margaret A. Amstutz, "Elizabeth Stoddard as Returned Californian: A Reading of the *Daily Alta California* Columns," in *American Culture, Canons, and the Case of Elizabeth Stoddard,* ed. Robert McClure Smith and Ellen Weinauer (Tuscaloosa: University of Alabama Press, 2003), esp. 68–69; and Susan Belasco, "Elizabeth Barrow Stoddard, the *Daily Alta California,* and the Tradition of American Humor," *American Periodicals* 10 (2000): 1–26.

26. Elizabeth Stoddard, "Collected by a Valetudinarian," in Stoddard, *The Morgesons and Other Writings,* 290–91, 307.

27. Barbara A. Bardes and Suzanne Gossett, "Sarah J. Hale, Selective Promoter of Her Sex," in *A Living of Words: American Women in Print Culture,* ed. Susan Albertine (Knoxville: University of Tennessee Press, 1995), 26. As Bardes and Gossett

point out, this final section included 119 total entries; Hale was more comfortable including writers than political activists and intellectuals.

28. "Authorship in America," *Atlantic Monthly* 51 (June 1883): 808.

29. See Burton J. Bledstein, *The Culture of Professionalism: The Middle Class and the Development of Higher Education in America* (New York: Norton, 1976) for an overview of this movement.

30. Rayne, 30.

31. Stowe, quoted in Susan Belasco, "The Writing, Reception, and Reputation of *Uncle Tom's Cabin*," in *Approaches to Teaching Stowe's* Uncle Tom's Cabin, ed. Elizabeth Ammons and Susan Belasco (New York: Modern Language Association of America, 2000), 28.

32. Michael Winship, "'The Greatest Book of Its Kind': A Publishing History of *Uncle Tom's Cabin*," *Proceedings of the American Antiquarian Society*, n.s. 112 (2002): 309–32.

33. Harriet Beecher Stowe, "How May I Know That I Can Make a Writer?," *Hearth and Home* 1 (January 20, 1869): 88, and "Faults of Inexperienced Writers," *Hearth and Home* 1 (January 23, 1869): 72. For another discussion of these essays and their deployment of professionalism within the context of gender constraints, see Sarah Robbins, "Gendering Gilded Age Periodical Professionalism: Reading Harriet Beecher Stowe's Hearth and Home Prescriptions for Women's Writing," in *"The Only Efficient Instrument": American Women Writers and the Periodical, 1837–1916*, ed. Aleta Feinsod Cane and Susan Alves (Iowa City: University of Iowa Press, 2001), 45–65.

34. Rose Terry Cooke, "A Letter to Mary Ann," *Sunday Afternoon* 3 (January 1879): 79–83. Subsequent citations to this work will be given parenthetically in the text. For a discussion of Cooke's bitterness in this article, see Elizabeth Ammons, "Introduction" to Cooke's *"How Celia Changed Her Mind" and Selected Stories*, ed. Ammons (New Brunswick, N.J.: Rutgers University Press, 1986), xviii.

35. Hawthorne to William D. Ticknor, January 19,1855, in Hawthorne, *The Letters, 1853–1856*, ed. Woodson et al., vol. 17 of *The Centenary Edition of the Works of Nathaniel Hawthorne*, ed. Charvat et al., 304.

36. "Woman in the Domain of Letters," *American Monthly Knickerbocker* 64 (July 1864): 86.

37. Thomas Wentworth Higginson, *Atlantic Essays* (Boston: James R. Osgood, 1874), 71.

38. Il Secretario, "American Letters—Their Character and Advancement," *American Review: A Whig Journal of Politics, Literature, Art, and Science* 1 (June 1845): 580.

39. Mary Abigail Dodge to Grace Greenwood, Hartford, Conn., April 15, 1857, in Gail Hamilton, *Gail Hamilton's Life in Letters*, ed. H. Augusta Dodge (Boston: Lee and Shepard, 1901), 1:139.

40. Naomi Sofer, "'Carry[ing] a Yankee Girl to Glory': Redefining Female Authorship in the Postbellum United States," *American Literature* 75 (March 2003): 43.

41. "Gossip of Authors and Writers," *Current Literature* 8 (September 1891): 16–17.

42. Helen Gray Cone, "Woman in American Literature," *Century Illustrated Magazine* 40 (October 1890): 924, 928, 921.

43. Annie Nathan Meyer, "Woman's Place in Letters," in *The Congress of Women: Held in the Woman's Building, World's Columbian Exposition, Chicago, U.S.A., 1893*, ed. Mary Kavanaugh Oldham Eagle (Chicago: American Publishing House, 1894), 135.

44. Rayne, 36.

45. Mary Temple Bayard, "Woman in Journalism," in *The Congress of Women*, 435.

46. Lawrence Buell, *New England Literary Culture* (Cambridge: Cambridge University Press, 1986), 379.

47. "Gossip of Authors and Writers," 24–25.

48. Cone, 930.

49. Davis, "Women in Literature," 2.

50. William Alfred Jones, "Female Novelists," *United States Magazine and Democratic Review* 14 (May 1844): 484–89.

51. "Female Authors," 41.

52. "Woman in the Domain of Letters," 84.

53. "Literary Women," *Living Age* (June 25, 1864): 609. This article was reprinted from a London review and referred to George Eliot in particular.

54. W. L. Courtney, *The Feminine Note in Fiction* (London: Chapman and Hall, 1904), xxxii. Courtney's main interest is in British novelists, although he does include Margaret Fuller, Mary Wilkins (Freeman), and Edith Wharton in his study.

55. Quoted in Belasco, "The Writing, Reception, and Reputation of *Uncle Tom's Cabin*," 31.

56. Mary E. Bryan, "How Should Women Write?," in *American Literature, American Culture*, ed. Gordon Hutner (New York: Oxford University Press, 1999), 120.

57. Fern, 170.

58. Neal, 147.

59. Virginia Penny, *How Women Can Make Money, Married or Single, in All Branches of the Arts and Sciences, Professions, Trades, Agricultural and Mechanical Pursuits* (Springfield, Mass.: D. E. Fisk, 1870), 4.

60. Harriet Beecher Stowe, "How Shall I Learn to Write?," *Hearth and Home* 1 (January 16, 1869): 49.

61. Naomi Schor, *Reading in Detail: Aesthetics and the Feminine* (New York: Routledge, 1989), 11–22. In America even authors, such as Hawthorne, who appreciated Dutch art tended to categorize the "feminine achievements in literature" as "pretty fancies of snow and moonlight." Of course, Hawthorne also associated his own mode of romance with moonlight, but the implication seems to be that the greatest contribution that women could make to literature is to invest themselves in the "small" and "familiar" or "weary common-place of daily life" (*The Marble Faun*, vol. 4 of *The Centenary Edition of the Works of Nathaniel Hawthorne*, ed. William Charvat et al. [Columbus: Ohio State University Press, 1968], 40, 61, 90).

62. Courtney, x.

63. Frank Norris, *The Responsibilities of the Novelist and Other Literary Essays* (New York: Doubleday, 1903), 236–37.

64. Stowe, "How Shall I Learn to Write?," 49.

65. Michael T. Gilmore, *Surface and Depth: The Quest for Legibility in American Culture* (Oxford: Oxford University Press, 2003).

66. Stephen Crane, *Maggie: A Girl of the Streets*, ed. Thomas A. Gullason (New York: Norton, 1979), 14, 15; [William Dean Howells], "Editor's Study," *Harper's Monthly* 74 (February 1887): 485.

67. Henry James, "The Art of Fiction," in *The Art of Criticism: Henry James on the Theory and Practice of Fiction*, ed. William Veeder and Susan M. Griffin (Chicago: University of Chicago Press, 1986), 172. For an earlier formulation of the connection between realism and female authorship, see James's review in the *Nation* 1 (September 14, 1865): 345, in which he states that "the greatest successes

in this line [of realism] are reserved for that branch of the school which contains the most female writers; for if women are unable to draw, they notoriously can at all events paint, and this is what realism requires."

68. Henry James, *The Portrait of a Lady*, ed. Jan Cohn (Boston: Houghton Mifflin, 2001), 85, 84.

69. Richard H. Brodhead, *The School of Hawthorne* (New York: Oxford University Press, 1986), 35.

70. Kristie Hamilton, *America's Sketchbook: The Cultural Life of a Nineteenth-Century Literary Institution* (Athens: Ohio University Press, 1998), 24.

71. Herman Melville, "Hawthorne and His Mosses," in Melville, *The Piazza Tales and Other Prose Pieces, 1839–1860*, ed. Harrison Hayford et al., vol. 9 of *The Writings of Herman Melville* (Evanston and Chicago: Northwestern University Press and the Newberry Library, 1987), 247. To be sure, there were some women who rejected imitation as vociferously as Melville did. Maria J. McIntosh, for example, criticized women for being "servile imitators" in their social and cultural lives (*Woman in America: Her Work and Her Reward* [New York: D. Appleton, 1850], 560).

72. Il Secretario, 576.

73. "Novels and Novelists," *North American Review* 76 (January 1853): 123, 109. See also the *New York Tribune* 10 (December 27, 1850), which describes *The Wide, Wide World* as "indicat[ing] more than common observation of life and manner" (6).

74. For an important exploration of the specific contributions of one female author to literary realism and of the resulting reperiodization of the genre, see Sharon M. Harris, *Rebecca Harding Davis and American Realism* (Philadelphia: University of Pennsylvania Press, 1991).

75. Melissa J. Homestead, *American Women Authors and Literary Property, 1822–1869* (Cambridge: Cambridge University Press, 2005); Isabel Marcus, "Coverture," in *The Reader's Companion to U.S. Women's History*, ed. Wilma Mankiller et al. (Boston: Houghton Mifflin, 1998), 136–37.

76. As one commentator put it, "The assumption in copyright is that the nation has a final proprietorship in its literature; it grants a monopoly for a term as an encouragement and protection to its authors" ("Authorship in America," 816).

77. H[enry] C[harles] Carey, *The International Copyright Question Considered, with Special Reference to the Interests of American Authors, American Printers and Publishers, and American Readers* (Philadelphia: Henry Carey Baird, 1872), 6, 19.

78. Cone, 924; Neal, 148. See also "Pay of Authors," which reports that "many an American author counts his readers by thousands, and his receipts by units" (*Littell's Living Age* 13 [May 8, 1847]: 257).

79. F. Wharton, "Authorship in America," *North American Review* 52 (April 1841): 385–404. The attribution to Wharton is given in *Poole's Index*.

80. "Authors and Writers," 346.

81. Rosemary J. Coombe, *The Cultural Life of Intellectual Properties: Authorship, Appropriation, and the Law* (Durham, N.C.: Duke University Press, 1998), 245. My use of the term "cultural commons" is indebted to Susan T. West, i and passim.

82. "Literary Women," 610; "Novels and Novelists," 109.

83. As Jennifer Cognard-Black points out, such a model—while a part of the overall "culture of professionalism"—also "made the mothering implicit in metaphoric femininity . . . into the indispensable element of perfect professionalism" (11).

84. Bryan, 118.

85. On authorship as "ethical technique," see David Saunders and Ian Hunter,

"Lessons from the 'Literatory': How to Historicise Authorship," *Critical Inquiry* 17 (spring 1991): 479–509.

86. Linda Kerber, *No Constitutional Right to Be Ladies: Women and the Obligations of Citizenship* (New York: Hill and Wang, 1998), xxiii.

87. Neal, 147.

Chapter 2

1. The best study of the parlor to date is Katherine C. Grier's *Culture and Comfort: Parlor Making and Middle-Class Identity, 1850–1930* (Washington, D.C.: Smithsonian Institution, 1988). For an important study of parlor rhetoric, see Nan Johnson, *Gender and Rhetorical Space in American Life, 1866–1910* (Carbondale and Edwardsville: Southern Illinois University Press, 2002).

2. Mary Kelley, "'A More Glorious Revolution': Women's Antebellum Reading Circles and the Pursuit of Public Influence," *New England Quarterly* 76 (June 2003): 168; Elizabeth McHenry, *Forgotten Readers: Recovering the Lost History of African-American Literary Societies* (Durham, N.C.: Duke University Press, 2002), chap. 5. See also Nancy F. Cott, *The Bonds of Womanhood: 'Woman's Sphere' in New England, 1780–1835* (New Haven, Conn.: Yale University Press, 1977).

3. Larry J. Reynolds, "From *Dial* Essay to New York Book: The Making of *Woman in the Nineteenth Century*," in *Periodical Literature in Nineteenth-Century America*, ed. Kenneth M. Price and Susan Belasco Smith (Charlottesville: University Press of Virginia, 1995), 20–22.

4. Jean Fagan Yellin, introduction to Harriet Jacobs, *Incidents in the Life of a Slave Girl*, ed. Yellin (Cambridge, Mass.: Harvard University Press, 1987), xix; Joan D. Hedrick, *Harriet Beecher Stowe: A Life* (New York: Oxford University Press, 1994), 107. Stowe had already published a geography text book, but Hedrick makes a convincing case for the importance of the epistolary form to Stowe's subsequent writings.

5. Nina Baym, *American Women Writers and the Work of History, 1790–1860* (New Brunswick, N.J.: Rutgers University Press, 1995), 93, 104, 132–33.

6. William Merrill Decker gives an overview of such epistolary literature in *Epistolary Practices: Letter Writing in America before Telecommunications* (Chapel Hill: University of North Carolina Press, 1998), 23–25. Decker emphasizes the difference between such printed letters and the "authentic correspondences" between real people, arguing that printed letters have distinct "conventions and expectations," particularly about narrative closure.

7. H. Hastings Weld, "Some Thoughts on Letter Writing," *Godey's Lady's Book* 44 (April 1852): 249.

8. Sophia Hawthorne to Nathaniel Peabody, February 27, 1853, in Nancy Luanne Jenkins Hurst, "Selected Literary Letters of Sophia Peabody Hawthorne, 1842–1853" (Ph.D. diss., Ohio State University, 1992), 310. For more on the collection of letters from Cuba, see Clare Badaracco, "Sophia Peabody Hawthorne's Cuba Journal: Volume Three, 31 October 1834–15 March 1835," *Essex Institute Historical Collections* 118 (1982): 280–315.

9. Marion Harland, *Marion Harland's Autobiography: The Story of a Long Life* (New York: Harper and Brothers, 1910), 241–42.

10. Hedrick, 81, 79. For more on the Semi-Colon Club, see Nicole Tonkovich, "Writing in Circles: Harriet Beecher Stowe, the Semi-Colon Club, and the Construction of Women's Authorship," in *Nineteenth-Century Women Learn to*

Write, ed. Catherine Hobbs (Charlottesville: University Press of Virginia, 1995), 145–75.

11. "Letter-Writing," *Atlantic Monthly* 2 (June 1858): 46; "A Chapter upon Letters and Letter-Writers," *Ladies' Repository* 16 (February 1856): 70.

12. The phrase is Louis J. Budd's, describing Stowe's *Oldtown Folks* in "The American Background," in *The Cambridge Companion to American Realism and Naturalism,* ed. Donald Pizer (Cambridge: Cambridge University Press, 1995), 40. See also Alfred Habegger, *Gender, Fantasy, and Realism in American Literature* (New York: Columbia University Press, 1982), who says that James and Howells "were born to, and then established themselves against, the maternal tradition of Anglo-American women's fiction" (ix). Brook Thomas offers a different view, arguing that domestic novels were "ordered by their authors' faith in a transcendental, usually religious, social order" and that "The realists' technical innovations helped to free their presentations from subordination to such an order" (*American Literary Realism and the Failed Promise of Contract* [Berkeley and Los Angeles: University of California Press, 1997], 10–11).

13. N. Johnson, 14, 79, 98, 85.

14. Mary La Fayette Robbins, "Introduction" to Robbins, *Alabama Women in Literature* (Selma, Ala.: Selma Printing Company, 1895), n.p.

15. Robert S. Levine, "In and Out of the Parlor," *American Literary History* 7 (winter 1995): 675.

16. Harriet Beecher Stowe, "Can I Write?," *Hearth and Home* 1 (January 9, 1869): 40.

17. For a summary of Alcott's experience with James Redpath, the editor of *Hospital Sketches,* see Daniel Shealy, "The Author-Publisher Relationships of Louisa May Alcott" (Ph.D. diss., University of South Carolina, 1985), 13–34.

18. Rayne, 14, 30.

19. This memoir is discussed in greater detail in Nicole Tonkovich, *Domesticity with a Difference: The Nonfiction of Catharine Beecher, Sarah J. Hale, Fanny Fern, and Margaret Fuller* (Jackson: University Press of Mississippi, 1997), 146–47. The memoir appears in Charles Edward Stowe and Lyman Beecher Stowe, *Harriet Beecher Stowe: The Story of Her Life* (Boston: Houghton Mifflin, 1911), 87–89.

20. "Literary Women," 610.

21. Rayne, 14.

22. See Jane Weiss, ed., "'Many Things Take My Time': The Journal of Susan Warner" (Ph.D. diss., City University of New York, 1995), 249; and Sarah Elbert, *A Hunger for Home: Louisa May Alcott's Place in American Culture* (New Brunswick, N.J.: Rutgers University Press, 1987), 163. For a discussion of the ways in which Afro-Protestant newspapers encouraged their readers to contribute to their pages, see also Frances Smith Foster, "African Americans, Literature, and the Nineteenth-Century Afro-Protestant Press," in *Reciprocal Influences: Literary Production, Distribution and Consumption in America,* ed. Steven Fink and Susan S. Williams (Columbus: Ohio State University Press, 1999), 28–29.

23. Caroline Kirkland, *A Book for the Home Circle* (New York: Scribner, 1853), 80.

24. Ibid., 78.

25. "Woman in the Domain of Letters," 83–86.

26. John Greenleaf Whittier to Gail Hamilton, October 31, 1877, in Whittier, *The Letters of John Greenleaf Whittier,* ed. John B. Pickard, 3 vols. (Cambridge, Mass.: Belknap Press of Harvard University Press, 1975), 3:380.

27. Decker, 94, 102.

28. Rebecca Harding Davis, "Life in the Iron Mills," in Davis, *A Rebecca Harding Davis Reader*, ed. Jean Pfaelzer (Pittsburgh: University of Pittsburgh Press, 1995), 4–5; Robyn R. Warhol, "Toward a Theory of the Engaging Narrator: Earnest Interventions in Gaskell, Stowe, and Eliot," *PMLA* 101 (October 1986): 811–17.

29. "Female Authors," 152.

30. Fern, *Ruth Hall*, 200. Subsequent citations will be to this edition and will be included parenthetically in the text.

31. Melissa J. Homestead, "'Every Body Sees the Theft': Fanny Fern and Literary Proprietorship in Antebellum America," *New England Quarterly* 74 (June 2001): 210–37.

32. *New York Ledger*, August 10, 1867, quoted in Tonkovich, *Domesticity with a Difference*, xi.

33. *Una* 2 (August 1854): 320, reprinted in Ann Russo and Cheris Kramarae, eds., *The Radical Women's Press of the 1850s* (New York: Routledge, 1991), 60–61.

34. William G. Rowland, *Literature and the Marketplace: Romantic Writers and Their Audiences in Great Britain and the United States* (Lincoln: University of Nebraska Press, 1996), gives this summary of the romantic solitary genius:

The major romantic writers experienced the general feeling of being cut off from "developed social relations" alternately as freedom and as despair. They felt free to explore the growth of their own minds (*The Prelude*) or to create inner apocalypses (*Prometheus Unbound, Jerusalem, The Confidence-Man*), but they sometimes despaired of communicating their insights to the public. Romantic literature, which both reflected and perpetuated the idea of the individual as isolated, thus penetrated deeply into the lived experiences of the members of industrial society, particularly the middle class. The romantics produced a great literature because their activity as writers forced them to confront a general experience of their historical period: the feeling of being cut off from other people and from the social and historical processes that determine one's life. (16)

35. Quoted in Susan S. Williams, "Widening the World: Susan Warner, Her Readers, and the Assumption of Authorship," *American Quarterly* 42 (December 1990): 573.

36. Quoted in Janet S. Zehr, "The Response of Nineteenth-Century Audiences to Louisa May Alcott's Fiction," *American Transcendental Quarterly* 1 (n.s.) (December 1987): 324.

37. Eugenia Sadler to Susan Warner, July 6, 1864, quoted in S. Williams, "Widening the World," 574.

38. Lydia Sigourney, *Letters of Life* (New York: Appleton, 1866), 377–78.

39. Elizabeth Stuart Phelps, *Chapters from a Life* (Boston: Houghton, Mifflin, 1897), 122, 123, 128.

40. On Melville and Hawthorne, see Elizabeth Hewitt, *Correspondence and American Literature, 1770–1865* (Cambridge: Cambridge University Press, 2004), chap. 3; on Emerson and Whitman, see Jay Grossman, "Rereading Emerson/Whitman," in *Reciprocal Influences*, ed. Fink and Williams, 75–97; on James and Howells see Michael Anesko, *Letters, Fictions, Lives: Henry James and William Dean Howells* (New York: Oxford University Press, 1997).

41. One contribution to such a study is Jennifer Cognard-Black and Elizabeth MacLeod Walls, eds., *Kindred Hands: Letters on Writing by Women Authors, 1860–1920* (Iowa City: University of Iowa Press, 2006).

42. Harland, 263. Harland also reports receiving letters from H. W. Longfellow, George Prentice, and James Redpath.

43. Lydia Sigourney to Mary Abigail Dodge, March 21, 1863, Mary Abigail Dodge Papers, folder 5, Peabody Essex Museum, Salem, Mass.

44. Rose Terry Cooke to Mary Abigail Dodge, February 15, 1878, Dodge Papers, folder 7.

45. It is also true that writers frequently acknowledged their personal "fraternity of Authors" by alluding in print to writers who had been particularly influential on them: Susan Warner's Ellen Montgomery reads the works of Maria Edgeworth; Jo March reads the works of Warner and of Charlotte Yonge; Avis Dobell reads Elizabeth Barrett Browning; and so on.

46. A copy of this portrait can be found in William S. McFeely, *Frederick Douglass* (New York: Norton, 1991), following 274.

47. The most influential account of this paradoxical situation for women writers remains Mary Kelley's *Private Woman, Public Stage: Literary Domesticity in Nineteenth-Century America* (New York: Oxford University Press, 1984).

48. For a helpful discussion of the culture of sincerity in antebellum America, and of its particular manifestation in letter writing, see Karen Halttunen, *Confidence Men and Painted Women* (New Haven, Conn.: Yale University Press, 1982).

49. John S. Hart, *The Female Prose Writers of America* (Philadelphia: E. H. Butler, 1852), 76. Hart specifically praises Sigourney's ability to blend her domestic and professional life: "She has sacrificed no womanly or household duty, no office of friendship or benevolence for the society of the muses. That she is able to perform so much in so many varied departments of literature and social obligation, is owing to her diligence" (81).

50. E. B. Huntington, "Lydia H. Sigourney," in *Eminent Women of the Age, Being Narratives of the Lives and Deeds of the Most Prominent Women of the Present Generation*, ed. James Parton et al. (Hartford, Conn: S. M. Betts, 1868), 96.

51. On "self" and "type," see Susan K. Harris, *19th-Century American Women's Novels: Interpretive Strategies* (New York: Cambridge University Press, 1990), esp. 29. For a related discussion of "schema" and "literal description" in visual portraits, see Richard Brilliant, *Portraiture* (London: Reaktion Books, 1991), 38.

52. Hart, v–vi.

53. White, 7.

54. Graves, 190.

55. Amy Kaplan, "Manifest Domesticity," *American Literature* 70 (September 1998): 582.

56. Peterson discusses the iconography of Sojourner Truth in relation to other black women writers in *"Doers of the Word,"* 40–45. The 1894 photo of Jacobs is on the cover of her *Incidents in the Life of a Slave Girl,* ed. Yellin.

57. For more on Lothrop, see "Contributions to Trade History, No. XXX, D. Lothrop and Co.," *American Bookseller,* n. s. 199 (1886): 281–83. A representative example of a winner in the five-hundred-dollar series is Grace Middlebrook's *One Year of My Life. Eleanor Winthrop's Diary for 1869* (Boston: D. Lothrop, 1870). Titles in the thousand-dollar series include D. S. Erickson's *The Wadsworth Boys; or, Agnes' Decision* (1872) and Julia A. Eastman's *Striking for the Right* (1872).

58. Rayne, 14, 31–32. As Johnson points out, Rayne's emphasis on Whitney's domestic space is consistent with her overall method, which is to discuss the accomplishments of women in higher education and the professions but then end with "the conservative cultural cliché that 'the glory of woman' lies in being an inspiration to her husband's public rhetorical life rather than pursuing one of her own" (149).

59. Mrs. A. D. T. Whitney, *Sights and Insights: Patience Strong's Story of Over the Way*, 2 vols. (Boston: Houghton, Mifflin, 1879), 1:2.

60. Constance Fenimore Woolson to John Hay, December 26, 1885, in Alice Hall Petry, ed. "'Always, Your Attached Friend': The Unpublished Letters of Constance Fenimore Woolson to John and Clara Hay," *Books at Brown* 29–30 (1982–83): 80.

61. R. H. Stoddard et al., *Poets' Homes: Pen and Pencil Sketches of American Poets and Their Homes*, 2 vols. (Boston: D. Lothrop, 1879), 2:98.

62. Louisa May Alcott, *Louisa May Alcott: Her Life, Letters and Journals*, ed. Ednah P. Cheney (Boston: Roberts Brothers, 1890), iv.

63. Ibid., 364.

64. Barbara Hochman, noting this change, argues that it led writers to adopt more impersonal narrative strategies that discouraged "reading for the author." See her *Getting at the Author: Reimagining Books and Reading in the Age of American Realism* (Amherst: University of Massachusetts Press, 2001), esp. chaps. 1 and 2.

Chapter 3

Portions of this chapter appeared in an earlier form in the *New England Quarterly* 69 (June 1996): 179–200.

1. Unidentified newspaper clipping in the Cummins Family Papers, folder 3, Phillips Library, Peabody Essex Museum, Salem, Mass. (hereafter cited as Cummins Papers). See also Nina Baym's introduction to *The Lamplighter*, which suggests that Sedgwick would have taught Maria "that a woman did not need to be ashamed of being unmarried" and that writing was "a way of making a contribution to society" (New Brunswick, N.J.: Rutgers University Press, 1988, xv).

2. "A Revived Novel," unattributed newspaper column in a Boston paper (probably following Houghton Mifflin's reissue of *The Lamplighter* in 1891), Cummins Papers, folder 3.

3. "The Lamplighter," *Littell's Living Age* 5 (April 1, 1854): 28; "Literary Notices," *Harper's New Monthly Magazine* 8 (April 1854): 714.

4. "Literary Notices," *Knickerbocker, or New York Monthly Magazine* 43 (May 1854): 509–10.

5. Advertisement in *Norton's Literary Gazette*, April 1, 1854, 180.

6. Michel Foucault, "What Is an Author," in Foucault, *Language, Counter-Memory, Practice*, 127, 126.

7. Asabel Huntington to Maria Cummins, March 6, 1854, Cummins Papers, folder 2.

8. "Literary Notices," *Universalist Quarterly and General Review* 11 (April 1854): 220. See also "Books, Publishers, Authors," *United States Magazine of Science, Art, Manufactures, Agriculture, Commerce and Trade* 1 (May 15, 1854), which reported that "'The Lamplighter' has brought to light a new lady author, in the person of Miss Cummings, somewhere in the neighborhood of Boston" (28).

9. Kelley, *Private Woman, Public Stage*, 128. For Cummins's invitations from newspaper editors, see letters from John H. Eastburn, March 16, 1854; F. B. Fitts, March 14, 1854; and William Roderick Lawrence, November 13, 1854, Cummins Papers, folder 2.

10. James Joyce, *Ulysses* (New York: Vintage, 1986), 298.

11. Nathaniel Hawthorne, *The Letters, 1853–1856*, ed. Thomas Woodson et al., vol. 17 of Hawthorne, *The Centenary Edition of the Works of Nathaniel Hawthorne*, 304.

12. Nina Baym, "Again and Again, the Scribbling Women," in *Hawthorne and Women: Engendering and Expanding the Hawthorne Tradition*, ed. John L. Idol, Jr., and Melinda M. Ponder (Amherst: University of Massachusetts Press, 1999), 20–35.

13. "Publications," *Monthly Religious Magazine* 11 (April 1854): 239.

14. Review of *The Lamplighter* and *The Barclays of Boston*, clipping, probably from a Boston newspaper, 1854, Cummins Papers, folder 3.

15. Contract between John P. Jewett and Co. and Maria S. Cummins, February 1, 1854, in Cummins Papers, folder 2.

16. Michael Winship notes that in 1856, "the most common rate of royalty paid by Ticknor and Fields was 10 percent of the retail price," although he stresses that there were other arrangements as well (*American Literary Publishing in the Mid-Nineteenth Century: The Business of Ticknor and Fields* [Cambridge: Cambridge University Press, 1995], 134).

17. For an overview of the Jewett Company, see Lynne P. Shackelford and Everett C. Wilkie, Jr., "John P. Jewett and Company," in *American Literary Publishing Houses, 1638–1899* (*Dictionary of Literary Biography*, vol. 49), ed. Peter Dzwonkowski (Detroit: Gale Research Press, 1986), 226. For a specific analysis of Stowe's financial arrangements with Jewett, see Susan Geary, "Harriet Beecher Stowe, John P. Jewett, and Author-Publisher Relations in 1853," *Studies in the American Renaissance* (1977): 345–67.

18. See letter of C. Summer to Cummins, March 25, 1854, Cummins Papers, folder 2; and "Theatrical Chronicle," *Boston Evening Gazette*, April 1, 1854, Cummins Papers, folder 3.

19. Quoted by William B. Todd and Ann Bowden in *Tauchnitz International Editions in English, 1841–1955: A Bibliographical History* (New York: Bibliographical Society of America, 1988), 86.

20. Letter to Maria Susanna Cummins from the proofreader of *The Lamplighter*, n.d., Maria S. Cummins Papers, 1850–1865, Accession #7076, 7076-a, 7076-b, in the Clifton Waller Barrett Library of American Literature, Special Collections, University of Virginia, Charlottesville.

21. Robert J. Griffin, "Introduction" to his *The Faces of Anonymity* (New York: Palgrave, 2003), 4, 10. For a discussion of the circumstantial conversion of romantic and legal constructions of the author-subject, see David Saunders, "Dropping the Subject," in *Of Authors and Origins: Essays on Copyright Law*, ed. Brad Sherman and Alain Strowel (Oxford: Clarendon Press, 1994), 93–110.

22. The story of Davis's interactions with the two magazines is spelled out in greater detail in Sharon M. Harris, esp. 125–29; and in Ellen C. Pratofiorito, "Selling the Vision: Marketability and Audience in Antebellum American Literature" (Ph.D. diss., Rutgers University, 1998), 61–89. Harris points out that Davis also broke her exclusivity agreement with Ticknor and Fields by agreeing to write for the *Galaxy*.

23. See, e.g., *Norton's Literary Gazette*, February 15, 1854, 87; and *Bode's United States Review*, April 1854, 3.

24. Donald E. Pease, "Author," in *Critical Terms for Literary Study*, ed. Frank Lentricchia and Thomas McLaughlin (Chicago: University of Chicago Press, 1995), 108.

25. *Norton's Literary Gazette*, April 1, 1854, 180; May 1, 1854, 236; and October 16, 1854, 538.

26. *Norton's Literary Gazette*, May 1, 1854, 236; and December 15, 1854, 636.

27. *Hingham Journal*, December 15, 1854, Cummins Papers, folder 3. As with

the original edition, the illustrated *Lamplighter* was a more modest enterprise than the illustrated edition of *Uncle Tom's Cabin*, which featured one hundred new illustrations by Hammatt Billings.

28. Maria Susanna Cummins, *The Lamplighter Picture Book*, by a Lady (Boston: John P. Jewett, 1856), 30.

29. Ibid., 3, 28.

30. Jacob Blanck, ed., *The Bibliography of American Literature*, 9 vols. (New Haven, Conn.: Yale University Press, 1955–91), 2:366.

31. Quoted in Stephen A. Hirsch, "Uncle Tomitudes: The Popular Reaction to *Uncle Tom's Cabin*," *Studies in the American Renaissance* 2 (1978): 318.

32. On Boston as an abolitionist publishing center, see Eric Gardner, "'This Attempt of Their Sister': Harriet Wilson's *Our Nig* from Printer to Readers," *New England Quarterly* 66 (June 1993): 228–33. Gardner's research suggests that most of the original readers of *Our Nig* were children under the age of twenty; like *The Lamplighter Picture Book*, its blend of religion and abolition appealed to a young audience.

33. Paul D. Swanwick to Cummins, July 28, 1854, Cummins Papers, folder 2.

34. John P. Jewett to Cummins, December 13, 1854, Cummins Papers, folder 2.

35. "Publications," 240.

36. Other reviews also employed this nationalist rhetoric; the editors of *Godey's Lady's Book*, for example, noted their pleasure on seeing that the book had sold thirty-five thousand copies while also calling it "one of the best and purest of its class that has emanated from an American mind" ("Literary Notices," *Godey's Magazine and Lady's Book* 49 [July 1854]: 84).

37. Maria Cummins to Maria Franklin Kittredge Cummins, April 9 and 13, 1860, reprinted in Heidi L. M. Jacobs, "Maria Susanna Cummins's London Letters: April 1860," *Legacy* 19 (2002): 245–50.

38. Charles A. Madison, *Irving to Irving: Author-Publisher Relations, 1800–1974* (New York: R. R. Bowker, 1974), 27–28.

39. Contract between Maria S. Cummins and William D. Ticknor and Co., March 20, 1860; and contract between Maria S. Cummins and J. E. Tilton and Co., March 22, 1864, and April 20, 1864, Cummins Papers, folder 2.

40. Financial statements sent to Thomas Cummins from Houghton Mifflin indicate that he received $12.00 for their sales of *The Lamplighter* in 1896, $7.10 for seventy-one copies in 1897; and $9.40 for ninety-four copies in 1898 (Cummins Papers, folder 4).

41. *The Bibliography of American Literature* indicates that no new editions of *The Lamplighter* appeared after Jewett's bankruptcy, though *The National Union Catalog* indicates that Houghton Mifflin reprinted the novel in 1882, 1883, 1887, 1888, 1891, and 1894, along with the New York publishers J. B. Alden (1888), W. L. Allison (1889), Butler Brothers (189[?]), T. Y. Crowell (189[?]), Grosset and Dunlap (1890[?]), F. M. Lupton (1898[?]), and the Chicago publisher D. C. Cook (189[?]).

42. James J. Barnes, *Authors, Publishers and Politicians: The Quest for an Anglo-American Copyright Agreement, 1815–1854* (Columbus: Ohio State University Press, 1974), 172.

43. *Bibliography of American Literature*, 2:364.

44. William Seaman, *The Lamplighter, or, The Blind Girl and Little Gerty* (London: T. H. Lacy, 1854), 72.

45. See Yvonne Wellink, "American Sentimental Bestsellers in Holland in the Nineteenth Century," in *Something Understood: Studies in Anglo-Dutch Literary*

Translation, ed. Bart Westerweel and Theo D'haen (Amsterdam: Rodopi, 1990), 276–80, 287. Wellink discusses translations of *The Lamplighter* published in 1878 and 1902.

46. Tighe Hopkins, "'The Tauchnitz' Edition: The Story of a Popular Publisher," *Pall Mall Magazine* 25 (1901): 200. The article quotes another letter from Cummins praising Tauchnitz for his "uniform courtesy."

47. Henry James, *A Small Boy and Others* (New York: Scribner's, 1913), 77–78.

48. A review quoted in one of Jewett's advertisements, for example, notes that "it is quite equal, to say the least, to 'Wide, Wide World,' though not what would be called a religious novel" (*Christian Review* 19 [April 1854]: 158).

49. Baym, "Introduction" to *The Lamplighter*, xvii.

50. Orm Øverland, Introduction to Drude Krog Janson, *A Saloonkeeper's Daughter*, tr. Gerald Thorson (Baltimore: Johns Hopkins University Press, 2002), xxvii–iii; Buell, *New England Literary Culture*, 82; Habegger, 202–3.

51. All citations are to the Rutgers edition of *The Lamplighter*, cited in note 1 above, and will be given parenthetically.

52. "A Chapter upon Letters and Letter-Writers," *Ladies' Repository* 16 (February 1856): 70.

53. Grier, 32.

54. Bell, *Culture, Genre, and Literary Vocation*, 153; Jennifer Camden, "Domestic Gothic: Plot and Providence in *The Lamplighter*," unpublished paper delivered at the SSAWW conference, Forth Worth, Tex., September 23, 2003; Amy Schrager Lang, *The Syntax of Class: Writing Inequality in Nineteenth-Century America* (Princeton, N.J.: Princeton University Press, 2003); Cindy Weinstein, "'A Sort of Adopted Daughter': Family Relations in *The Lamplighter*," *ELH* 68 (2001): 1023–47.

55. Weinstein, 1023, 1042.

56. Weinstein, 1025. Kaplan's own comments are in "Manifest Domesticity," 601.

57. This ancestral home bears striking similarity to that to which Holgrave and Phoebe retire at the end of Hawthorne's *The House of the Seven Gables*; indeed, Cummins's enunciation of the burden of history is complementary to Hawthorne's, although Hawthorne is more concerned about the effects of trying to repress the past.

Chapter 4

1. Bronson Alcott, *The Journals of Bronson Alcott*, ed. Odell Shepard (Boston: Little Brown, 1938), 337.

2. For a detailed reading of the parlor theatricals in "Behind a Mask" and others of Alcott's works, see Alan L. Ackerman, *The Portable Theater: American Literature and the Nineteenth-Century Stage* (Baltimore: Johns Hopkins University Press, 1999), 155–80.

3. Louisa May Alcott, *Hospital Sketches*, in Louisa May Alcott, *Alternative Alcott*, ed. Elaine Showalter (New Brunswick, N.J.: Rutgers University Press, 1988), 43. The significance of this scene is underscored by the fact that James Redpath reprinted it in *On Picket Duty and Other Tales* (1864), a collection of Alcott stories that he published as part of a dime novel series designed for Union soldiers.

4. Ibid., 62.

5. Louisa May Alcott to Miss Churchill, Christmas Day [1878?], in L. M. Alcott, *Selected Letters*, 232.

6. Louisa May Alcott to Mary Elizabeth Waterman, November 6, 1863, in L. M. Alcott, *Selected Letters*, 95.

7. Louisa May Alcott, "Happy Women," in L. M. Alcott, *Alternative Alcott*, 205.

8. Louisa May Alcott, *Work*, in L. M. Alcott, *Alternative Alcott*, 336, 339–40, 344–45.

9. Debra Bernardi has provided one way to theorize such a collapse in her concept of "domestic horror," which she suggests can lead to a reading of *Little Women* that is both sensational and domestic ("'A Bit Sensational' or 'Simple and True': Domestic Horror and the Politics of Genre," *Legacy* 16 [1999]: 138–39).

10. Elaine Showalter, "Introduction" to L. M. Alcott, *Alternative Alcott*, ix.

11. Judith Fetterley, "*Little Women*: Alcott's Civil War," *Feminist Studies* 5 (1979): 369; Elizabeth Young, *Disarming the Nation: Women's Writing and the American Civil War* (Chicago: University of Chicago Press, 1999), 71; Lora Romero, "Domesticity and Fiction," in *The Columbia History of the American Novel*, ed. Emory Elliott (New York: Columbia University Press, 1991), 121.

12. Alice Fahs contextualizes *Hospital Sketches* in *The Imagined Civil War: Literature of the North and South, 1861–1865* (Chapel Hill: University of North Carolina Press, 2001), and in her excellent introduction to her edition of the text (Boston: Bedford/St. Martin's, 2004, 1–49).

13. Although my emphasis here will be on realism rather than "genius," I am sympathetic to Gustavus Stadler's reading of Alcott's authorship as bringing together genius and sentiment, and, more specifically, finding in *Little Women* a "hybridization of the tragic sentimental heroine and the tragic romantic genius" that in turn creates "a model of authorship in which 'consumption' becomes productive, becomes the position of authorship" ("Louisa May Alcott's Queer Geniuses," *American Literature* 71 [December 1999]: 670–71).

14. Madeleine Stern, "Introduction" to Louisa May Alcott, *Behind a Mask: The Unknown Thrillers of Louisa May Alcott*, ed. Madeleine Stern (New York: William Morrow, 1975), xx–xxi.

15. Ibid., xix.

16. For the full text of the Ostend Manifesto and a summary of attempts to annex Cuba, see the University of Virginia's on-line *American History Leaflets* at http://xroads.virginia.edu/~HYPER/HNS/Ostend/ostend.html. See also Antonio de la Cova, "Filibusters and Freemasons: The Sworn Obligation," *Journal of the Early Republic* 17 (spring 1997): 95–120; and Allan Nevins, *Ordeal of the Union: A House Dividing 1852–1857* (New York: Scribners, 1947), chap. 10.

17. Louisa May Alcott, "Pauline's Passion," in L. M. Alcott, *Behind a Mask*, 119. All subsequent citations to this story are to this edition and will be given parenthetically in the text.

18. *Hospital Sketches* also alludes to Young America when Periwinkle describes Thomas Crawford's "Armed Liberty" at the Capitol, which stands "flat in the mud, with Young America most symbolically making dirt pies, and chip forts, in its shadows" (L. M. Alcott, *Alternative Alcott*, 54). For more on Young America, see Edward L. Widmer, *Young America: The Flowering of Democracy in New York City* (New York: Oxford University Press, 2000).

19. Louisa May Alcott, *Louisa May Alcott on Race, Sex, and Slavery*, ed. Sarah Elbert (Boston: Northeastern University Press, 1997), xxiv. Elbert, who is specifically discussing Alcott's story "M. L.," in turn draws on Susan Gillman's essay "The Mulatto, Tragic or Triumphant? The Nineteenth-Century Race Melodrama," in *The Culture of Sentiment*, ed. Shirley Samuels (New York: Oxford, 1992), 224–25.

20. Gilbert also specifically asks why he allows himself to stay in the presence

of Pauline "to wound and be wounded by the hand that once caressed me" (126), and Pauline explains to Manuel how to "wound" Gilbert "deeply" through "daily torment" (135).

21. Young, 72. Young admits that this is a temporary freedom: *Little Women* and its sequels constitute a return to themes of discipline and constraint, with a matriarchy in which the wounded soldier becomes the dying female child (Beth) and the heroic soldier a masculinized woman (Jo when she cuts her hair).

22. Ibid., 87.

23. Louisa May Alcott to Alfred Whitman, June 22, 1862, in L. M. Alcott, *Selected Letters*, 79.

24. T. P. [Louisa May Alcott] to Mrs. Chick [Caroline Dall], September 21, [1864], reprinted in Helen R. Deese, ed., "Louisa May Alcott's *Moods*: A New Archival Discovery," *New England Quarterly* 76 (September 2003): 454.

25. Louisa May Alcott, *Moods*, ed. Sarah Elbert (New Brunswick, N.J.: Rutgers University Press, 1991), 8, 10. All subsequent citations to this edition (which reprints the entire first edition and excerpts from the revised edition) will be given parenthetically in this text.

26. Elbert, "Introduction" to L. M. Alcott, *Moods*, xv–xvi.

27. Ibid., xxxix.

28. For a discussion of the daguerreotype as a fictional talisman, see Susan S. Williams, *Confounding Images: Photography and Portraiture in Antebellum American Fiction* (Philadelphia: University of Pennsylvania Press, 1997).

29. Herman Melville, *Typee*, ed. John Bryant (New York: Penguin, 1996), 248.

30. Louisa May Alcott to Abigail May Alcott, December 25, 1864, in L. M. Alcott, *Selected Letters*, 106.

31. Henry James, review of Alcott's *Moods*, *North American Review* 101 (July 1865), reprinted in L. M. Alcott, *Moods*, 223–24.

32. T. P. [Louisa May Alcott] to Mrs. Chick [Caroline Dall], September 13, 1864, in Deese, 451.

33. Courtney, xiii.

34. Sarah Elbert makes this connection, noting that Richter's novel *Jubelsnoir* includes a similarly beautiful and simple anniversary celebration (*Hunger for Home*, 127).

35. *Hospital Sketches* similarly critiques art that is not realistic. Entering Washington for the first time, Tribulation Periwinkle meditates "upon the perfection which Art had attained in America—having just passed a bronze statue of some hero, who looked like a black Methodist minister, in a cocked hat, above the waist, and a tipsy squire below; while his horse stood like an opera dancer, on one leg" (L. M. Alcott, *Alternative Alcott*, 18). The sarcasm here stems from the fact that the statue is visually incongruent (mixing races and class hierarchies) and that the "hero," although common, bears no resemblance to real life. The statuary in the Capitol Rotunda she finds equally unsatisfying; it is "massive and concrete" but so generic that one could not discern whether the subject was "Columbus, Cato, or Cockelorum Tibby, the tragedian." The portraits of "expiring patriots," meanwhile, were nothing more than a blur of "ruffled shirts," "torn banners, bomb shells, and buff and blue arms and legs" (54).

36. Louisa May Alcott, "The Hawthorne," in *Louisa May Alcott: An Intimate Anthology* (New York: Doubleday, 1997), 147–49.

37. For a full discussion of this falling-out, see Claudia Durst Johnson, "Discord in Concord," in Idol and Ponder, 104–20. Johnson points out that *Hospital Sketches* was published shortly after Hawthorne's "Chiefly about War Matters,"

with Alcott's pro-Union piece being much more successful than Hawthorne's more skeptical account. Hawthorne also remained loyal to his friend Franklin Pierce at a time when abolitionists such as the Alcotts saw Pierce as a traitor to the Union cause.

38. Brodhead, *The School of Hawthorne*, 9, 11.

39. "Literary," *Harper's Weekly* 9 (January 21, 1865): 35; B. Alcott, 396.

40. L. M. Alcott, *Moods*, 224.

41. See letters to Annie Maria Lawrence, February 3, 1865; Moncure Daniel Conway, February 18, 1865; and Mr. Ayer, March 19, 1865, in L. M. Alcott, *Selected Letters*, 107–10.

42. In 1863, the year before she published *Moods*, Alcott acknowledged that her stilted use of African American dialect in her short story "My Contraband" resulted in part from her reliance on a faulty source. She used a letter written by Frances Dana Barker Gage about slaves in the Sea Islands of South Carolina and knew that "perhaps she was mistaken, in the locality, [as] women often are inaccurate when their sympathies are at work." See letter to Thomas Wentworth Higginson, November 12, 1863, in L. M. Alcott, *Selected Letters*, 96.

43. Nancy Schnog has shown how Alcott and other women writers used the economy of moods to tap into masculine romantic ideals that in turn allowed them to "put behind them the legacy of the woman writer as domestic moralist or professional hack" (105). See "Changing Emotions: Moods and the Nineteenth-Century American Woman Writer," in *Inventing the Psychological*, ed. Joel Pfister and Nancy Schnog (New Haven, Conn.: Yale University Press, 1997), 84–109.

44. Nathaniel Hawthorne, *The Scarlet Letter*, Vol. 1 of Hawthorne, *The Centenary Edition of the Works of Nathaniel Hawthorne*, ed. William Charvat et al. (Columbus: Ohio State University Press, 1962), 37.

45. Henry James, *The American* (New York: Charles Scribner's, 1922), xvii–viii.

46. Brodhead, *School of Hawthorne*, 154.

47. Henry James, "Alphonse Daudet," quoted in Brodhead, *School of Hawthorne*, 154.

48. For a comprehensive survey of this credo, particularly in relation to language, see Madeleine Stern, "Louisa Alcott's Self-Criticism," *Studies in the American Renaissance* 10 (1985): 333–43.

49. Louisa May Alcott to Mary E. Channing Higginson, October 18, 1868, in L. M. Alcott, *Selected Letters*, 118.

50. Margaret R. Higonnet, "Civil Wars and Sexual Territories," in *Arms and the Woman: War, Gender, and Literary Representation*, ed. Helen M. Cooper, Adrienne Auslander Munich, and Susan Merrill Squier (Chapel Hill: University of North Carolina Press, 1989), 89.

51. Louisa May Alcott, *Little Women*, ed. Anne Hiebert Alton (Peterborough, Ontario: Broadview Press, 2001), 191. All citations to *Little Women* will be to this edition and will be given parenthetically in the text. Young reads this metaphorical amputation as a counterpoint to the amputations that Alcott describes in *Hospital Sketches*. In the sketches soldiers are feminized amputees attended by masculinized nurses, while Jo here becomes more masculine by virtue of a symbolic amputation (100).

52. Nancy Glazener discusses the distinction between "domestic realism" and "high realism" in *Reading for Realism*.

53. Higonnet, 81.

54. Mary P. Ryan, *The Empire of the Mother: American Writing about Domesticity 1830–1860* (Binghamton, N.Y.: Haworth Press, 1982). For other important discussions

about the connection between domesticity and imperialism, see Kaplan, 581–606; and Baym, *American Women Writers.*

55. Sofer, "Carry[ing] a Yankee Girl to Glory," 42. Sofer sees this move as more feminist than I do since she thinks that it caters to women especially; the evocation of "genius" with "fellows," however, seems to reinscribe antebellum associations between masculinity and genius.

Chapter 5

1. Gail Hamilton, *A Battle of the Books* (Cambridge: Hurd and Houghton, 1870), 281. Subsequent citations will be to this edition and will be given parenthetically in the text. Excerpts of this book are also included in Gail Hamilton, *Gail Hamilton: Selected Writings,* ed. Susan Coultrap-McQuin (New Brunswick, N. J.: Rutgers University Press, 1992).

2. See, for instance, Katherine Adams, "Freedom and Ballgowns: Elizabeth Keckley and the Work of Domesticity," *Arizona Quarterly* 57 (winter 2001): 45–87; and Xiomara Santamarina, "Behind the Scenes of Black Labor: Elizabeth Keckley and the Scandal of Publicity," *Feminist Studies* 28 (fall 2002): 515–37. Adams focuses on Keckley's role in constructing national domestic ideals by, for example, making the dresses in which Mary Lincoln would appear with the "first family"; Santamarina focuses on Keckley's "literary reformulation of black female agency along the lines of labor" by making her work produce "social, rather than simply monetary, value and credibility" (519, 521).

3. Adams, 58.

4. Thomas, 38, 41. The text of the Fourteenth Amendment can be found online at http://www.law.cornell.edu/constitution/constitution.amendmentxiv.html.

5. Fanny Fern's essay "Gail Hamilton" tries to dispel this characterization of Dodge as antidomestic: "She is also a living, breathing, brilliant refutation of the absurd notion that a woman with brains must necessarily be ignorant of, or disdain, the every-day domestic virtues. When she writes of house-keeping and kindred matters, she knows what she is talking about. All the New England virtues of thrift, executiveness, thoroughness—in short, '*faculty*'—are exemplified in her daily practice. Well may there be sunshine inside her house" (Parton et al., 219).

6. Sophia Hawthorne to Annie Fields, August 3, 1868, in Randall Stewart, "Mrs. Hawthorne's Financial Difficulties," *More Books* 21 (February 1946): 51.

7. Elizabeth Keckley, *Behind the Scenes: Thirty Years a Slave and Four Years in the White House,* ed. Frances Smith Foster (Urbana and Chicago: University of Illinois Press, 2001), 52. Subsequent citations to this text will be to this edition and will be given parenthetically within the text.

8. Peterson; Frances Smith Foster, *Written by Herself: Literary Production by African American Women, 1746–1892* (Bloomington: Indiana University Press, 1993).

9. M. P. Ryan, 14.

10. Patricia J. Williams, "Alchemical Notes: Reconstructing Ideals from Deconstructed Rights," in *Feminist Legal Theory: Foundations,* ed. D. Kelly Weisberg (Philadelphia: Temple University Press, 1993), 498; and *The Alchemy of Race and Rights* (Cambridge: Harvard University Press, 1991), 21.

11. Jennifer Fleischner, *Mrs. Lincoln and Mrs. Keckly* (New York: Broadway Books, 2003). This biography posits that Mary Lincoln and Keckley were related by marriage; that Keckley's biological father was her master; and that Keckley really

signed her name Keckly and hence has a different published and personal "voice." I am retaining the published spelling since it is in that form that Keckley presented herself as a public author.

12. Jennifer Fleischner, *Mastering Slavery: Memory, Family, and Identity in Women's Slave Narratives* (New York: New York University Press, 1996), 93.

13. Rafia Zafar, *We Wear the Mask: African Americans Write American Literature, 1760–1870* (New York: Columbia University Press, 1997), 182.

14. For a particularly fine reading of Keckley's rhetoric of inversion, see Lori Merish, *Sentimental Materialism: Gender, Commodity Culture, and Nineteenth-Century American Literature* (Durham, N.C.: Duke University Press, 2000), 251–58; see also Fleischner's discussion of Mrs. Lincoln's "deployment as Other" in *Mastering Slavery*, esp. 101–3. Young points out that Keckley also employs rhetorical doubling with the president; see 128–32.

15. Foster includes a copy of the *Chicago Evening Journal* letter in her edition of Keckley's *Behind the Scenes*, 51.

16. Priscilla Wald, *Constituting Americans: Cultural Anxiety and Narrative Form* (Durham, N.C.: Duke University Press, 1995), 69.

17. Young, 129.

18. As Thomas puts it, "When two people, of whatever social class, shake hands to seal an agreement, they symbolically enact an equal standing, at least in terms of this particular transaction. Indeed, by handing over their reputations as trustworthy people to one another, they submit themselves to be measured by the same standard of accountability. This ritual act dramatizes a crucial aspect of contract's promise" (32–33).

19. P. J. Williams, "Alchemical Notes," 498–99.

20. Harriet Jacobs, 45; Michele Birnbaum, *Race, Work and Desire in American Literature, 1860–1930* (Cambridge: Cambridge University Press, 2003), 39.

21. Foster cites a contemporary report of James Redpath meeting with Keckley on a daily basis to work on *Behind the Scenes*: "everybody in the [boarding]-house knew that Mrs. Keckley was writing a book on Mrs. Lincoln and that Mr. Redpath was helping her compile it" (Letter from Mrs. John Brooks to John E. Washington, quoted in "Historical Introduction" to Keckley *Behind the Scenes*, li). This letter supercedes previous scholarly assertions that Keckley worked with the abolitionist Jane Grey Swisshelm or the journalist Hamilton Busbey (see, for example, Justin G. Turner and Linda Levitt Turner, *Mary Todd Lincoln: Her Life and Letters* [New York: Alfred E. Knopf, 1972], 471 n. 1).

22. For an account of Warner and Putnam, see Ezra Greenspan, *George Palmer Putnam: Representative American Publisher* (University Park: Pennsylvania State University Press, 2000), 255–58; Louisa May Alcott to James Redpath, [July? 1863], in Alcott, *The Selected Letters*, 86.

23. For a reading of this letter that identifies Keckley as "curator" of her own collection, see Michael Berthold, "Not 'Altogether' the 'History of Myself': Autobiographical Impersonality in Elizabeth Keckley's *Behind the Scenes. Or, Thirty Years a Slave and Four Years in the White House*," *American Transcendental Quarterly* 13 (June 1999): 116.

24. Interestingly, the name J. Ball recalls the pen name, John Ball, Jr., that James Redpath used in writing reports about antebellum slaves in the abolitionist press. I have not yet been able to determine whether a real J. Ball actually existed, but the similarity provides a suggestive link between Redpath and Keckley.

25. See Fleischner, *Mastering Slavery*.

26. For fuller accounts of the reception of the book, see Fleischner, *Mrs. Lincoln*

and Mrs. Keckly, 316–18, and Foster, "Historical Introduction" to Keckley, *Behind the Scenes*, lvi.

27. Birnbaum, 30.

28. Ibid., 32.

29. Betsey Kickley, pseud., *Behind the Seams; by a Nigger Woman Who Took in Work from Mrs. Lincoln and Mrs. Davis* (New York: National News Company, 1868), 24.

30. P. J. Williams, "Alchemical Notes," 504.

31. M. P. Ryan points out that in 1855 Harper's publishing house employed "300 females to operate [the] simple levers" of the machines that produced their books (115). Herman Melville critiques this use of female labor in "The Tartarus of Maids," in which women's reproductive vitality is substituted for the nine-minute process of producing paper.

32. Fanny Fern, "Gail Hamilton—Miss Dodge," in *Eminent Women of the Age*, ed. Parton et al., 204–5. In order to avoid confusion, I, like Susan Coultrap-McQuin, refer to Dodge by her legal name rather than her pen name (see Coultrap-McQuin, *Doing Literary Business*).

33. "The Pay of Authors," *Congregationalist and Boston Recorder*, October 10, 1867, 184.

34. Gail Hamilton, "My Book," in G. Hamilton, *Skirmishes and Sketches* (Boston: Ticknor and Fields, 1866), 404.

35. Mary Abigail Dodge to Mr. Wood, May 28, 1860, in G. Hamilton, *Gail Hamilton's Life in Letters*, 2 vols., ed. H. Augusta Dodge (Boston: Lee and Shepard, 1901), 1:287.

36. Gail Hamilton, *Twelve Miles from a Lemon* (New York: Harper, 1874), 181, cited in Janice G. Pulsifer, "Gail Hamilton: 1833–1896," *Essex Institute Historical Collections* 104 (1968): 179.

37. Mary Abigail Dodge to Mr. French, February 10, 1864, in G. Hamilton, *Life in Letters*, 1:372.

38. Mary Abigail Dodge to Henry James, Sr., May 7, 1864, in G. Hamilton, *Life in Letters*, 1:407.

39. B. W. Williams to Mary Abigail Dodge, October 24, 1860, in Mary Abigail Dodge Papers, folder 5, Peabody Essex Museum, Salem, Mass.

40. Nathaniel Hawthorne to James T. Fields, July 1, 1863, in Hawthorne, *The Letters, 1857–1864*, ed. Thomas Woodson, James A. Rubino, L. Neal Smith, and Norman Holmes Pearson, vol. 18 of *The Centenary Edition of the Works of Nathaniel Hawthorne* (Columbus: Ohio State University Press, 1987), 579; Sophia Hawthorne to Mary Abigail Dodge, December 1, 1865, Dodge Papers. For an inventory of Sophia Hawthorne's correspondence (though one that does not include her correspondence with Dodge), see Edwin Haviland Miller, "A Calendar of the Letters of Sophia Peabody Hawthorne," *Studies in the American Renaissance* 11 (1986): 199–281.

41. Nathaniel Hawthorne, "Civic Banquets," *Atlantic Monthly* 12 (August 1863): 195–212; Gail Hamilton, "Side-Glances at Harvard Class-Day," *Atlantic Monthly* 12 (August 1863): 242–51.

42. Mary Abigail Dodge to Sophia Hawthorne, July 14, 1863, Berg Collection of English and American Literature, The New York Public Library, Astor, Lenox and Tilden Foundations. In an earlier letter to her sister Elizabeth Peabody, Sophia describes a portrait of Hawthorne that she also finds dark: "It is very melancholy & contemplative, without the unfathomable sunshine, but it is like him sometimes—& bears a wonderful resemblance to the sad reserved face of his father in the miniature" (March 6, 1851, in Hurst, 234).

43. Sophia Hawthorne to Mary Abigail Dodge, November 26, 1865, Dodge Papers. Earlier letters indicate that Sophia found in this "King" a soul mate as well as someone to admire: "No two minds were ever more completely independent & individual than Mr. Hawthorne's & mine," she wrote to her mother in 1843 (Hurst, 70).

44. Coultrap-McQuin, *Doing Literary Business*, 125.

45. Rebecca Harding Davis to James T. Fields, November [1867], in Sharon M. Harris, 139.

46. Dodge in turn quotes Mary Russell Mitford (whom she renames "Mitbridge" in *A Battle*), who makes this observation in a letter to Mrs. Jennings in *The Life of Mary Russell Mitford*, ed. A. G. K. L'Estrange, 2 vols. (New York: Harper, 1870): 2:346.

47. Sophia Hawthorne to Mary Abigail Dodge, August 20, 1868, Dodge Papers.

48. Julie E. Hall, "'Coming to Europe,' Coming to Authorship: Sophia Hawthorne and Her *Notes in England and Italy*," *Legacy* 19 (June 2003): 139. Hall cites a letter from Nathaniel Hawthorne to Francis Bennoch dated November 29, 1859.

49. Mary Abigail Dodge to Sophia Hawthorne, September 2, 1868, Berg Collection.

50. P. J. Williams, "Alchemical Notes," 499; P. J. Williams, *Alchemy of Race and Rights*, 146.

51. "Current Literature," *Overland Monthly* 4 (June 1870): 581.

52. "Editor's Literary Record," *Harper's Monthly Magazine* 40 (May 1870): 929.

53. "Literature of the Day," *Lippincott's Magazine* 5 (June 1870): 686.

54. "Literature and Art," *Galaxy* 9 (May 1870): 710.

55. Sophia Hawthorne to Elizabeth Peabody, December 4, 1868, Ohio State Libraries Rare Book Collection, Columbus, Ohio.

56. Hall, 143–44; Annamaria Formichella Elsden, *Roman Fever: Domesticity and Nationalism in Nineteenth-Century American Women's Writing* (Columbus: Ohio State University Press, 2004), 71–94. Elsden specifically sees her as presenting "herself as the artist she wanted to be" (94).

57. Mary Abigail Dodge to James Redpath, August 13, 1886, and October 14, 1886, Dodge Papers, folder 3.

58. Gail Hamilton, "An American Queen," *North American Review* 143 (October 1886): 329–45.

59. Dodge to Redpath, August 13, 1886, Dodge Papers, folder 3.

60. Thomas, 34–38.

61. P. J. Williams, *Alchemy of Race and Rights*, 233–34.

62. Berthold, 111.

63. Gail Hamilton, *Biography of James G. Blaine* (Norwich, Conn.: Henry Bill, 1895), 142.

64. Sylvia D. Hoffert, "Jane Grey Swisshelm, Elizabeth Keckley, and the Significance of Race Consciousness in American Women's History," *Journal of Women's History* 13 (2001): 27.

65. William Charvat, *The Profession of Authorship in America, 1800–1870* (New York: Columbia University Press, 1992), 296.

Chapter 6

1. Elizabeth Stuart Phelps Ward, "The Rejected Manuscript," *Harper's New Monthly Magazine* 86 (January 1893): 282–94. Subsequent citations will be to this

edition. The story was also reprinted in Phelps's *The Empty House and Other Stories* (Boston: Houghton Mifflin, 1910), 238–73.

2. Elizabeth Stuart Phelps, *Chapters from a Life* (Boston: Houghton, Mifflin, 1896), 11. Subsequent citations will be given parenthetically in the text.

3. See Susan Coultrap-McQuin, "Elizabeth Stuart Phelps: The Cultural Context of a Nineteenth-Century Professional Writer" (Ph.D. diss., University of Iowa, 1979), 203; and letter from Elizabeth Stuart Phelps Ward to Henry Oscar Houghton, May 4, 1894, Houghton Papers, Houghton Library, bMS Am 1648 (903). This and subsequent letters from this collection are published by permission of the Houghton Library, Harvard University, Cambridge, Mass.

4. James D. Hart, *The Popular Book: A History of America's Literary Taste* (New York: Oxford University Press, 1950), 163, 170.

5. Elizabeth Stuart Phelps Ward to William Hayes Ward, August 5, 1893, Elizabeth Stuart Phelps Ward Papers (MSS 229), Peabody Essex Museum, Salem, Mass. For an overview of Phelps's relation to her publishers, see Coultrap-McQuin, *Doing Literary Business*, 168–92.

6. In the only other reading of this story that I know, Anne Boyd emphasizes a more univocal reading of the image, claiming that this illustration is a "potent image of the lifeless woman writer, killed by neglect and the exhaustion of motherhood," that "remains the dominant one of the story" (*Writing for Immortality*, 176).

7. In addition to Coultrap-McQuin, see, for example, Ellen Ballou, *The Building of the House: Houghton Mifflin's Formative Years* (Boston: Houghton Mifflin, 1970), 424–25, who mentions the "critical and demanding" Phelps in the context of writers "plaguing" Henry Mifflin about advertising.

8. George Bainton, ed., *The Art of Authorship* (New York: D. Appleton, 1890), 67.

9. Phelps does not mention the death of Thompson directly in *Chapters from a Life*, although the serialized version of the book included a photograph of the Andover class of 1861, which includes "Lieutenant S. H. Thompson, son of the late Professor William Thompson of East Windsor Seminary" ("Chapters from a Life," *McClures Magazine* 6 [March 1896]: 362). His identity is made clear in a retrospective of her work that reports, "Elizabeth was only seventeen when her first deep attachment was formed. The object of her affection, a handsome and spirited boy of nineteen, a son of Dr. Thompson of Hartford, enlisted in the Civil War and was killed" ("The Fragile Genius of Elizabeth Stuart Phelps," *Current Literature* 50 [March 1911]: 1).

10. Austin Phelps, "Memorial," in H. Trusta [Elizabeth Stuart Phelps], *The Last Leaf from the Sunny Side* (Boston: Phillips, Sampson, 1853), 83. In *Chapters from a Life*, Phelps reports, "My first distinct vision of this kind of a mother gives her by the nursery lamp, reading to us her own stories, written for ourselves, never meant to go beyond that little public or two, and illustrated in colored crayons by her own pencil" (13).

11. Elizabeth Stuart Phelps, "A Sacrifice Consumed," *Harper's New Monthly Magazine* 28 (January 1864): 235–40; "The Bend," *Harper's New Monthly Magazine* 29 (August 1864): 323–35; "My Refugees," *Harper's New Monthly Magazine* 29 (November 1864): 754–63. Subsequent citations to these stories will be given parenthetically in the text. Interestingly, one of Phelps's last stories was another Civil War tale that appeared in *Harper's*, although in this case the focus is on Civil War veterans and the need to memorialize the dead ("Comrades," *Harper's New Monthly Magazine* 123 [August 1911]: 398–406).

12. Gail Hamilton, "A Call to My Country-Women," *Atlantic Monthly* 11 (March 1863): 347.

13. 1 Kings 18:38, King James version. See also 2 Chron. 7:1: "Now when Solomon had made an end of praying, the fire came down from heaven, and consumed the burnt offering and the sacrifices; and the glory of the Lord filled the house." The first meaning of "holocaust," according to the OED, is "A sacrifice wholly consumed by fire; a whole burnt offering."

14. Jeremiah Taylor, *The Sacrifice Consumed: Life of Edward Hamilton Brewer, Lately a Soldier in the Army of the Potomac* (Boston: Henry Hoyt, 1863), viii, 70, 69.

15. The fact that John dies at Antietam "'long with Burnside down by the Bridge" (239) makes this endurance somewhat ironic; Burnside unwittingly created a large number of unnecessary casualties by ordering his unit across the bridge, where they became standing targets, rather than across the river.

16. Higonnet, 89.

17. See Alcott, *Hospital Sketches*, 106.

18. See, for example, Nancy Schnog, "'The Comfort of My Fancying': Loss and Recuperation in *The Gates Ajar*," *Arizona Quarterly* 49 (1993): 127–54; Lisa Long, "'The Corporeity of Heaven': Rehabilitating the Civil War Body in *The Gates Ajar*," *American Literature* 69 (1997): 781–811; Gail Smith, "From the Seminary to the Parlor: The Popularization of Hermeneutics in *The Gates Ajar*," *Arizona Quarterly* 54 (summer 1998): 99–133; and Nina Baym, introduction to Elizabeth Stuart Phelps, *Three Spiritualist Novels*, ed. Baym (Urbana: University of Illinois Press, 2000), vii–xxiii.

19. Charles Lamb, "Distant Correspondents," in *Essays of Elia, First Series*, ed. George Armstrong Wauchope (Boston: Ginn, 1904), 192.

20. In *Chapters from a Life*, Phelps reports that she had gone to Lawrence only as a tourist, "a place to drive to" for ice cream (88). But the "curdling horror" of the fires had made her want to learn and write about the place in detail. Like the narrator in Rebecca Harding Davis's "Life in the Iron Mills," she had previously seen the mill only through a high-art, aestheticizing vision: "We did not think about the mill-people; they seemed as far from us as the coal-miners of a vague West" (89). Like that narrator, her goal in "The Tenth of January" was to make her readers see and feel the tragedy. Davis created that vision by focusing on a frustrated male artist, while Phelps focused on a mill girl killed in the fire. Asenath (Sene) Martyn, like Deb in "Iron Mills," is physically deformed, with a scarred face and a hunched back. Although Deb loves Hugh Wolfe, he never recognizes her love or sees her as a sexual woman, focusing instead on the female statue he sculpts out of the refuse of the iron mill. Sene, on the other hand, is allowed to fall in love with her beloved Dick, although in the end she allows her more beautiful sister to escape the fire—and into Dick's arms. For a discussion of the story's relation to "Iron Mills," see Mari Jo Buhle and Florence Howe, "Afterword" to Phelps, *The Silent Partner and "The Tenth of January"* (Old Westbury, N.Y.: Feminist Press, 1983), 373.

21. Elizabeth Stuart Phelps, "Whittier," *Century Magazine* 45 (January 1893): 363.

22. Importantly, Avis learns about this wounding by reading about it in the newspaper. The actual line reads, "Ostrander, Philip, surgeon: in the lungs." See Phelps, *The Story of Avis*, ed. Carol Farley Kessler (New Brunswick, N. J.: Rutgers University Press, 1985), 85. Subsequent citations will be to this edition and will be cited parenthetically in the text.

23. Naomi Sofer, *Making the "America of Art": Cultural Nationalism and Nineteenth-Century American Women Writers* (Columbus: Ohio State University Press, 2005),

195. Sofer relates this war effort, and Avis's inability to do art after her marriage, to Phelps's critique of the cultural nationalism being promoted at this time by male Northern intellectuals.

24. Sir William Hamilton, *The Metaphysics of Sir William Hamilton*, ed. Francis Bowen (Cambridge, Mass.: Sever, Francis, 1868), 523.

25. Austin Phelps, "Christian Character a Power in the Redemption of the World," quoted in Daniel Day Williams, *The Andover Liberals* (Morningside Heights, N.Y.: King's Crown Press, 1941), 25.

26. For more on Phelps's notion of "feminine strength," see Cognard-Black, *Narrative in the Professional Age*. On the connection between benevolence and individualism, see Susan Ryan, *The Grammar of Good Intentions: Benevolence and Racial Identity in Antebellum American Literature* (Ithaca, N.Y.: Cornell University Press, 2003).

27. Higonnet, 81.

28. Baym, introduction to Phelps, *Three Spiritualist Novels*, xii.

29. Elizabeth Stuart Phelps to George Eliot, February 26, 1873, reprinted in George V. Griffith, "An Epistolary Friendship: The Letters of Elizabeth Stuart Phelps to George Eliot," *Legacy* 18 (fall 2001): 95.

30. Ibid., 96.

31. Taylor, 74, 77.

32. Lyde Cullen Sizer, *The Political Work of Northern Women Writers and the Civil War, 1850–1872* (Chapel Hill: University of North Carolina Press, 2000), 77.

33. Annie Nathan Meyer, "The Problem of the Novel," *Arena* 87 (February 1897): 451. Meyer helped found Barnard College and was herself a novelist as well as an essayist.

34. Elizabeth Stuart Phelps [Ward] to Henry Oscar Houghton, August 12, 1894, Houghton Papers, Houghton Library, bMS Am 1648.

35. "Fragile Genius of Elizabeth Stuart Phelps," 2.

36. On the Andover Controversy, see Francis L. Patton, "Is Andover Romanizing?" *Forum* 3 (June 1887): 327–38; Gail Hamilton, "That Everlasting Andover Controversy," *North American Review* 144 (May 1887): 477–86; and D. D. Williams, 26–30.

37. Elizabeth Stuart Phelps to John Greenleaf Whittier, April 5, 1878, Houghton Library, bMS Am 1844 (325).

38. Meyer, "Problem of the Novel," 453. Meyer goes on to list *The Story of Avis* specifically as a perfect example of the "language of the novel; the language that wrings our heart, that moves our soul, that rouses all that is most powerful in us" (455). She also cautions against overly photographic realism, on the one hand, and "false realism," on the other.

39. Quoted in Donald Pizer, "Introduction" to Pizer, ed., *Documents of American Realism and Naturalism* (Carbondale: Southern Illinois University Press, 1998), 6.

40. A review of *Chapters from a Life* contested this notion, claiming that Phelps was "an idealist of the old school, the school of Ouida on the one hand and Ruskin on the other; an idealist of the kind that is sternly opposed to the realist with an impassable bar between" ("The Autobiography of an Idealist," *Dial* 22 [January 16, 1897]: 58). However, as the reviews of *A Singular Life* indicate, this was far from a majority opinion.

41. "Book Notes," *Peterson Magazine* 6 (November 1896): 1207; "Books Received," *Godey's Magazine* 132 (February 1896): 209.

42. "The Library Table: Glimpses of the New Books," *Current Literature* 19 (April 1896): 370.

43. William Morton Payne, "Recent Fiction," *Dial* 20 (February 1, 1896): 80.

44. "Book Notes," 1211, 1207.

45. Thomas, 89. Thomas discusses *The Silent Partner* in particular.

46. Michael Davitt Bell, *The Problem of American Realism: Studies in the Cultural History of a Literary Idea* (Chicago: University of Chicago Press, 1993), 172. For a related view, see Ammons, who argues that late nineteenth-century women were united by their "avowed ambition . . . to be artists" (4).

47. Elizabeth Stuart Phelps to William Dean Howells, September 24, 1874, Houghton Library, bMS Am 1784 (515).

48. Elizabeth Stuart Phelps to William Dean Howells, February 9, 1881, Houghton Library, bMS Am 1784 (515).

49. Elizabeth Stuart Phelps to William Dean Howells, November 2, 1887, Houghton Library, bMS Am 1784 (515).

50. "Talks about the New Books," *Frank Leslie's Popular Monthly* 43 (February 1897): 237.

51. Elizabeth Stuart Phelps, *Friends: A Duet*, quoted in Carol Farley Kessler, *Elizabeth Stuart Phelps* (Boston: Twayne, 1982), 96. Kessler also points out that Phelps wrote in a letter to Richard Watson Gilder that her novella *Jack the Fisherman* owed more than half of its success "to its great moral story; as with 'Uncle Tom' on the larger plan." The review is from *The Union Signal*, quoted in Munroe Stevens, *The 'A Singular Life' Reviewed and Gloucester Vindicated* (N.p.: privately printed, 1897), 7.

52. See, for example, reviews in *Galaxy* 24 (December 1877): 855, which calls *Avis*'s "study of womanhood . . . unnatural and not attractive"; in *Harper's Monthly Magazine* 56 (January 1878): 310, which says that *Avis* is not "altogether a wholesome story" and does not give "the kind of interior experience which it is desirable that our young girls should have portrayed before them as the ideal of true love"; and in *Scribner's Monthly* 15 (December 1877): 281, which calls "Avis and the people about her . . . so superior that the mind of New York cowers before them."

53. H[enry] M[ills] Alden to Elizabeth Stuart Phelps Ward, September 22, 1905, Miscellaneous Manuscripts "A," box 1, folder 3, American Antiquarian Society, Worcester, Mass. Ironically, in the next letter in this collection, dated May 29, 1906, Alden rejects a story that Phelps had sent him.

54. Vernon Parrington, *Main Currents in American Thought*, 3 vols. (New York: Harcourt Brace, 1930), 3:61.

55. The programs for the 2001 and 2003 SSAWW conferences are archived at http://www.unl.edu/legacy/SSAWW_conf.html. The program for the 1996 Hartford conference is reprinted in *Legacy* 15 (1998): 10–14.

56. Baym, "Rewriting the Scribbling Women," 9.

57. "Fragile Genius of Elizabeth Stuart Phelps," 1.

Chapter 7

1. Constance Fenimore Woolson to John Hay, December 26, 1885, in Petry, 80.

2. Henry James to William Dean Howells, February 21, 1884, in Anesko, 243–44.

3. Constance Fenimore Woolson to Paul Hamilton Hayne, February 13, 1876, quoted in Anne E. Boyd, "Anticipating James, Anticipating Grief: Constance Fenimore Woolson's 'Miss Grief,'" in *Constance Fenimore Woolson's Nineteenth Century: Essays*, ed. Victoria Brehm (Detroit: Wayne State University Press, 2001), 196.

4. Woolson, who was a few years older than James, appears to have valued his judgments and experience while also expressing her own opinions. On her frequent solitary walks in Florence, she did not hesitate to pronounce the interior of the Duomo a "great gloomy space," but when she went there with James, she tried to admire it as he did. Similarly, she told James that she disliked the "distracted" look of the reclining statues in the Sacristy of San Lorenzo but then had to put up with his moving off to look at a fresco, "(probably) to recover from my horrible ignorance." These examples are taken from the excerpts of Woolson's journals reprinted in Clare Benedict, *Constance Fenimore Woolson*, vol. 2 of *Five Generations (1785–1923)* (London: Ellis, 1929), 187–88. For his part, James clearly admired Woolson as an author and a person. In his sister's eyes, at least, it was a romantic attachment: "Henry is somewhere on the continent flirting with Constance," Alice wrote to their brother William in 1888 (Alice James to William James, November 4, 1888, in Alice James, *The Death and Letters of Alice James*, ed. Ruth Bernard Yeazell [Los Angeles: University of California Press, 1981], 149).

5. Cheryl B. Torsney, *Constance Fenimore Woolson: The Grief of Artistry* (Athens: University of Georgia Press, 1989), 77; Boyd, "Anticipating James," 194. See also Sharon L. Dean, *Constance Fenimore Woolson: Homeward Bound* (Knoxville: University of Tennessee Press, 1995), 82–88; and Joan Myers Weimer, "The 'Admiring Aunt' and the 'Proud Salmon of the Pond': Constance Fenimore Woolson's Struggle with Henry James," in *Critical Essays on Constance Fenimore Woolson*, ed. Cheryl B. Torsney (New York: G. K. Hall, 1992), 203–16.

6. See, for example, Constance Fenimore Woolson, *Women Artists, Women Exiles: "Miss Grief" and Other Stories*, ed. Joan Weimer (New Brunswick, N.J.: Rutgers University Press, 1988); James E. Miller, ed., *Heritage of American Literature* (San Diego: Harcourt Brace Jovanovich, 1991); Eileen Barrett and Mary Cullinan, eds., *American Women Writers: Diverse Voices in Prose since 1845* (New York: St. Martin's Press, 1992); Susan Koppelman, ed., *Two Friends and Other Nineteenth-Century Lesbian Stories by American Women Authors* (New York: Meridian, 1994); Karen L. Kilcup, ed., *Nineteenth-Century American Women Writers An Anthology* (Oxford: Blackwell Publishers, 1997); Elaine Showalter, ed., *Scribbling Women: Short Stories by 19th-Century American Women* (New Brunswick, N.J.: Rutgers University Press 1997).

7. Torsney, 75. Torsney discusses the publication history of "Miss Grief" on pages 70–72.

8. Weimer, *Women Artists, Women Exiles*, xxxix.

9. For discussions of these reciprocal influences, see Sharon Dean, "Constance Fenimore Woolson and Henry James: The Literary Relationship," *Massachusetts Studies in English* 7 (1980): 1–9; Lynda S. Boren, "'Dear Constance,' 'Dear Henry': The Woolson/James Affair—Fact, Fiction, or Fine Art?" *American Studies* 27 (1982): 457–66; Mary P. Edwards Kitterman, "Henry James and the Artist-Heroine in the Tales of Constance Fenimore Woolson," in *Nineteenth-Century Women Writers of the English-Speaking World*, ed. Rhoda B. Nathan (New York: Greenwood Press, 1986), 45–59; and Rayburn S. Moore, "The Strange Irregular Rhythm of Life: James's Late Tales and Constance Woolson," *South Atlantic Bulletin* 41 (1976): 86–93.

10. Rayburn S. Moore makes this connection in his introduction to Woolson's *For the Major and Selected Short Stories by Constance Fenimore Woolson* (New Haven, Conn.: New College and University Press, 1967), 16. As Boyd notes, there has been some implication among subsequent scholars that Woolson wrote the story after meeting James, but this is impossible, given that they met in April 1880 and the story appeared in the May issue of *Lippincott's* (192).

11. *Atlantic Monthly* 43 (January 1879), reprinted in Benedict, 54–62.

12. Henry James, "Miss Woolson," in *The American Essays*, ed. Leon Edel (Princeton, N.J.: Princeton University Press, 1956), 164, 167.

13. *Harper's Weekly* 30 (June 5, 1886): 366, quoted in Petry, 91.

14. [Henry James], "The Schönberg-Cotta Family," *Nation* 1 (September 14, 1865), 344–45.

15. For an important reading of this development, see Glazener.

16. Meyer, "Woman's Place in Letters," 135.

17. Constance Fenimore Woolson to Henry James, May 7, 1883, in Henry James, *Letters*, 4 vols., ed. Leon Edel (Cambridge, Mass.: Belknap Press of Harvard University Press, 1974–84), 3:552; Constance Fenimore Woolson to John Hay, December 26, 1885, in Petry, 80. "I am not a subject for a sculptor," she added in the letter to James; "as far as possible from it." For that reason, when she consented to sit for a portrait medallion made by Larkin G. Mead, William Dean Howells's brother-in-law, she considered it a "great sacrifice" and found the process of sitting "acutely disagreeable." The only pose that she approved of was when she was photographed from behind, with her head turned in profile. Indeed, in the same letter in which she complains to James about her portrait, she also creates a verbal picture of herself that concludes with "the back view of me as I depart from you . . . not very clearly seen" (549). For another discussion of the James letter, see Boren, 463–64. She speculates that Woolson agreed to the portrait-medallion because she anticipated that James would have one done too: "Obviously, if she cannot secure James's love, she will, by association, link their medallioned portraits in her own mind with the two Greek coins she wishes him to wear close to his heart" (464).

18. Contance Fenimore Woolson to John Hay, December 20, 1890, in Petry, 102.

19. Constance Fenimore Woolson to Clara Louise Stone Hay, March 16, 1883, in Petry, 31.

20. Constance Fenimore Woolson, "Miss Grief," in *Nineteenth-Century American Women Writers*, ed. Kilcup, 303. Further citations will refer to this edition and will be given within the text.

21. Kristin M. Comment, "Lesbian 'Impossibilities' of Miss Grief's 'Armor,'" in *Constance Fenimore Woolson's Nineteenth Century*, 213–15.

22. Torsney, focusing on Aaron's superior verbal powers, goes so far as to say that Aaronna is a messianic figure who is "a harbinger of an artistic era yet to come, when powerful women will direct their own creative destinies" (77). See also Weimer's introduction to Woolson, *Women Artists, Women Exiles*, xxxviii.

23. Brodhead, *The School of Hawthorne*, 30, 27.

24. James, *Letters*, 3:550.

25. Yet, Hawthorne's sense of his ideal reader was less a devotee like Hilda than an idealized "gentle reader"—such as John Lothrop Motley—who understood better than the average public exactly how his works ought to be taken. See Susan S. Williams, "Manufacturing Intellectual Equipment: The Tauchnitz Edition of *The Marble Faun*," in *Reading Books*, 137.

26. See Schnog, "Changing Emotions," 84–109.

27. In this sense, his reading corresponds to Woolson's private reading of James; in one letter she writes of her "despair" upon discovering "that, added to your other perfections, was the gift of writing as you do, at the first draft" (Henry James, *Letters*, 3:539). She labors at her writing, and particularly at the copying of her manuscripts, while his "gift" enables him to produce his pieces wholesale—"like the work of dreams."

28. "Introduction" to Henry James, *The Notebooks of Henry James*, ed. F. O. Matthiessen and Kenneth B. Murdock (Chicago: University of Chicago Press, 1981), xvi.

29. Paul Crumbley, "Haunting the House of Print: The Circulation of Disembodied Texts in 'Collected by a Valetudinarian' and 'Miss Grief,'" in *American Culture, Canons, and the Case of Elizabeth Stoddard*, ed. Robert McClure Smith and Ellen Weinauer (Tuscaloosa: University of Alabama Press, 2003), 95, 83–84.

30. The image of books as children for women writers has a long history in American literature, beginning with Anne Bradstreet's "The Author to Her Book." It has also been used by Cheryl Torsney to help explain Woolson's suicide: Woolson may have been suffering a "postpartum-like stress" following her completion of her novel *Horace Chase* (15).

31. Henry James, *Letters*, 3:539.

32. Ibid.,163.

33. Henry James, "The Real Thing," in *The Portable American Realism Reader*, ed. James Nagel and Tom Quirk (New York: Penguin, 1997), 254. Subsequent citations will be to this edition and will be given in the text.

34. Henry James, *Notebooks*, 102.

35. Ibid., 103.

36. See Susan Stewart, *On Longing: Narratives of the Miniature, the Gigantic, the Souvenir, the Collection* (Baltimore: Johns Hopkins University Press, 1984).

37. Sigourney, 368; Kirkland, 70.

38. Grier, 213–14.

39. For a strong reading of this passage that links the glance to the overall structure of narrative effacement in the story and to the narrator's last words, see Sam Whitsitt, "A Lesson in Reading: Henry James's 'The Real Thing,'" *Henry James Review* 16 (fall 1995): 309–11. It is also worth noting that Woolson frequently uses the word "charming" in relation to James, although sometimes with a bit of an edge to her tone. In one letter, for instance, she comments that when she writes long letters, he writes curt replies, but that when she writes a short one, "I have received a very charming letter in reply" (Henry James, *Letters*, 3:542). It is not clear here whether she, like Mrs. Monarch, wants to claim responsibility for producing this charm or whether she is condemning their letters, like the narrator of "Miss Grief," to writing charming "domestic interiors."

40. These haunting presences are akin to James's response to visiting Woolson's grave site, a "very particular spot" that he finds "tremendously, inexhaustibly touching—its effect never fails to overwhelm" (Henry James, *Letters*, 4:460).

41. Henry James, *Letters*, 3:529. Woolson was also direct and honest with James about his audacity of subject: "How did you ever dare write a portrait of a lady?" she asked (535).

42. Lawrence Buell, "American Civil War Poetry and the Meaning of Literary Commodification: Whitman, Melville, and Others," in *Reciprocal Influences*, ed. Fink and Williams, 131,132.

43. Hall, 138. Hall's essay provides an overview of critical assessments of Sophia Hawthorne.

44. John Carlos Rowe, "Nineteenth-Century United States Literary Culture and Transnationality," *PMLA* 118 (January 2003): 88

Bibliography

Ackerman, Alan L. *The Portable Theater: American Literature and the Nineteenth-Century Stage.* Baltimore: Johns Hopkins University Press, 1999.

Adams, Katherine. "Freedom and Ballgowns: Elizabeth Keckley and the Work of Domesticity." *Arizona Quarterly* 57 (winter 2001): 45–87.

Alcott, Bronson. *The Journals of Bronson Alcott.* Ed. Odell Shepard. Boston: Little Brown, 1938.

Alcott, Louisa May. *Alternative Alcott.* Ed. Elaine Showalter. New Brunswick, N.J.: Rutgers University Press, 1988.

———. *Behind a Mask: The Unknown Thrillers of Louisa May Alcott.* Ed. Madeleine Stern. New York: William Morrow, 1975.

———. "The Hawthorne." In *Louisa May Alcott: An Intimate Anthology,* 147–49. New York: Doubleday, 1997.

———. *Hospital Sketches.* Ed. Alice Fahs. Boston: Bedford/St. Martin's, 2004.

———. *Little Women.* Ed. Anne Hiebert Alton. Peterborough, Ontario: Broadview Press, 2001.

———. *Louisa May Alcott: Her Life, Letters and Journals.* Ed. Ednah P. Cheney. Boston: Roberts Brothers, 1890.

———. *Louisa May Alcott on Race, Sex, and Slavery.* Ed. Sarah Elbert. Boston: Northeastern University Press, 1997.

———. *Moods.* Ed. Sarah Elbert. New Brunswick, N.J.: Rutgers University Press, 1991.

———. *On Picket Duty, and Other Tales.* Boston: James Redpath, 1864.

———. *The Selected Letters of Louisa May Alcott.* Ed. Joel Myerson and Daniel Shealy. Boston: Little, Brown, 1987.

Ammons, Elizabeth. *Conflicting Stories: American Women Writers at the Turn into the Twentieth Century.* New York: Oxford University Press, 1992.

Amstutz, Margaret A. "Elizabeth Stoddard as Returned Californian: A Reading of the *Daily Alta California* Columns." In *American Culture, Canons, and the Case of Elizabeth Stoddard,* ed. Smith and Weinauer, 65–82.

Anesko, Michael. *Letters, Fictions, Lives: Henry James and William Dean Howells.* New York: Oxford University Press, 1997.

"Authors and Writers." *United States Literary Gazette* 1 (March 1, 1825): 346–47.

"Authorship in America." *Atlantic Monthly* 51 (June 1883): 808–18.

"The Autobiography of an Idealist." *Dial* 22 (January 16, 1897): 58.

Badaracco, Clare. "Sophia Peabody Hawthorne's Cuba Journal: Volume Three,

31 October 1834–15 March 1835." *Essex Institute Historical Collections* 118 (1982): 280–315.

Bainton, George, ed. *The Art of Authorship.* New York: D. Appleton, 1890.

Ballou, Ellen. *The Building of the House: Houghton Mifflin's Formative Years.* Boston: Houghton Mifflin, 1970.

Bardes, Barbara A., and Suzanne Gossett. "Sarah J. Hale, Selective Promoter of Her Sex." In *A Living of Words: American Women in Print Culture,* ed. Susan Albertine, 18–34. Knoxville: University of Tennessee Press, 1995.

Barnes, James J. *Authors, Publishers and Politicians: The Quest for an Anglo-American Copyright Agreement, 1815–1854.* Columbus: Ohio State University Press, 1974.

Barrett, Eileen, and Mary Cullinan, eds. *American Women Writers: Diverse Voices in Prose since 1845.* New York: St. Martin's Press, 1992.

Barthes, Roland. "The Death of the Author." In *The Book History Reader,* ed. Finkelstein and McCleery, 221–24.

Battersby, Christine. *Gender and Genius: Towards a Feminist Aesthetics.* Bloomington: Indiana University Press, 1989.

Bayard, Mary Temple. "Woman in Journalism." In *The Congress of Women,* ed. Eagle, 435–37.

Baym, Nina. "Again and Again, the Scribbling Women." In *Hawthorne and Women,* ed. Idol and Ponder, 20–35.

———. *American Women Writers and the Work of History, 1790–1860.* New Brunswick, N.J.: Rutgers University Press, 1995.

———. "Melodramas of Beset Manhood: How Theories of American Fiction Exclude Women Authors." *American Quarterly* 33 (1981): 123–39.

———. "Rewriting the Scribbling Women." *Legacy* 2 (1985): 3–12.

———. *Women's Fiction: A Guide to Novels by and about Women in America, 1820–1870.* Ithaca, N.Y.: Cornell University Press, 1984.

Belasco, Susan. "Elizabeth Barrow Stoddard, the *Daily Alta California,* and the Tradition of American Humor." *American Periodicals* 10 (2000): 1–26.

———. "The Writing, Reception, and Reputation of *Uncle Tom's Cabin.*" In *Approaches to Teaching Stowe's Uncle Tom's Cabin,* ed. Elizabeth Ammons and Susan Belasco, 21–36. New York: Modern Language Association of America, 2000.

Bell, Michael Davitt. *Culture, Genre, and Literary Vocation: Selected Essays on American Literature.* Chicago: University of Chicago Press, 2001.

———. *The Problem of American Realism: Studies in the Cultural History of a Literary Idea.* Chicago: University of Chicago Press, 1993.

Benedict, Clare. *Constance Fenimore Woolson.* Vol. 2 of *Five Generations (1785–1923).* London: Ellis, 1929.

Bernardi, Debra. "'A Bit Sensational' or 'Simple and True': Domestic Horror and the Politics of Genre." *Legacy* 16 (1999): 135–53.

Berthold, Michael. "Not 'Altogether' the 'History of Myself': Autobiographical Impersonality in Elizabeth Keckley's *Behind the Scenes. Or, Thirty Years a Slave and Four Years in the White House.*" *American Transcendental Quarterly* 13 (June 1999): 105–19.

Birnbaum, Michele. *Race, Work and Desire in American Literature, 1860–1930.* Cambridge: Cambridge University Press, 2003.

Blanck, Jacob, ed. *The Bibliography of American Literature.* 9 vols. New Haven, Conn.: Yale University Press, 1955–91.

Bledstein, Burton J. *The Culture of Professionalism: The Middle Class and the Development of Higher Education in America.* New York: Norton, 1976.

"Book Notes." *Peterson Magazine* 6 (November 1896): 1207–11.

"Books, Publishers, Authors." *United States Magazine of Science, Art, Manufacturers, Agriculture, Commerce, and Trade* 1 (May 15, 1854): 27–28.

"Books Received." *Godey's Magazine* 132 (February 1896): 209–10.

Boren, Lynda S. "'Dear Constance,' 'Dear Henry': The Woolson/James Affair—Fact, Fiction, or Fine Art?" *American Studies* 27 (1982): 457–66.

Bourdieu, Pierre. *The Field of Cultural Production.* Ed. Randal Johnson. New York: Columbia University Press, 1993.

Boyd, Anne E. "Anticipating James, Anticipating Grief: Constance Fenimore Woolson's 'Miss Grief.'" In *Constance Fenimore Woolson's Nineteenth Century,* ed. Brehm, 191–206.

———. *Writing for Immortality: Women and the Emergence of High Literary Culture in America.* Baltimore: Johns Hopkins University Press, 2004.

Brehm, Victoria, ed. *Constance Fenimore Woolson's Nineteenth Century: Essays.* Detroit: Wayne State University Press, 2001.

Brilliant, Richard. *Portraiture.* London: Reaktion Books, 1991.

Brodhead, Richard H. *Cultures of Letters: Scenes of Reading and Writing in Nineteenth-Century America.* Chicago: University of Chicago Press, 1993.

———. *The School of Hawthorne.* New York: Oxford University Press, 1986.

Bryan, Mary. "How Should Women Write?" In *American Literature, American Culture,* ed. Gordon Hutner, 118–21. New York: Oxford University Press, 1999.

Budd, Louis J. "The American Background." In *The Cambridge Companion to American Realism and Naturalism,* ed. Donald Pizer, 21–46. Cambridge: Cambridge University Press, 1995.

Buell, Lawrence. "American Civil War Poetry and the Meaning of Literary Commodification: Whitman, Melville, and Others." In *Reciprocal Influences,* ed. Fink and Williams, 123–38.

———. *New England Literary Culture.* Cambridge: Cambridge University Press, 1986.

Buhle, Mari Jo, and Florence Howe. "Afterword." In Phelps, *The Silent Partner and "The Tenth of January,"* 355–86.

"Cacoethes Scribendi." *Boston Medical Intelligencer* 2 (August 3, 1824): 50.

"Cacoethes Scribendi." *Harvardiana* 2 (September 1, 1835): 21–26.

Carey, H[enry] C[harles]. *The International Copyright Question Considered, with Special Reference to the Interests of American Authors, American Printers and Publishers, and American Readers.* Philadelphia: Henry Carey Baird, 1872.

"A Chapter upon Letters and Letter-Writers." *Ladies' Repository* 16 (February 1856): 70–71.

Charvat, William. *The Profession of Authorship in America, 1800–1870.* New York: Columbia University Press, 1992.

Cheney, Ednah D. *Louisa May Alcott: The Children's Friend.* Boston: L. Prang, 1888.

Cognard-Black, Jennifer. *Narrative in the Professional Age: Transatlantic Readings of Harriet Beecher Stowe, George Eliot, and Elizabeth Stuart Phelps.* New York: Routledge, 2004.

Cognard-Black, Jennifer, and Elizabeth MacLeod Walls, eds. *Kindred Hands: Letters on Writing by Women Authors, 1860–1920.* Iowa City: University of Iowa Press, 2006.

Comment, Kristin M. "Lesbian 'Impossibilities' of Miss Grief's 'Armor.'" In *Constance Fenimore Woolson's Nineteenth Century,* ed. Brehm, 207–24.

Cone, Helen Gray. "Woman in American Literature." *Century Illustrated Magazine* 40 (October 1890): 921–31.

"Conference Program." *Legacy* 15 (1998): 10–14.

"Contributions to Trade History, No. XXX, D. Lothrop and Co." *American Bookseller,* n.s. 199 (1886): 281–83.

Cooke, Rose Terry. *"How Celia Changed Her Mind" and Selected Stories.* Ed. Elizabeth Ammons. New Brunswick, N.J.: Rutgers University Press, 1986.

————. "A Letter to Mary Ann." *Sunday Afternoon* 3 (January 1879): 79–83.

Coombe, Rosemary J. *The Cultural Life of Intellectual Properties: Authorship, Appropriation, and the Law.* Durham, N.C.: Duke University Press, 1998.

Cott, Nancy F. *The Bonds of Womanhood: 'Woman's Sphere' in New England, 1780–1835.* New Haven, Conn.: Yale University Press, 1977.

Coultrap-McQuin, Susan. *Doing Literary Business: American Women Writers in the Nineteenth Century.* Chapel Hill: University of North Carolina Press, 1990.

————. "Elizabeth Stuart Phelps: The Cultural Context of a Nineteenth-Century Professional Writer." Ph.D. diss., University of Iowa, 1979.

Courtney, W. L. *The Feminine Note in Fiction.* London: Chapman and Hall, 1904.

Crane, Stephen. *Maggie: A Girl of the Streets.* Ed. Thomas A. Gullason. New York: Norton, 1979.

Crumbley, Paul. "Haunting the House of Print: The Circulation of Disembodied Texts in 'Collected by a Valetudinarian' and 'Miss Grief.'" In *American Culture, Canons, and the Case of Elizabeth Stoddard,* ed. Smith and Weinauer. 83–104.

"Culture and Progress." *Scribner's Monthly* 15 (December 1877): 277–84.

Cummins, Maria Susanna. *The Lamplighter.* Ed. Nina Baym. New Brunswick, N.J.: Rutgers University Press, 1988.

[————.] *The Lamplighter Picture Book, or the Story of Uncle True and Little Gerty, Written for the Little Folks.* Boston: Jewett, 1856.

"Current Literature." *Galaxy* 24 (December 1877): 851–63.

"Current Literature." *Overland Monthly* 4 (June 1870): 580–84.

Darnton, Robert. "What Is the History of Books?" In *The Book History Reader,* ed. Finkelstein and McCleery, 9–26.

Davis, Rebecca Harding. *A Rebecca Harding Davis Reader.* Ed. Jean Pfaelzer. Pittsburgh: University of Pittsburgh Press, 1995.

————. "Women in Literature." *Independent,* May 7, 1891, 2.

de la Cova, Antonio. "Filibusters and Freemasons: The Sworn Obligation." *Journal of the Early Republic* 17 (spring 1997): 95–120.

Dean, Sharon L. *Constance Fenimore Woolson: Homeward Bound.* Knoxville: University of Tennessee Press, 1995.

————. "Constance Fenimore Woolson and Henry James: The Literary Relationship." *Massachusetts Studies in English* 7 (1980): 1–9.

Decker, William Merrill. *Epistolary Practices: Letter Writing in America before Telecommunications.* Chapel Hill: University of North Carolina Press, 1998.

Deese, Helen R., ed. "Louisa May Alcott's *Moods:* A New Archival Discovery." *New England Quarterly* 76 (September 2003): 439–55.

Derby, J. C. *Fifty Years among Authors.* New York: Carleton, 1884.

Donovan, Josephine. *New England Local Color Literature: A Women's Tradition.* New York: Continuum, 1983.

Eagle, Mary Kavanaugh Oldham, ed. *The Congress of Women: Held in the Woman's Building, World's Columbian Exposition, Chicago, U.S.A., 1893.* Chicago: American Publishing House, 1894.

Eastman, Julia A. *Striking for the Right.* Boston: D. Lothrop, 1872.

"Editor's Literary Record." *Harper's Monthly Magazine* 40 (May 1870): 925–30.

"Editor's Literary Record." *Harper's Monthly Magazine* 56 (January 1878): 307–13.

Edwards Kitterman, Mary P. "Henry James and the Artist-Heroine in the Tales of Constance Fenimore Woolson." In *Nineteenth-Century Women Writers of the English-Speaking World*, ed. Rhoda B. Nathan, 45–59. New York: Greenwood Press, 1986.

Elbert, Sarah. *A Hunger for Home: Louisa May Alcott's Place in American Culture.* New Brunswick, N.J.: Rutgers University Press, 1987.

Erickson, D. S. *The Wadsworth Boys; or, Agnes' Decision.* Boston: D. Lothrop, 1872.

Evans, Augusta J. *St. Elmo.* New York: Grosset and Dunlap, n.d.

Fahs, Alice. *The Imagined Civil War: Literature of the North and South, 1861–1865.* Chapel Hill: University of North Carolina Press, 2001.

"Female Authors." *North American Review* 72 (January 1851): 151–77.

"Female Authorship." *Littell's Living Age* 9 (May 23, 1846): 345–48.

"Female Authorship." *National Era* 11 (August 6, 1857): 126.

Fern, Fanny. "Gail Hamilton—Miss Dodge." In *Eminent Women of the Age*, ed. Parton et al., 202–20.

———. *Ruth Hall.* Ed. Susan Belasco Smith. New York: Penguin, 1997.

———. *Ruth Hall and Other Writings.* Ed. Joyce W. Warren. New Brunswick, N.J.: Rutgers University Press, 1986.

Fetterley, Judith. "Commentary: Nineteenth-Century American Women Writers and the Politics of Recovery." *American Literary History* 6 (autumn 1994): 600–11.

———. "*Little Women*: Alcott's Civil War." *Feminist Studies* 5 (1979): 369–83.

———. "Plenary Remarks." *Legacy* 19 (March 2002): 5–9.

———, ed. *Provisions: A Reader from 19ᵗʰ-Century American Women.* Bloomington: Indiana University Press, 1985.

Fetterley, Judith, and Marjorie Pryse. *Writing out of Place: Regionalism, Women, and American Literary Culture.* Urbana: University of Illinois Press, 2003.

Fink, Steven, and Susan S. Williams, eds. *Reciprocal Influences: Literary Production, Distribution and Consumption in America.* Columbus: Ohio State University Press, 1999.

Finkelstein, David, and Alistair McCleery, eds. *The Book History Reader.* London: Routledge, 2002.

Fleischner, Jennifer. *Mastering Slavery: Memory, Family, and Identity in Women's Slave Narratives.* New York: New York University Press, 1996.

———. *Mrs. Lincoln and Mrs. Keckly.* New York: Broadway Books, 2003.

Formichella Elsden, Annamaria. *Roman Fever: Domesticity and Nationalism in Nineteenth-Century American Women's Writing.* Columbus: Ohio State University Press, 2004.

Forten, Charlotte. *The Journals of Charlotte Forten Grimké.* Ed. Brenda Stevenson. New York: Oxford University Press, 1988.

Foster, Frances Smith. "African Americans, Literature, and the Nineteenth-Century Afro-Protestant Press." In *Reciprocal Influences*, ed. Fink and Williams, 24–35.

———. *Written by Herself: Literary Production by African American Women, 1746–1892.* Bloomington: Indiana University Press, 1993.

Foucault, Michel. *Language, Counter-Memory, Practice.* Ed. Donald F. Bouchard. Ithaca, N.Y.: Cornell University Press, 1977.

"The Fragile Genius of Elizabeth Stuart Phelps." *Current Literature* 50 (March 1911): 318–19.

Gallagher, Catherine. *Nobody's Story: The Vanishing Acts of Women Writers in the Marketplace, 1670–1820.* Berkeley: University of California Press, 1994.

Gardner, Eric. "'This Attempt of Their Sister': Harriet Wilson's *Our Nig* from Printer to Readers." *New England Quarterly* 66 (June 1993): 226–46.

Geary, Susan. "Harriet Beecher Stowe, John P. Jewett, and Author-Publisher Relations in 1853." *Studies in the American Renaissance* 1 (1977): 345–67.

Gibson, William L. "Writers behind Barbed Wire." *New York Review of Books* 10 (March 14, 1968): 35.

Gilbert, Sandra, and Susan Gubar. *The Madwoman in the Attic: The Woman Writer and the Nineteenth-Century Literary Imagination.* New Haven, Conn.: Yale University Press, 1979.

Gillman, Susan. "The Mulatto, Tragic or Triumphant? The Nineteenth-Century Race Melodrama." In *The Culture of Sentiment,* ed. Shirley Samuels, 221–43. New York: Oxford, 1992.

Gilmore, Michael T. *American Romanticism and the Marketplace.* Chicago: University of Chicago Press, 1985.

———. *Surface and Depth: The Quest for Legibility in American Culture.* Oxford: Oxford University Press, 2003.

Glazener, Nancy. *Reading for Realism: The History of a U.S. Literary Institution.* Durham, N.C.: Duke University Press, 1997.

"Gossip of Authors and Writers." *Current Literature* 8 (September 1891): 16–27.

Grasso, Linda. *The Artistry of Anger: Black and White Women's Literature in America, 1820–1860.* Chapel Hill: University of North Carolina Press, 2002.

Graves, Mrs. A. J. *Woman in America: Being an Examination into the Moral and Intellectual Condition of American Female Society.* New York: Harper and Brothers, 1847.

Greenspan, Ezra. *George Palmer Putnam: Representative American Publisher.* University Park: Pennsylvania State University Press, 2000.

Grier, Katherine C. *Culture and Comfort: Parlor Making and Middle-Class Identity, 1850–1930.* Washington, D.C.: Smithsonian Institution, 1988.

Griffin, Robert J., ed. *The Faces of Anonymity.* New York: Palgrave, 2003.

Griffith, George V. "An Epistolary Friendship: The Letters of Elizabeth Stuart Phelps to George Eliot." *Legacy* 18 (fall 2001): 94–100.

Grossman, Jay. "Rereading Emerson/Whitman." In *Reciprocal Influences,* ed. Fink and Williams, 75–97.

Groves, Jeffrey D. "Judging Literary Books by Their Covers: House Styles, Ticknor and Fields, and Literary Promotion." In *Reading Books,* ed. Moylan and Stiles, 75–100.

Habegger, Alfred. *Gender, Fantasy, and Realism in American Literature.* New York: Columbia University Press, 1982.

Hall, Julie E. "'Coming to Europe,' Coming to Authorship: Sophia Hawthorne and Her *Notes in England and Italy.*" *Legacy* 19 (June 2003): 137–51.

Halttunen, Karen. *Confidence Men and Painted Women.* New Haven, Conn.: Yale University Press, 1982.

Hamilton, Gail. "An American Queen." *North American Review* 143 (October 1886): 329–45.

———. *A Battle of the Books.* Cambridge: Hurd and Houghton, 1870.

———. *Biography of James G. Blaine.* Norwich, Conn.: Henry Bill, 1895.

———. "A Call to My Country-Women." *Atlantic Monthly* 11 (March 1863): 345–50.

———. *Gail Hamilton: Selected Writings.* Ed. Susan Coultrap-McQuin. New Brunswick, N.J.: Rutgers University Press, 1992.

———. *Gail Hamilton's Life in Letters.* 2 vols. Ed. H. Augusta Dodge. Boston: Lee and Shepard, 1901.

———. "My Book." In Hamilton, *Skirmishes and Sketches*, 399–447. Boston: Ticknor and Fields, 1866.

———. "Side-Glances at Harvard Class-Day." *Atlantic Monthly* 12 (August 1863): 242–51.

———. "That Everlasting Andover Controversy." *North American Review* 144 (May 1887): 477–86.

———. *Twelve Miles from a Lemon.* New York: Harper, 1874.

Hamilton, Kristie. *America's Sketchbook: The Cultural Life of a Nineteenth-Century Literary Institution.* Athens: Ohio University Press, 1998.

Hamilton, Sir William. *The Metaphysics of Sir William Hamilton.* Ed. Francis Bowen. Cambridge, Mass.: Sever, Francis, 1868.

Harland, Marion. *Marion Harland's Autobiography: The Story of a Long Life.* New York: Harper and Brothers, 1910.

Harris, Sharon M. *Rebecca Harding Davis and American Realism.* Philadelphia: University of Pennsylvania Press, 1991.

Harris, Susan K. *19th-Century American Women's Novels: Interpretive Strategies.* New York: Cambridge University Press, 1990.

Hart, James D. *The Popular Book: A History of America's Literary Taste.* New York: Oxford University Press, 1950.

Hart, John S. *The Female Prose Writers of America.* Philadelphia: E. H. Butler, 1852.

Hawthorne, Nathaniel. *The Centenary Edition of the Works of Nathaniel Hawthorne.* Ed. William Charvat et al. 23 vols. Columbus: Ohio State University Press, 1962–94.

———. "Civic Banquets." *Atlantic Monthly* 12 (August 1863): 195–212.

Hedrick, Joan D. *Harriet Beecher Stowe: A Life.* New York: Oxford University Press, 1994.

Hewitt, Elizabeth. *Correspondence and American Literature, 1770–1865.* Cambridge: Cambridge University Press, 2004.

Higginson, Thomas Wentworth. *Atlantic Essays.* Boston: James R. Osgood, 1874.

Higonnet, Margaret R. "Civil Wars and Sexual Territories." In *Arms and the Woman: War, Gender, and Literary Representation,* ed. Helen M. Cooper, Adrienne Auslander Munich, and Susan Merrill Squier, 80–96. Chapel Hill: University of North Carolina Press, 1989.

Hirsch, Stephen A. "Uncle Tomitudes: The Popular Reaction to *Uncle Tom's Cabin.*" *Studies in the American Renaissance* 2 (1978): 303–30.

Hochman, Babara. *Getting at the Author: Reimagining Books and Reading in the Age of American Realism.* Amherst: University of Massachusetts Press, 2001.

Hoffert, Sylvia D. "Jane Grey Swisshelm, Elizabeth Keckley, and the Significance of Race Consciousness in American Women's History." *Journal of Women's History* 13 (2001): 8–33.

Homestead, Melissa J. *American Women Authors and Literary Property, 1822–1869.* Cambridge: Cambridge University Press, 2005.

———. "'Every Body Sees the Theft': Fanny Fern and Literary Proprietorship in Antebellum America." *New England Quarterly* 74 (June 2001): 210–37.

Hopkins, Tighe. "'The Tauchnitz' Edition: The Story of a Popular Pubisher." *Pall Mall Magazine* 25 (1901): 197–208.

Howe, Julia Ward. "Women in Politics." *Independent,* May 7, 1891, 1.

[Howells, William Dean.] "Editor's Study." *Harper's Monthly* 74 (February 1887): 482–86.

Huntington, E. B. "Lydia H. Sigourney." In *Eminent Women of the Age,* ed. Parton et al., 85–101.

Hurst, Nancy Luanne Jenkins. "Selected Literary Letters of Sophia Peabody Hawthorne, 1842–1853." Ph.D. diss., Ohio State University, 1992.

Idol, John L., Jr., and Melinda M. Ponder, eds. *Hawthorne and Women: Engendering and Expanding the Hawthorne Tradition.* Amherst: University of Massachusetts Press, 1999.

Il Secretario. "American Letters—Their Character and Advancement." *American Review: A Whig Journal of Politics, Literature, Art, and Science* 1 (June 1845): 575–81.

Jacobs, Harriet. *Incidents in the Life of a Slave Girl.* Ed. Jean Fagan Yellin. Cambridge, Mass.: Harvard University Press, 1987.

Jacobs, Heidi L. M. "Maria Susanna Cummins's London Letters: April 1860." *Legacy* 19 (2002): 245–50.

James, Alice. *The Death and Letters of Alice James.* Ed. Ruth Bernard Yeazell. Los Angeles: University of California Press, 1981.

James, Henry. *The American.* New York: Charles Scribner's, 1922.

———. "The Art of Fiction." In *The Art of Criticism: Henry James on the Theory and Practice of Fiction*, ed. William Veeder and Susan M. Griffin, 165–83. Chicago: University of Chicago Press, 1986.

———. *Letters.* Ed. Leon Edel. 4 vols. Cambridge, Mass.: Belknap Press of Harvard University Press, 1974–84.

———. "Miss Woolson." In *The American Essays*, ed. Leon Edel, 162–74. Princeton, N.J.: Princeton University Press, 1956.

———. *The Notebooks of Henry James.* Ed. F. O. Matthiessen and Kenneth B. Murdock. Chicago: University of Chicago Press, 1981.

———. *The Portrait of a Lady.* Ed. Jan Cohn. Boston: Houghton, Mifflin, 2001.

———. "The Real Thing." In *The Portable American Realism Reader*, ed. James Nagel and Tom Quirk. New York: Penguin, 1997.

[———.] "The Schönberg-Cotta Family." *Nation* 1 (September 14, 1865): 344–45.

———. *A Small Boy and Others.* New York: Scribner's, 1913.

Janson, Drude Krog. *A Saloonkeeper's Daughter.* Ed. Orm Øverland. Baltimore: Johns Hopkins University Press, 2002.

Johnson, Claudia Durst. "Discord in Concord." In *Hawthorne and Women*, ed. Idol and Ponder, 104–20.

Johnson, Nan. *Gender and Rhetorical Space in American Life, 1866–1910.* Carbondale and Edwardsville: Southern Illinois University Press, 2002.

Jones, William Alfred. "Female Novelists." *United States Magazine and Democratic Review* 14 (May 1844): 484–89.

Joyce, James. *Ulysses.* New York: Vintage, 1986.

Kaplan, Amy. "Manifest Domesticity." *American Literature* 70 (September 1998): 581–606.

Keckley, Elizabeth. *Behind the Scenes: Thirty Years a Slave and Four Years in the White House.* Ed. Frances Smith Foster. Urbana and Chicago: University of Illinois Press, 2001.

Kelley, Mary. "'A More Glorious Revolution': Women's Antebellum Reading Circles and the Pursuit of Public Influence." *New England Quarterly* 76 (June 2003): 163–96.

———. *Private Women, Public Stage: Literary Domesticity in Nineteenth-Century America.* New York: Oxford University Press, 1984.

Kerber, Linda. *No Constitutional Right to Be Ladies: Women and the Obligations of Citizenship.* New York: Hill and Wang, 1998.

Kessler, Carol Farley. *Elizabeth Stuart Phelps.* Boston: Twayne, 1982.

Kickley, Betsey, pseudo. *Behind the Seams; by a Nigger Woman Who Took in Work from Mrs. Lincoln and Mrs. Davis.* New York: National News Company, 1868.

Kilcup, Karen, ed. *Nineteenth-Century American Women Writers: An Anthology.* Oxford: Blackwell Publishers, 1997.

Kirkland, Caroline. *A Book for the Home Circle.* New York: Scribner, 1853.

Koppelman, Susan, ed. *Two Friends and Other Nineteenth-Century Lesbian Stories by American Women Authors.* New York: Meridian, 1994.

Lamb, Charles. "Distant Correspondents." In *Essays of Elia, First Series,* ed. George Armstrong Wauchope, 189–95. Boston: Ginn, 1904.

"The Lamplighter." *Littell's Living Age* 5 (April 1, 1854): 28.

Lang, Amy Schrager. *The Syntax of Class: Writing Inequality in Nineteenth-Century America.* Princeton, N.J.: Princeton University Press, 2003.

[Lee, Hannah Farnham Sawyer.] "Female Authorship." *Monthly Miscellany of Religion and Letters* 2 (May 1840): 248–53; 3 (September 1840): 151–54.

"Letter-Writing." *Atlantic Monthly* 2 (June 1858): 43–48.

Levine, Robert S. "In and Out of the Parlor." *American Literary History* 7 (winter 1995): 669–80.

Lewis, R. W. B. *Edith Wharton: A Biography.* New York: Harper and Row, 1975.

"The Library Table: Glimpses of the New Books." *Current Literature* 19 (April 1896): 368–70.

"Literary." *Harper's Weekly* 9 (January 21, 1865): 35.

"Literary Notices." *Godey's Magazine and Lady's Book* 49 (July 1854): 81–85.

"Literary Notices." *Harper's New Monthly Magazine* 8 (April 1854): 714–17.

"Literary Notices." *Knickerbocker; or New York Monthly Magazine* 43 (May 1854): 507–17.

"Literary Notices." *Universalist Quarterly and General Review* 11 (April 1854): 205–20.

"Literary Success of Female Writers." *Harvard Register* 2 (April 1827): 50–59.

"Literary Women." *Living Age* 81 (June 25, 1864): 609–10.

"Literature and Art." *Galaxy* 9 (May 1870): 709–16.

"Literature of the Day." *Lippincott's Magazine* 5 (June 1870): 685–88.

Long, Lisa. "'The Corporeity of Heaven': Rehabilitating the Civil War Body in *The Gates Ajar.*" *American Literature* 69 (December 1997): 781–811.

Lulie. "Persevere: Or, Life with an Aim." *Godey's Lady's Book* 68 (March 1864): 254–58.

Madison, Charles A. *Irving to Irving: Author-Publisher Relations, 1800–1974.* New York: R. R. Bowker, 1974.

Marcus, Isabel. "Coverture." In *The Reader's Companion to U.S. Women's History,* ed. Wilma Mankiller et al., 136–37. Boston: Houghton Mifflin, 1998.

Mathews, Fannie Aymar. "When I Was a Man: A True Story." *New Peterson Magazine* 2 (October 1893): 1033–35.

McCann, Sean. "Reintroduction of the Specialists." *American Quarterly* 49 (March 1997): 183–92.

McFeely, William S. *Frederick Douglass.* New York: Norton, 1991.

McGill, Meredith. *American Literature and the Culture of Reprinting, 1834–1853.* Philadelphia: University of Pennsylvania Press, 2003.

McHenry, Elizabeth. *Forgotten Readers: Recovering the Lost History of African-American Literary Societies.* Durham, N.C.: Duke University Press, 2002.

McIntosh, Maria J. *Woman in America: Her Work and Her Reward.* New York: D. Appleton, 1850.

Melville, Herman. "Hawthorne and His Mosses." In Melville, *The Piazza Tales and*

Other Prose Pieces, 1839–1860, ed. Harrison Hayford et al. Vol. 9 of *The Writings of Herman Melville.* Evanston and Chicago: Northwestern University Press and the Newberry Library, 1987.

———. *Typee.* Ed. John Bryant. New York: Penguin, 1996.

Merish, Lori. *Sentimental Materialism: Gender, Commodity Culture, and Nineteenth-Century American Literature.* Durham, N.C.: Duke University Press, 2000.

Meyer, Annie Nathan. "The Problem of the Novel." *Arena* 87 (February 1897): 451–60.

———. "Woman's Place in Letters." In *The Congress of Women,* ed. Eagle, 135–37.

Middlebrook, Mrs. Grace. *One Year of My Life: Eleanor Winthrop's Diary for 1869.* Boston: D. Lothrop, 1870.

Miller, Edwin Haviland. "A Calendar of the Letters of Sophia Peabody Haw-thorne." *Studies in the American Renaissance* 10 (1986): 199–281.

Miller, James E., ed. *Heritage of American Literature.* San Diego: Harcourt Brace Jovanovich, 1991.

Mitford, Mary Russell. *The Life of Mary Russell Mitford.* Ed. A. G. K. L'Estrange. 2 vols. New York: Harper, 1870.

Moore, Rayburn S. "The Strange Irregular Rhythm of Life: James's Late Tales and Constance Woolson." *South Atlantic Bulletin* 41 (1976): 86–93.

Mott, Frank Luther. *Golden Multitudes.* New York: Macmillan, 1947.

———. *A History of American Magazines, 1865–1885.* Cambridge, Mass.: Harvard University Press, 1938.

Moylan, Michele, and Lane Stiles, eds. *Reading Books: Essays on the Material Text and Literature in America.* Amherst: University of Massachusetts Press, 1996.

"National Literature, and the International Copy-Right Treaty." *United States Review* 2 (August 1853): 97–117.

Neal, Alice. "American Female Authorship." *Godey's Magazine and Lady's Book* 44 (February 1852): 145–48.

Nevins, Allan. *Ordeal of the Union: A House Dividing 1852–1857.* New York: Scrib-ners, 1947.

"New Publications." *New York Tribune,* 28 March 1854, 6.

Newbury, Michael. *Figuring Authorship in Antebellum America.* Stanford, Calif.: Stan-ford University Press, 1997.

Norris, Frank. *The Responsibilities of the Novelist and Other Literary Essays.* New York: Doubleday, 1903.

"Novels and Novelists." *North American Review* 76 (January 1853): 104–23.

Parrington, Vernon. *Main Currents in American Thought.* 3 vols. New York: Har-court Brace, 1930.

Parton, James, et al., eds. *Eminent Women of the Age, Being Narratives of the Lives and Deeds of the Most Prominent Women of the Present Generation.* Hartford, Conn.: S. M. Betts, 1868.

Patton, Francis L. "Is Andover Romanizing?" *Forum* 3 (June 1887): 327–38.

"The Pay of Authors." *Congregationalist and Boston Recorder,* October 10, 1867, 184.

"Pay of Authors." *Littell's Living Age* 13 (May 8, 1847): 257–58.

Payne, William Morton. "Recent Fiction." *Dial* 20 (February 1, 1896): 76–81.

Pease, Donald E. "Author." In *Critical Terms for Literary Study,* ed. Frank Lentric-chia and Thomas McLaughlin, 105–17. Chicago: University of Chicago Press, 1995.

Penny, Virginia. *How Women Can Make Money, Married or Single, in All Branches of the Arts and Sciences, Professions, Trades, Agricultural and Mechanical Pursuits.* Springfield, Mass.: D. E. Fisk, 1870.

Peterson, Carla L. *"Doers of the Word": African-American Women Speakers and Writers in the North (1830–1880)*. New York: Oxford University Press, 1995.

Petry, Alice Hall, ed. "'Always, Your Attached Friend': The Unpublished Letters of Constance Fenimore Woolson to John and Clara Hay." *Books at Brown* 29–30 (1982–83): 11–107.

Phelps, Austin. "Memorial." In H. Trusta [Elizabeth Stuart Phelps]. *The Last Leaf from the Sunny Side*, 5–112. Boston: Phillips, Sampson, 1853.

Phelps, Elizabeth Stuart. "The Bend." *Harper's New Monthly Magazine* 29 (August 1864): 323–35.

———. "Chapters from a Life." *McClures Magazine* 6 (March 1896): 361–68.

———. *Chapters from a Life*. Boston: Houghton, Mifflin, 1897.

———. *The Empty House and Other Stories*. Boston: Houghton Mifflin, 1910.

———. "My Refugees." *Harper's New Monthly Magazine* 29 (November 1864): 754–63.

———. "A Sacrifice Consumed." *Harper's New Monthly Magazine* 28 (January 1864): 235–40.

———. *The Silent Partner and "The Tenth of January."* Old Westbury, N.Y.: Feminist Press, 1983.

———. *The Story of Avis*. Ed. Carol Farley Kessler. New Brunswick, N.J.: Rutgers University Press, 1985.

———. *Three Spiritualist Novels*. Ed. Nina Baym. Urbana: University of Illinois Press, 2000.

———. "Whittier." *Century Magazine* 45 (January 1893): 363–68.

Pizer, Donald, ed. *Documents of American Realism and Naturalism*. Carbondale: Southern Illinois University Press, 1998.

Pratofiorito, Ellen C. "Selling the Vision: Marketability and Audience in Antebellum American Literature." Ph.D. diss., Rutgers University, 1998.

"Publications." *Monthly Religious Magazine* 11 (April 1854): 239–40.

Pulsifer, Janice G. "Gail Hamilton: 1833–1896." *Essex Institute Historical Collections* 104 (1968): 165–216.

Rayne, Mrs. M. L. *What Can a Woman Do; or, Her Position in the Business and Literary World*. Detroit: F. B. Dickerson, 1883.

Robbins, Mary La Fayette. *Alabama Women in Literature*. Selma, Ala.: Selma Printing Company, 1895.

Robbins, Sarah. "Gendering Gilded Age Periodical Professionalism: Reading Harriet Beecher Stowe's *Hearth and Home* Prescriptions for Women's Writing." In *"The Only Efficient Instrument": American Women Writers and the Periodical, 1837–1916*, ed. Aleta Feinsod Cane and Susan Alves, 45–65. Iowa City: University of Iowa Press, 2001.

Rodman, Ella. "A Fragment of Autobiography." *Graham's American Monthly Magazine of Literature, Art, and Fashion* 45 (November 1854): 436–51.

Romero, Lora. "Domesticity and Fiction." In *The Columbia History of the American Novel*, ed. Emory Elliott, 110–29. New York: Columbia University Press, 1991.

Rowe, John Carlos. "Nineteenth-Century United States Literary Culture and Transnationality." *PMLA* 118 (January 2003): 78–89.

Rowland, William G. *Literature and the Marketplace: Romantic Writers and Their Audiences in Great Britain and the United States*. Lincoln: University of Nebraska Press, 1996.

Russo, Ann, and Cheris Kramarae, eds. *The Radical Women's Press of the 1850s*. New York: Routledge, 1991.

Ryan, Mary P. *The Empire of the Mother: American Writing about Domesticity, 1830–1860.* Binghamton, N.Y.: Haworth Press, 1982.

Ryan, Susan. *The Grammar of Good Intentions: Benevolence and Racial Identity in Antebellum American Literature.* Ithaca, N.Y.: Cornell University Press, 2003.

Santamarina, Xiomara. "Behind the Scenes of Black Labor: Elizabeth Keckley and the Scandal of Publicity." *Feminist Studies* 28 (fall 2002): 515–37.

———. "Black Hairdresser and Social Critic: Eliza Potter and the Labors of Femininity." *American Literature* 77 (March 2005): 151–77.

Saunders, David. "Dropping the Subject." In *Of Authors and Origins: Essays on Copyright Law,* ed. Brad Sherman and Alain Strowel, 93–110. Oxford: Clarendon Press, 1994.

Saunders, David, and Ian Hunter. "Lessons from the 'Literatory': How to Historicise Authorship." *Critical Inquiry* 17 (spring 1991): 479–509.

Schnog, Nancy. "Changing Emotions: Moods and the Nineteenth-Century American Woman Writer." In *Inventing the Psychological,* ed. Joel Pfister and Nancy Schnog, 84–109. New Haven, Conn.: Yale University Press, 1997.

———. "'The Comfort of My Fancying': Loss and Recuperation in *The Gates Ajar.*" *Arizona Quarterly* 49 (1993): 127–54.

Schor, Naomi. *Reading in Detail: Aesthetics and the Feminine.* New York: Routledge, 1989.

Seaman, William. *The Lamplighter, or, The Blind Girl and Little Gerty.* London: T. H. Lacy, 1854.

Sedgwick, Catharine. "Cacoethes Scribendi." In *Provisions,* ed. Fetterley, 49–59.

Shackelford, Lynne P., and Everett C. Wilkie, Jr. "John P. Jewett and Company." In *American Literary Publishing Houses, 1638–1899,* ed. Peter Dzwonkowski. Vol. 49 of *Dictionary of Literary Biography.* Detroit: Gale Research Press, 1986.

Shealy, Daniel. "The Author-Publisher Relationships of Louisa May Alcott." Ph.D. diss., University of South Carolina, 1985.

Shields, Carol. *Unless.* London: Fourth Estate/HarperCollins, 2002.

Showalter, Elaine, ed. *Scribbling Women: Short Stories by 19th-Century American Women.* New Brunswick, N.J.: Rutgers University Press, 1997.

Sigourney, Lydia. *Letters of Life.* New York: Appleton, 1866.

Sizer, Lyde Cullen. *The Political Work of Northern Women Writers and the Civil War, 1850–1872.* Chapel Hill: University of North Carolina Press, 2000.

Smith, Gail. "From the Seminary to the Parlor: The Popularization of Hermeneutics in *The Gates Ajar.*" *Arizona Quarterly* 54 (summer 1998): 99–133.

Smith, Robert McClure, and Ellen Weinauer, eds. *American Culture, Canons, and the Case of Elizabeth Stoddard.* Tuscaloosa: University of Alabama Press, 2003.

Sofer, Naomi. "'Carry[ing] a Yankee Girl to Glory': Redefining Female Authorship in the Postbellum United States." *American Literature* 75 (March 2003): 31–60.

———. *Making the "America of Art": Cultural Nationalism and Nineteenth-Century Women Writers.* Columbus: Ohio State University Press, 2005.

Stadler, Gustavus. "Louisa May Alcott's Queer Geniuses." *American Literature* 71 (December 1999): 657–77.

Stern, Madeleine. "Louisa Alcott's Self-Criticism." *Studies in the American Renaissance* 9 (1985): 333–82.

Stevens, Munroe. *The 'A Singular Life' Reviewed and Gloucester Vindicated.* N.p.: Privately printed, 1897.

Stewart, Randall. "Mrs. Hawthorne's Financial Difficulties." *More Books* 21 (February 1946): 43–52.

————. "Mrs. Hawthorne's Quarrel with James T. Fields." *More Books* 21 (September 1946): 254–63.

Stewart, Susan. *On Longing: Narratives of the Miniature, the Gigantic, the Souvenir, the Collection.* Baltimore: Johns Hopkins University Press, 1984.

Stoddard, Elizabeth. *The Morgesons and Other Writings, Published and Unpublished.* Ed. Lawrence Buell and Sandra A. Zagarell. Philadelphia: University of Pennsylvania Press, 1984.

Stoddard, R. H., et al. *Poets' Homes: Pen and Pencil Sketches of American Poets and Their Homes.* 2 vols. Boston: D. Lothrop, 1879.

Stowe, Charles Edward, and Lyman Beecher Stowe. *Harriet Beecher Stowe: The Story of Her Life.* Boston: Houghton Mifflin, 1911.

Stowe, Harriet Beecher. "Can I Write?" *Hearth and Home* 1 (January 9, 1869): 40–41.

————. "Faults of Inexperienced Writers." *Hearth and Home* 1 (January 23, 1869): 72.

————. "How May I Know That I Can Make a Writer?" *Hearth and Home* 1 (January 30, 1869): 88.

————. "How Shall I Learn to Write?" *Hearth and Home* 1 (January 16, 1869): 49.

"Talks about the New Books." *Frank Leslie's Popular Monthly* 43 (February 1897): 237–38.

Talmon, Thrace. "The Latest Crusade: Lady Authors and Their Critics." *National Era* 11 (June 5, 1857): 101.

Taylor, Jeremiah. *The Sacrifice Consumed: Life of Edward Hamilton Brewer, Lately a Soldier in the Army of the Potomac.* Boston: Henry Hoyt, 1863.

Thomas, Brook. *American Literary Realism and the Failed Promise of Contract.* Berkeley and Los Angeles: University of California Press, 1997.

Thorne, P. "Cacoethes Scribendi; and What Came of It." *Lippincott's Magazine of Literature, Science, and Education* 6 (December 1870): 639–45.

Todd, William B., and Ann Bowden. *Tauchnitz International Editions in English, 1841–1955: A Bibliographical History.* New York: Bibliographical Society of America, 1988.

Tonkovich, Nicole. *Domesticity with a Difference: The Nonfiction of Catharine Beecher, Sarah J. Hale, Fanny Fern, and Margaret Fuller.* Jackson: University Press of Mississippi, 1997.

————. "Writing in Circles: Harriet Beecher Stowe, the Semi-Colon Club, and the Construction of Women's Authorship." In *Nineteenth-Century Women Learn to Write,* ed. Catherine Hobbs, 145–75. Charlottesville: University Press of Virginia, 1995.

Torsney, Cheryl B. *Constance Fenimore Woolson: The Grief of Artistry.* Athens: University of Georgia Press, 1989.

"True Republicanism." *Current Literature* 37 (November 1904): 470–71.

Trusta, H. [Elizabeth Stuart Phelps]. *The Last Leaf from the Sunny Side, with a Memorial of the Author, by Austin Phelps.* Boston: Phillips, Sampson, 1853.

Turner, Justin G., and Linda Levitt Turner. *Mary Todd Lincoln: Her Life and Letters.* New York: Alfred E. Knopf, 1972.

Unsworth, John. "Reconsidering and Revising the MLA Committee on Scholarly Editions' Guidelines for Scholarly Editions." http://www.iath.virginia.edu/~jmu2m/sts2001.html. Accessed January 30, 2004.

"The Victim of a Proof-Reader." *Atkinson's Casket* 9 (September 1835): 486–88.

Wald, Priscilla. *Constituting Americans: Cultural Anxiety and Narrative Form.* Durham, N.C.: Duke University Press, 1995.

Walker, Cheryl. "Feminist Literary Criticism and the Author." *Critical Inquiry* 16 (spring 1990): 551–71.

Walker, Nancy. *The Disobedient Writer: Women and Narrative Tradition.* Austin: University of Texas Press, 1995.

Ward, Elizabeth Stuart Phelps. "Comrades." *Harper's New Monthly Magazine* 123 (August 1911): 398–406.

———. "The Rejected Manuscript." *Harper's New Monthly Magazine* 86 (January 1893): 282–94.

Warhol, Robyn R. "Toward a Theory of the Engaging Narrator: Earnest Interventions in Gaskell, Stowe, and Eliot." *PMLA* 101 (October 1986): 811–17.

Weimer, Joan Myers. "The 'Admiring Aunt' and the 'Proud Salmon of the Pond': Constance Fenimore Woolson's Struggle with Henry James." In *Critical Essays on Constance Fenimore Woolson,* ed. Cheryl B. Torsney. New York: G. K. Hall, 1992.

Weinstein, Cindy. "'A Sort of Adopted Daughter': Family Relations in *The Lamplighter*." *ELH* 68 (2001): 1023–47.

Weiss, Jane, ed. "'Many Things Take My Time': The Journal of Susan Warner." Ph.D. diss., City University of New York, 1995.

Weld, H. Hastings. "Some Thoughts on Letter Writing." *Godey's Lady's Book* 44 (April 1852): 249–52.

Wellink, Yvonne. "American Sentimental Bestsellers in Holland in the Nineteenth Century." In *Something Understood: Studies in Anglo-Dutch Literary Translation,* ed. Bart Westerweel and Theo D'haen, 271–89. Amsterdam: Rodopi, 1990.

West, Susan T. "From Owning to Owning Up: Authorial Rights and Rhetorical Responsibilities." Ph.D. diss., Ohio State University, 1997.

Wharton, F. "Authorship in America." *North American Review* 52 (April 1841): 385–404.

White, Barbara A. "Notes toward a Bibliography: Some Sources for the Study of Women's Fiction, 1790–1865." *Legacy* 2 (spring 1985): 6–8.

Whitney, Mrs. A. D. T. *Sights and Insights: Patience Strong's Story of Over the Way.* 2 vols. Boston: Houghton, Mifflin, 1879.

Whitsitt, Sam. "A Lesson in Reading: Henry James's 'The Real Thing.'" *Henry James Review* 16 (fall 1995): 304–14.

Whittier, John Greenleaf. *The Letters of John Greenleaf Whittier.* Ed. John B. Pickard. 3 vols. Cambridge, Mass.: Belknap Press of Harvard University Press, 1975.

Widmer, Edward L. *Young America: The Flowering of Democracy in New York City.* New York: Oxford University Press, 2000.

Williams, Daniel Day. *The Andover Liberals.* Morningside Heights, N.Y.: King's Crown Press, 1941.

Williams, Patricia J. "Alchemical Notes: Reconstructing Ideals from Deconstructed Rights." In *Feminist Legal Theory: Foundations,* ed. D. Kelly Weisberg, 496–506. Philadelphia: Temple University Press, 1993.

———. *The Alchemy of Race and Rights.* Cambridge, Mass.: Harvard University Press, 1991.

Williams, Susan S. *Confounding Images: Photography and Portraiture in Antebellum American Fiction.* Philadelphia: University of Pennsylvania Press, 1997.

———. "Manufacturing Intellectual Equipment: The Tauchnitz Edition of *The Marble Faun*." In *Reading Books,* ed. Moylan and Stiles, 117–50.

———. "Widening the World: Susan Warner, Her Readers, and the Assumption of Authorship." *American Quarterly* 42 (December 1990): 565–86.

Winship, Michael. *American Literary Publishing in the Mid-Nineteenth Century: The Business of Ticknor and Fields.* Cambridge: Cambridge University Press, 1995.

————. "'The Greatest Book of Its Kind': A Publishing History of *Uncle Tom's Cabin*." *Proceedings of the American Antiquarian Society*, n.s. 112 (2002): 309–32.

"Woman in the Domain of Letters." *American Monthly Knickerbocker* 64 (July 1864): 83–86.

Woolson, Constance Fenimore. *For the Major and Selected Short Stories by Constance Fenimore Woolson*. Ed. Rayburn S. Moore. New Haven, Conn.: New College and University Press, 1967.

————. "'Miss Grief." In *Nineteenth-Century American Women Writers*, ed. Kilcup, 302–15.

————. *Women Artists, Women Exiles: "Miss Grief" and Other Stories*. Ed. Joan Weimer. New Brunswick, N.J.: Rutgers University Press, 1988.

Young, Elizabeth. *Disarming the Nation: Women's Writing and the American Civil War*. Chicago: University of Chicago Press, 1999.

Zafar, Rafia. *We Wear the Mask: African Americans Write American Literature, 1760–1870*. New York: Columbia University Press, 1997.

Zboray, Ronald J., and Mary Saracino Zboray. *Literary Dollars and Social Sense: A People's History of the Mass Market Book*. New York: Routledge, 2005.

Zehr, Janet S. "The Response of Nineteenth-Century Audiences to Louisa May Alcott's Fiction." *American Transcendental Quarterly* 1 (n.s.) (December 1987): 323–42.

Index

Acknowledgments

This book, like many academic second books, has evolved over some years, and I have many people to thank for their assistance in that evolution. I was introduced to the subject of nineteenth-century American authorship by Richard Brodhead, whose enthusiasm for the work of Susan Warner and Louisa May Alcott inspired my own. Early on, I also had productive conversations about female authorship with Nancy Schnog, who made me feel that I had something important to offer.

The American Antiquarian Society (AAS) has been of indispensable help to this project from beginning to end. My participation in the 1990 Seminar on the History of the Book was crucial to my understanding of book history as a field as well and to the importance of working with archival materials in undertaking it. More materially, I carried out much of the initial research for this book as a Stephen Botein Fellow at the AAS in 1997. I am grateful to John Hench for his direction of these fellowships and to Joanne Chaison for her unparalleled research assistance and support. As I moved toward completing the work, I also benefited from the comments of Stephen Nissenbaum, Michael Winship, Scott Casper, and especially Jeff Groves on my contribution on nineteenth-century authorship to volume 3 of *The History of the Book in America*, the editorial office for which is housed at the AAS. Many of the questions that they asked me to think about for that chapter had ramifications for this study as well, and I appreciate their insights.

Significant research for this project was also conducted during a month-long residency at the Peabody Essex Museum in Salem, Massachusetts. I thank the museum staff for providing housing as well as a wealth of research support. I am also grateful to the museum for giving me permission to quote letters from Sophia Hawthorne and Mary Abigail Dodge. Other libraries and institutions have provided permission to reprint manuscript and visual material as well; I thank the AAS, the Houghton Library at Harvard University, the New York Public Library, the National Gallery of Scotland, U.S. Games Systems, Inc., the University of Virginia Library, and the Ohio State University Libraries, especially the Cartoon Research Library. Portions of Chapter 3 first appeared in the *New England Quarterly*, and I thank its editor, Linda Smith Rhoads, for her support of my work. For their help in obtaining images for this book, I also thank the University of Nebraska Press, Matthew Isenburg, and Paul Kotheimer of Humanities Information Systems at Ohio State University.

At Ohio State, I also received a variety of other kinds of invaluable material and intellectual support. Two Special Research Assignments from the College of Humanities and a Faculty Professional Leave from the Office of Academic Affairs allowed me to focus on my research and writing. James Phelan and Valerie Lee, the chairs of the English department while I was working on this project, provided unflagging support and helped keep me on a reasonable timetable. In addition, a grant from the Critical Difference for Women program of the Department of Women's Studies helped support my archival research. Steve Fink, Elizabeth Hewitt, James Phelan, and the graduate students enrolled in my 2004–5 dissertation seminar offered astute readings of chapters in progress. Steve also helped me hone some of my initial thoughts on Phelps as we team-taught a course, planned a colloquium, and then coedited a volume on the legacy of William Charvat: a collaborative venture that was invigorating as well as fun. My graduate research assistants—Jennifer Phegley, Kristin Risley, and Sharon Estes—were organized and innovative in tracking down materials. I particularly want to thank Sharon for helping me with the final stages of the manuscript preparation. I also thank the Office of Research at Ohio State, who awarded me an Arts and Humanities Seed Grant that helped fund Sharon's position. Ivonne Garcia and Teresa Kulbaga offered much-needed last-minute technological assistance, and a Grant-in-Aid from the College of Humanities helped fund preparation of the final manuscript.

My former and current colleagues and friends Nicholas Howe, Georgina Kleege, Cathy Shuman, John Norman, Kathleen Gagel, Luke Wilson, Chris Zacher, and Marlene Longenecker provided support at the moments I needed them most. My students at Ohio State have continually provided my main motivation for doing new reading, articulating my thoughts, and drawing connections. I particularly thank the following students: Ph.D. students Jennifer Cognard-Black, whose work in many ways dovetails with my own, and Jennifer Camden, Elizabeth Côté, and Jennifer Desiderio, who share my interest in *The Lamplighter*, the members of my English 756 course in spring and fall 2004; and the members of my English 592 (women writers) course in 2001 and 2002.

Jerry Singerman at the University of Pennsylvania Press patiently awaited the book's completion and provided expert editorial advice; I particularly appreciate his work in facilitating the editorial review process. The Press's two anonymous readers were encouraging and helpful in their suggestions for final revisions, and Suzanne Dorf and Erica Ginsburg were expeditious in guiding me through the production process.

Finally, I would like to thank members of my family, who have patiently waited for this book for a long time. Helen and Jerry Jacobson learned not to ask too much about it. My mother, Sue Williams, knew when to ask and when not to ask and also read part of the manuscript in progress. My father, Neil Williams, supported some much-needed vacation time and inspired me through his commitment to excellence. My husband, Jeff Jacobson, listened to me work through some of the ideas in this book and helped me think of its title. My son, Alex, has never known me when I was not at work on this book, and I thank him for his forbearance. I also thank all of his caregivers—Kathy Dill, Amber Neff, Sarah Steffen, Mary Garvin, and Debbie Brandeberry—whose hard work made my own possible; they are the unsung heroes of this book.